PRACTICAL DATA BASE MANAGEMENT

Practical
Data Base
Management

**edited by
AUERBACH Publishers Inc.**

 **Reston Publishing Company, Inc.
A Prentice-Hall Company
Reston, Virginia**

Library of Congress Cataloging in Publication Data

Main entry under title:

Practical data base management.

   1. Data base management.   I. Auerbach Publishers.
QA76.9.D3P7   001.64'068   81-5194
ISBN 0-8359-5591-5   AACR2

This book is dedicated to our President, I. L. Auerbach. His hard-driving, eye-on-the-ball managerial style makes us look beyond our horizons.

The AUERBACH Editorial Staff

2155554

Contents

PREFACE

The earliest implementations of data base technology go back more than twenty years. During the latter part of the 1970s we gained enough operational experience with the technology to assemble a reasonable body of practical knowledge. Pragmatic guidelines and well-considered advice are rarely based on the experience of having completed the task once. After years of working with the technology, the contributors and the consulting editors have assembled a host of practical recommendations under the title *Practical Data Base Management*.

The primary objective of this book is to provide an easy-to-read, organized guide to the practical issues of planning, designing, and implementing data-base-supported information systems. The "authors" of this book are the contributors to the *AUERBACH Data Base Management Series*. They are professionals with many years of experience in the effective use of data base technology.

The book's organization follows a conceptual model of a data base environment, comprised of five basic components:

- Data Bases
- Data Base Management Systems
- Data Dictionary/Directory Systems
- Data Base Administration
- User System Interfaces

This book is geared to the manager responsible for the planning, design, implementation, and maintenance of a data base environment. Because data base technology is a highly complex topic, material relevant only to the technologist has been omitted or reduced to a conceptual level. Technical detail relevant to the discussion is included to clarify for the reader the practical impact of that particular aspect. The book is not intended as a comprehensive tutorial. It is intended to present practical experience and insight for the practicing manager.

Part I introduces the concept of a data base environment and defines the five components. The chapters emphasize some management issues and the importance of planning.

Part II provides an in-depth exploration of the five components within the data base environment. A chapter is devoted to each.

Part III deals with evaluating and selecting the software components of the data base environment. Those components implemented as software are the Data Base Management System and the Data Dictionary/Directory System.

Part IV addresses the administration and control of the data base environment. This part contains job descriptions, organizational issues, and other related management topics.

Part V is devoted to the design and development of data bases. Practical insight is offered as well as guidance on methods and procedures related to design and development. Key trade-offs involved in data base design are explored.

Part VI presents a glimpse into the future of data base technology. Beginning with an overview of current trends, this section emphasizes the relevant aspects of distributed data bases and other state-of-the-art developments.

Many individuals have been instrumental in the development of this volume, most notably:

Gene Altshuler   Donna Sheppard Rund
Gene Lowenthal   Richard Chamberlein
James P. Fry   Jay-Louise Weldon
                               Warren Minami

Special credit is also due the editorial staff of AUERBACH
Publishers, who assiduously assembled and edited this volume.

Bernard K. Plagman
Consulting Editor
New York City

W. A. Sommerfield
Editor-in-Chief
AUERBACH Publishers Inc
Philadelphia PA

January 1981

PART I

Management Perspectives and Planning

Deciding to go data base requires rigorous planning. Objectives must be determined and corporate approval and funding obtained. Implementation cannot proceed without a well-conceived strategy.

Planning for the data base environment involves both management and technical issues. Although most attention focuses on technical considerations, management issues are more difficult to resolve and require more careful planning and coordination. Developing and gaining management commitment to the proposed strategy is essential to the successful implementation of data base technology. In addition, the potential impact of this implementation on the organization must be examined.

chapter 1

Planning for the Data Base Environment

INTRODUCTION

A "data base," from the viewpoint of an organization, may be defined as the central repository, in a logical sense, of all automated data available to the organization. The concept of a *data base environment* extends the definition to include the capture, storage, maintenance, and dissemination of data used within the organization in a controlled, consistent fashion. To many organizations, this approach represents a radical departure from present methods of handling data. Characteristic of many data environments today are:

- Fragmented (independent) application development
- Inadequate user service levels
- Uncontrolled data redundancy
- Inconsistent data definition
- Inconsistent data manipulation

The general objective, then, of a data base approach is the elimination of both data and processing redundancy and inconsistency, and the establishment of an environment capable of

3

responding to the varied needs of the end user. In essence, the data base approach demands a well-defined, centrally administered set of standards and procedures relative to all aspects of data used by the organization.

The data base approach implies a high degree of automation (though not exclusively so) and thus includes such software elements as an automated data dictionary, a generalized transaction control processor, the application systems, and the generalized Data Base Management System; however, a data base does not imply that an organization simply has to acquire a DBMS from a vendor and "turn it over" to the user groups within the organization. The key element of the data base environment is that of standards and procedures; without these standards and procedures the data base cannot function effectively.

Such a critical change in an organization's data processing environment demands a thorough, well-managed plan of implementation. The establishment of an effective planning team to map out the tasks required to evolve toward a data-base-supported environment is therefore imperative. As in any major systems development effort, poor planning and poor management will be reflected in the delivered product. The scope of this chapter, then, will include requirements planning, the identification of the major elements of the data-base-supported environment, a description of the key elements or tasks of the implementation plan, and a discussion of major considerations in setting up, staffing, and initiating the implementation plan.

PLANNING FOR DB REQUIREMENTS

The plan for a data base environment is actually a subset of the overall DP plan, which in turn is a subset of the even broader-scoped corporate plan. This interrelationship suggests that it would be futile to begin planning a data base environment without having both a corporate plan and a DP plan upon which to base the more specific topics of a DB plan.

A basic assumption of the discussion in this chapter is that an approved corporate plan exists and that there is a recognized DP plan as well. The corporate planning process has been relatively well defined in other literature and needs no further mention here. However, the DP planning process has been widely ignored and thus lacks universally recognized principles. While this chapter is not an exposition of DP planning, there are certain elements of a DP plan without which it would be literally futile to begin planning for a data base environment. An apt analogy is to build a "tool" without knowing what it is to be used for.

The elements of the DP planning process that are essential to the data base environment planning effort are directly related to the data/information situation of the enterprise. The questions which the DP plan must answer at this point are:

1. How is data/information being handled now?
2. How will this data/information be handled in the future?

The first question and its answer form the topic of the following section. The second question is the cornerstone of orderly development because it establishes the goals and objectives of the data base environment. It is discussed in the subsequent section.

What can be done in a case where there is no formal DP plan upon which to base the planning for a data base environment? Such a situation obviously cannot be ideal. Nevertheless, it may be both possible and appropriate to approach the discussion in the next two sections independent of a formal DP plan and then attempt to develop the necessary foundations for future development in the best possible way, given the existing situation.

CURRENT STATUS OF DATA/INFORMATION HANDLING

It usually comes as a vast surprise to most information system executives that no one within their organizations can provide quick, precise answers to the following supposedly simple questions: How many operational programs are there? Of these programs how many perform edit-validate functions, I/O functions, etc.? How many systems are there in production status? Most importantly, how many and what files are associated with each such system? All of these questions concern only the automated portion of a corporation's data resources. The answers to such questions such as how many basic data elements there are in use in the company and what is the extent of actual data sharing, manual or otherwise are rarely even contemplated. If answers cannot be given to these high-order questions, then how can one expect to start determining the answers to questions of the actual data existence and information usage?

Answers to questions like these are necessary since the essential benefit of a data base environment is to provide a central source of data available to all applications and users for automated systems and common utility software to access and manipulate this data. There is no way to determine the nature of the eventual implementation, let alone to scope the effort without definitive information on the existing data and information usage, i.e., systems.

The initial approach to determining the answers to these

questions involves a usually arduous manual effort. A complete catalog of all systems, the number and type of programs associated with each, and a determination of all files used and produced by each system must be established. All names and symbolic labels (for later use) should be noted, including very short English language descriptors of each data element, system, program, and file.

Much of this work can be delegated to the applications development groups with the planning group acting in a coordinating/ advisory role. A simple but well-formulated questionnaire should be established. Figure 1-1 shows a suggested form for this data collection procedure. Also required (but not shown) is a simple catalog containing each identified data file and its contents. In some high-volume situations it may even be desirable to implement an automated data dictionary at this early stage.

From this information a graphical representation can be drawn to show the interrelationship between existing systems, manual or otherwise, and the basic flow of information to and from each system. The primary purpose of this effort is to pinpoint central and functional use of data as information. Eventually these concentrations will be the focus of the entire data base

---

GENERAL INFORMATION

Generally describe the operation of your area of responsibility.
Is there a specific authority or regulation covering your area?

USE OF INFORMATION

1. From what areas (systems) do you receive information?
   Describe the basic data elements involved.
2. Is such information received at specific times?
3. What are the approximate transaction volumes?
4. What do you do with this information?
5. What security precautions must you take with respect to the information?
6. To what areas (systems) do you send information?
7. Does your processing have time constraints?
8. Are there contemplated changes to any existing procedures?

EXTENT OF AUTOMATION (for user areas only)

9. Describe, in general terms, the computer system (if any).
10. Are there changes to the system being currently considered?
11. What additional tasks would you like the computer to perform?
12. What new uses do you see for the computer?

Figure 1-1. Data Base Management: Guidelines for Collecting Data on Existing Use of Information

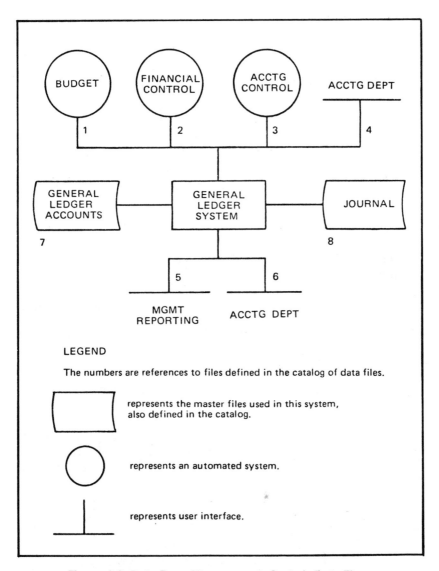

Figure 1-2. Data Base Management: System Data Flows

effort. Figure 1-2 is a pictorial representation of a single system with data flows (to and from other systems), both automated and manual. The end result of this first study is a complete set of these pictorial representations of data/information flow, supported by the catalog of data files in use.

FUTURE INFORMATION REQUIREMENTS

To attempt data base planning in the abstract is to doom it to failure. For a variety of reasons, to plan to establish such a plan based on the current environment or situation in a specific firm is equally inappropriate. The dynamics of the corporate milieu are neither well understood nor very apparent. It has been said that attempting to formulate a plan for a corporation today is like trying to hit a jet plane with a rock.

It is the responsibility of the corporate planning function to define or approximate the future environment and not that of the DP department. Nevertheless, it is the DP department's responsibility to assure that it will be positioned properly to service the future requirements of the corporation. The first step in this process is a careful review of the current corporate plans and a complete understanding of the goals and objectives set forth therein.

The task with regard to planning the data base environment is much simpler in terms of scale and scope, for the primary function of the data base planning effort is to assure that the future information requirement of the corporation will be satisfied. One viable approach to achieving this assurance is the establishment of an information system structure predicated in general on the corporate plan and in particular on existing state of data files and systems.

The information systems structure has as its conceptual base the rationale that information is structured and used in a hierarchical sense. Figure 1-3 shows an overly simplistic representation of this structure. The lowest level is the operational data of the firm. The data may be contained in automated or manual systems, both internal and external to the firm. This data relates to the transaction levels of the firm's business, e.g., order transactions, account transactions. The primary characteristic of this data is that it is grouped within specific systems which relate to single subfunctions that are typically bounded as a computer application.

Next is the functional level which involves grouping the operational level systems under primary corporate functions. Such functions as marketing, production, or financial activities are examples of this type of grouping. A key feature of this level is that rarely if ever does a single operational system feed, on a transaction basis, more than one functional grouping.

The top level is that of corporate information. The key to this level is that it involves decisions requiring data that cuts across all functional lines at one time or another. Decisions involving

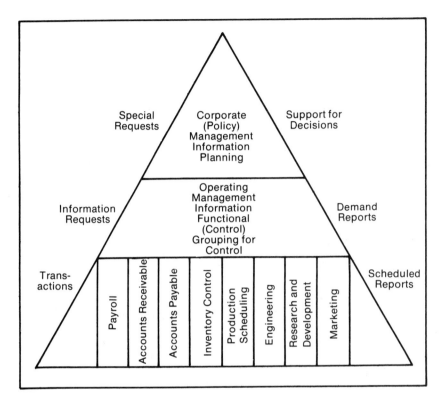

Figure 1-3. Data Base Management: Information System Structure

such things as corporate expansion, acquisition, and divestiture, fall into this range.

Viewing the future corporate information requirements as a tiered pyramid of this nature facilitates the necessary understanding to perform the more definitive identification of the pieces that will comprise the corporate information systems structure.

The establishment of this structure is likened to constructing a model, since many of the attendant benefits of the modeling process accrue: the identification of all interacting elements; creating order from chaos (i.e., the mere structuring of a large number of variables); and others. The goal of the information systems structure is to identify all existing and planned automated and manual information systems and their relationships to each other and to the previously identified functional and corporate information needs. Work already done to define existing data and information usage becomes indispensable as the next task of structuring is undertaken.

The next step is to design a conceptual schema. A conceptual schema for a bank is shown in Figure 1-4 as an example of information system structure. The illustration is reproduced here to present a concrete example of the application of this technique. The design technique is discussed in Part V.

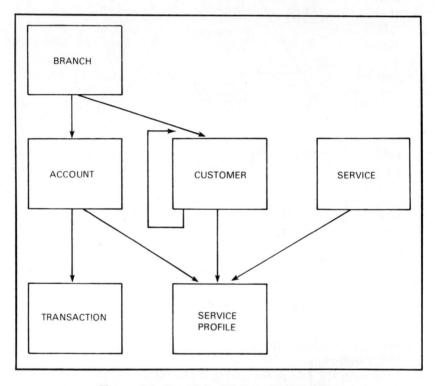

Figure 1-4. Conceptual Schema For a Bank

This structure shows the groupings and subsets of the information systems structure for a bank. Also shown are relationships among the groupings of data. Each grouping is clearly not a record per se, in the traditional sense of a collection of data elements, but is a true entity of the organization, being a data cluster composed of the attributes used to describe the entities.

The base upon which this conceptual schema is established is an evolving process. Basic business functions that must be accomplished represent the focal point of analysis at a higher level of detail and definition than during the design phase. The planner should not be expected to gather operational details from user departments nor should he be expected to define in detail the information systems that he is planning. He must be engaged, however, in the activities of fact gathering and information system design and should perform these activities only to the level of detail required to identify and define the conceptual schema of the systems and information processing environment at hand. He will rely to a great extent on the data gathered in defining the current environment, deviating when future requirements dictate.

In establishing this structure, it is recommended that two groups be formed to work independent of each other. The idea is to have a combination of "top-down" and "bottom-up" approaches, which would produce viable alternatives. The process is to begin concurrently by the two coordinated groups.

The first group works in an abstract top-down approach with the objective of developing a conceptual schema and a set of information systems which would satisfy the future requirements as specified by the users. The second group uses the specified existing information flow as a starting point with an objective similar to that of the first group. The ability of the two groups to converge to one structure is aided by the use of a standardized method of depicting the information system and its underlying conceptual schema.

FUNCTIONAL COMPONENTS
OF A DATA BASE ENVIRONMENT

The concepts of a data base environment are described in terms of its five functional components (see Figure 1-4). One point should be emphasized: *The data base environment is not a system; it is a concept under which systems are to be implemented.* This concept is to be utilized in the development, operation, and maintenance of the information system structure. Each component is uniquely affected by the specific nature of the conceptual schema and the information system plan of a corporation.

This section presents, from a planning viewpoint, some of the alternatives that must be evaluated with regard to the five components of the data base environment. Specific emphasis is on the manner in which these elements must support the implementation of the conceptual schema and plan.

Data Base Administration

This element is the human aspect of the data base environment concept. It is largely affected by the basic concept of centralization inherent in integration and less so by the specific nature of the conceptual schema on the information systems plan. It is for this reason that the data base administrator (DBA) is covered in much greater depth in Part II, Chapter 6 of this book.

In one regard, organizational placement, the data base administrator is affected by the information systems plan. The issue of organizational placement has been discussed in the literature. Almost without exception, the authors considering this problem call for the DBA to report to the highest full-time DP manager. In reality, however, few DBAs are aligned in this way.

In situations where the DP plan and the conceptual schema indicate a requirement for widespread sharing of data among diverse organizational entities (both internal and external to the DP department), the job of the DBA is significantly hampered if he does not obtain proper organizational placement. In this regard, the nature of the conceptual schema will to some degree affect the nature of the DBA component of the data base environment.

Data Dictionary/Directory System (DD/DS)

The DD/DS is possibly the single most important element of the data base environment, inasmuch as it provides for the control of the environment as a whole. Nevertheless, in implementing the DD/DS it is still necessary to decide what will be the major emphasis or objective of the DD/DS.

The DD/DS maintains information about data. This information, often referred to as metadata, can be used to standardize the use of data or simply to disseminate information about the use of data.

Analysis of the information systems requirements of a firm will provide some insight for this decision. If there is wide and prevalent sharing of data, then it will be necessary to utilize the DD/DS in a stricter sense to provide for standardization where appropriate. On the other hand, if there will not be a high degree of data sharing, then the necessity for standardization is minimized and there will be more emphasis on dissemination of information about data.

Another aspect of the DD/DS which must be decided early is whether or not the system need be automated. This issue will also be answered by the results of the analysis of information systems requirements in terms of the volume of information about data that needs to be collected and maintained.

There are three classes of potential users of the DD/DS, and the analysis of information systems requirements will help determine the extent to which each of these classes will require support.

- **The End User.** The end user can utilize the DD/DS to browse for information about what he needs to know. Depending on the degree of free-form query predicted as a result of the information systems requirements analysis, there will be a greater or lesser need for this type of support.
- **The Analyst-Designer.** The analyst or designer of applications can utilize the DD/DS to assist him in the analysis of new data requirements for his application. Depending on the amount of new information source identified in the analysis of information systems requirements and in the conceptual schema, this type of support will be of greater or lesser importance.
- **The DBMS Software.** The DBMS element relies on the DD/DS for parametric data, which facilitates the storage and retrieval of data from the data base. This interface will be of greater or lesser criticality depending on the absolute necessity for complete control in the DBMS environment. This, in turn, also depends on the relative amount of data sharing that will take place in the DB environment.

The DD/DS will often be the first component to be implemented. It should be designed with the results of the analysis of information systems requirements in mind.

User/System Interfaces (USI)

The study of information system requirements will have significant impact on the nature of the user/system interfaces, which will be necessary for the eventual success of the data base effort. A prime example in this regard is the case of the language interface.

In assessing the information requirements, i.e., the manner in which information is used, it should become apparent that there are several classes of users of information. In some cases, the user requires a totally problem-oriented language, completely independent of the data that he requires to access. In other cases, the language provided must be capable of supporting complex data structures. In still other situations, a parametric type of keyword "language" is all that is required. Analysis of information system requirements thus helps determine the types of languages that will serve best as user/system interfaces.

Data Base (DB)

There are three types of data bases which may comprise an organization's data resources:

- Central data base
- Functional data base
- Dedicated data base

As a direct result of the analysis performed in conjunction with assessing information requirements, it is possible to identify the distribution of data among these three types of data bases. In essence, the degree of data sharing that is identified as a result of information usage patterns will dictate the concentration of data in the functional and central data bases.

This is a key issue, for it is the nature of the shared data bases which, in the final analysis, determines the specific type of data base management support required.

Data Base Management System (DBMS)

One of the most important results of the study of information system requirements is the identification of objectives and requirements for the DBMS. Referring to the conceptual DB environment shown in Figure 1-5, it can be seen that there is interaction between all four other elements of the environment and the DBMS. This suggests that the combined requirements analysis of the four other elements forms the basis of the procurement process for

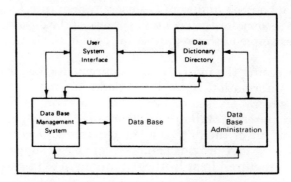

Figure 1-5. Conceptual DB Environment

the DBMS and eventually dictates the specific DBMS that ought to be selected for a particular DB environment.

An example from the results of one study of information systems requirements will illustrate what the cause and effect is in this regard. It was ascertained from the summation of individual requirements from a total of over 30 subsystems that the relative volume of data was not exceedingly high nor was the growth rate. Transactions involved, however, were high, and the complexity of data structures was significant. There was to be a heavy emphasis on ad hoc query, and there was an immediate necessity to implement a significant portion of the total information systems structure.

Just this broad-brush type of analysis dictates a certain class of DBMS software. The desired DBMS should support the complex data structure in a way conducive to flexible ad hoc inquiry. This suggests the network data structure is implemented using partially invented indices. Also, the DBMS should be easy to use and flexible in its implementation.

This is a cursory example of the type of analysis implied. In reality this process will be carried out in much greater detail and in a more rigorous manner.

SOFTWARE COMPONENTS OF THE DATA BASE ENVIRONMENT

Aside from the administrative aspects, and expanding on the software components, the data base environment may be defined as consisting of the following software elements:

- Transaction controller
- Application systems
- Data Base I/O interface (DBIO)
- Data Base Management System (DBMS)
- Data Dictionary/Directory System (DD/DS)

Figure 1-6 illustrates the interrelationships between these software components in a flow sense. A description of each component is given in the following paragraphs.

The Transaction Controller

The transaction controller is a user system interface and has two general functions: (1) the handling of transactions entering the data base environment and the distribution of messages/re-

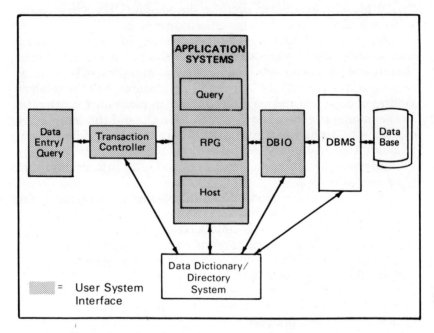

Figure 1-6. Elements of a Data Base Environment

sponses flowing from the environment; and (2) the scheduling and monitoring of application systems and subsystems within the environment.

The transaction controller may perform additional functions such as basic edit/validation (e.g., size check, range check), terminal and user password verification, transaction logging, and message/query checkpointing.

The Application Systems

Application systems user system interfaces are the problem-processing elements of the data base environment. Typically, the problem processors are the COBOL, FORTRAN, PL/1, Assembly, or other programming language programs designed and implemented to handle specific user requirements. These programs communicate with the DBMS through a language set embedded within (or "hosted" by) the program itself. The language set falls into two categories: the program's Data Description Language (DDL) and the Data Manipulation Language (DML).

User requirements may also be supported through higher level languages that are "self-contained" and do not require programming language (COBOL, FORTRAN, etc.) expertise to use. These languages are often employed by the end user for report generation (RPG) or query use. Such self-contained languages may also provide basic retrieval and update capabilities but typically do not support the comprehensive procedural facilities available in compiler-level languages. These languages are particularly valuable in supporting the one-time, ad hoc needs of end users, especially when turnaround time is critical.

Regardless of the language type used for requesting data from the data base, all these requests for data are processed by the DBMS. The actual physical addressing of data within the data base and any logical transformation of data are performed by the DBMS.

The Data Base I/O (DBIO) Interface

The DBIO interface is also a user system interface and is an optional element of the data base environment. Functionally, the DBIO acts as an intermediate process between the application program or process (host, query, or report writer language) and the DBMS. All "calls," or service requests, from an application program are made directly to the DBIO. The DBIO will further process the request, pass the request to the DBMS, and return all responses, both status and data, from the DBMS to the requesting application program.

The Data Base Management System (DBMS)

The DBMS is the software system that services all requests for data. The DBMS receives information relative to the content, structure, and physical characteristics from the data base designer via two languages—the data base DDL and the Device Media Control Language (DMCL). Requests for data against the data base may come from a host language DML call, a report writer language specification, or from a query language command.

The data base DDL is the language used to describe the full scope of the data base to the DBMS. The DBMS processes the schema specification and builds an internal *directory* containing complete information on data items, records, and record relationships. Physical device characteristics and physical storage strategies (grouping, page sizes, free space allocation, etc.) are entered via the DMCL.

Once the data base is defined and established, the DBMS processes all requests against the data base by first verifying the requester's authorization to manipulate the requested data. If the request is authorized, the DBMS then relates the subschema and the request to the data base schema, extracts the required data from the physical data base, transforms the data according to the program's data specification, and delivers the data back to the requester. If a DBIO interface exists, the DBMS functions as if the DBIO were the requesting application program.

The Data Dictionary/Directory System (DD/DS)

The DD/DS serves as a repository of *data about data, metadata*. The DD/DS interfaces with the data base administrator, the systems analyst, the programmer, the user, and the various software elements of the data base environment.

PLANNING FOR THE DATA BASE ENVIRONMENT

The commitment to a data base approach is a major organizational decision. Essential to the success of the implementation of the data base environment is full support of the user, management, and data processing groups.

The first step toward the achievement of a data base environment is the statement of objectives. These objectives must then be communicated to the user, management, and data processing groups. This communication, or education, consists of a full presentation of the goals and concepts of a data base approach, the estimates of costs, resources, and time required to develop a data base environment, and the responsibilities the users, management, and data processing will each have in the data base environment.

Following the general presentation of the goals, concepts, and planned approach, the data base environment planning team will be established. From this point on, the team will develop and execute the discrete tasks necessary to establish the data base environment, including activities relating to the hardware/software components and administrative procedures.

ONGOING SYSTEMS AND DATA BASE DESIGN
AND DEVELOPMENT

The final task of the data base environment planning and development effort is the integration, testing, and acceptance of the data base environment components. Upon completion of this task, the data base environment becomes production oriented. In the production mode, the Data Base Administrator will coordinate the systems and data base design functions according to the standards and procedures established by the DBA function.

ADMINISTRATION OF THE DATA BASE ENVIRONMENT

The development of a data-base-supported environment requires the standardization and coordination of data definition, capture, storage, maintenance, and dissemination, as discussed previously. This coordination aspect is reflected in the DBA function, with the Data Base Administrator being responsible not only for the coordination and control of the data base environment, but also for the establishment of the standards and procedures for coordination and control. A successful data base environment demands extensive communication between the users of the data base and the data processing group. Within the data processing group itself, clear communication is required between the operating entities of systems analysis, programming, and operations as well as the various support functions such as planning, education, documentation, etc. Therefore, it is strongly recommended that the DBA responsibility be placed, as a quasi-staff function, organizationally reporting directly to a senior Data Processing officer or his equivalent.

ELEMENTS OF THE LONG-RANGE PLAN

The long-range plan for the data base environment should be a subset of the overall DP plan; as such, the data base plan will rely heavily on the goals and objectives set forth for the organization. Nevertheless, a formal statement of the objectives of the data base environment is essential as the first task of the planning process. This will be followed by formulation of the tasks whose performance will bring the stated goals and objectives to fruition. At this stage in the planning process, the formulation of tasks should provide enough detail to allow the next step of resource estimation and allocation to be performed. In some cases, this may require detailed breakdowns of the tasks into activities. Finally, the tasks must be phased into chronological sequence to ensure orderly development of the data base environment.

The following paragraphs are devoted to detailed discussion of the tasks involved in the development of the data base environment. Figure 1-7 summarizes these tasks.

Define Goals

Development of the data base environment is based on a general statement of goals to be achieved with the environment. This statement must be based on the organization's long-range plan.

Establish the Data Base Administration (DBA) Function

An integrated data base environment demands thorough coordination. Coordination requires standards and procedures and a centralized function to administer these standards and procedures. This function is defined as the Data Base Administration function. A key responsibility of the DBA function, then, is the coordination and control of the ongoing data base environment. An important aspect of this coordination activity involves the development of the data base environment, including establishment of standards and procedures, analysis of requirements, and the evaluation and selection of the software required. These functions logically fall within the responsibilities of the DBA function. Therefore the establishment of the DBA function as early as possible in the data base environment development process is essential.

Define Operating Plan

Definition of the operating plan addresses the tasks and phasing required to establish the data base environment, as identified in the definition of goals. The plan represents the project plan that will result in an operational, integrated data base environment.

Develop Data Collection Standards

A key task in preparing for a data base environment is the identification and documentation of the *existing* and *projected* information needs of the corporation. This task is the initial effort following completion of the operating plan.

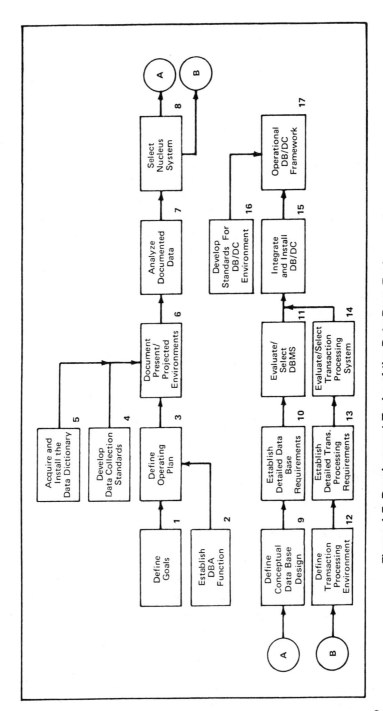

Figure 1-7. Development Tasks of the Data Base Environment

21

Acquire and Install the Data Dictionary/Directory System

One of the most important tools for the coordination and control of the data base environment is the data dictionary. The data dictionary, if implemented early, can be used also in the coordination and control of the development process. Thus, the dictionary can be used to facilitate the establishing of the standards and procedures to be employed in describing data within the existing and projected environments. These standards and procedures must address the methods of collecting information, the forms to be utilized, the data entities to be described, the data attributes to be described for each data entity, and the transactions that operate against these data entities. Establishment of the data dictionary and these standards and procedures is the responsibility of the Data Base Administrator.

Document the Present and Projected Data Environments

Utilizing the standards and procedures established in the foregoing task, the Data Base Administrator will coordinate the process of collecting information about data as it currently exists or is known to be desired. This collection effort may extend to the total data environment of the organization or to a defined subset of the data environment (i.e., one or more functional areas of the organization). Should this effort initially extend only to a defined subset of the total data environment, it should be noted that this process will be the initial task for all future plans to integrate additional functional areas into the data base environment.

Analyze Documented Data

Analysis of the data documented in the preceding task serves to identify common areas of information by use, as well as data redundancy and inconsistency, and provides a perspective on transaction flow and application interrelationships. This analysis will form the basis for selecting a target, or nucleus application area that will represent the first system development effort under the integrated data base environment.

Select the Nucleus System

Identification of a nucleus system serves two purposes:

1. Defining the initial application(s) to be implemented in the data base environment

2. Providing a basis for a detailed requirements analysis in preparation for selection of a DBMS package and a Transaction Processor (TP) package

Once the nucleus system is selected, efforts in the selection and acquisition of a DBMS and a TP system may begin. Both tasks may proceed in parallel.

Define the Conceptual Data Base Design

Utilizing the data collected and analyzed in earlier phases, the Data Base Administrator will combine data into logical groupings and combine these logical groupings into a general-level data base structure, relating the data in the hierarchical and/or network relationships that will serve the information needs of the organization.

Establish Detailed Data Base Requirements

Examination of the various transactions and activities that will be imposed against the data base structure will provide the Data Base Administrator with the data necessary to develop the selection criteria for a DBMS.

In balancing the requirements of all transactions against the data base, the Data Base Administrator will be able to select the optimum access method and storage strategy for each record, or record group, in the proposed data base structure. He or she should assume for the purposes of this analysis that all access methods and storage strategies are available. The results of such an analysis will be a *desired* set of capabilities that can be translated into selection criteria for a DBMS.

Evaluate and Select a DBMS

Utilizing the selection criteria developed in the previous task, the Data Base Administrator can develop a request for proposal to be delivered to the various DBMS vendors. In the selection process, the Data Base Administrator (or the evaluation team) should take into consideration the alternative of in-house development.

Define TP Requirements

The analysis of transaction processing requirements and the selection of a TP system may proceed in parallel with the evaluation and selection of a DBMS. Definition of transaction requirements will, in this phase, include identification of transaction characteristics, analysis of transaction response requirements, and determination of transaction volumes and frequencies.

Establish Detailed TP System Requirements

In this task, the requirements of a TP system are defined in greater detail. This analysis will address such factors as transaction loading on the system, priority requirements, scheduling, journaling, recovery and restart, terminal characteristics, and communications network requirements.

Evaluate and Select a TP System

Utilizing the requirements established in the previous task, a request for proposal will be issued to prospective vendors. Consideration should also be given to the alternative of in-house development.

Integrate and Install the DBMS and the TP System

In this phase, the DBMS and the TP system will be integrated, tested, and accepted. The Data Base Administrator is responsible for establishing the testing procedures and acceptance criteria.

Develop Standards and Procedures for the Data Base Environment

After selection of the software components for the data base environment, and in conjunction with the integration and installation of these components, the Data Base Administrator will begin the development of standards and procedures for managing and controlling the environment. These standards and procedures will encompass the following areas:

- Data collection and analysis
- Data dictionary/directory system
- Data identification conventions
- Validation rules
- DBMS usage
- TP system usage
- Data base design
- User chargeback

- Security/integrity
- Activity monitoring
- Application design specification
- Application documentation
- Application testing
- Operations
- Environment maintenance
- Environment documentation

Upon completion of the preceding tasks, the data base environment may be considered operational. At this point, design, development, and implementation of the nucleus system, identified during the establishment of the data base environment, can begin. Development of the nucleus application and all future applications within the data base environment will be coordinated by the Data Base Administrator and will conform to the standards and procedures established in previous tasks.

ESTABLISHING THE IMPLEMENTATION PLAN

Initiating the Planning Framework

Identification of the general objectives of a data-base-supported environment is the first task in establishing the long-range plan and is generally executed at the data processing directorate level, typically as a statement of long-term data processing objectives. From this statement, the DP planning committee will establish a formal document outlining the methodology to be employed in initiating action on the plan. Once approved through standard review cycles, the DP planning committee will integrate the data base implementation plan into the organization's overall long-range DP plan.

Integration of the data base implementation plan into the long-range DP plan must consider the following:

- Methodology of execution
- Phasing of execution
- Transition from implementation of the data base environment to a production environment

Assuming the DP function maintains a long-range plan for data processing, the recommended approach to detailing the elements of the data base plan includes first the setting of the long-term (5-7 years) goals of the DP function in general and the role of the data base within that projected environment. The long-range view addresses such factors as anticipated user needs, anticipated hardware support requirements, and projected DP manpower support levels.

At the second level of planning, the long-range DP plan addresses intermediate-term (2-3 years) goals. At this level, the plan should identify *prioritized* requirements and thus establish a general plan of phased development. At the data base implementation plan level, the intermediate-term tasks will be outlined in terms of major milestones/goals to be achieved within this time frame. Included in these milestones are the following:

- Initiation of the formal data base implementation plan
- Detailed statement of data base objectives
- Identification of the "pilot," or nucleus application
- Establishment of data base system requirements
- Evaluation and selection of the DBMS and related software, if appropriate (e.g., a teleprocessing system)
- Acquisition of the DBMS and related software, if appropriate.
- Implementation and testing of the "pilot," or nucleus application
- Final acceptance of the DBMS and related software, if appropriate
- Formalization of the ongoing system development procedure
- Formalization of DBA functions
- Cutover to a production data-base-supported environment

As the third, and final, step in the development of the long-range DP plan, the planning committee will focus on the near-term (1 year) aspects of the long-range plan. The near-term plan addresses manpower allocation, project budgeting, project initialization, and project control for the defined period. At the data base implementation plan level, the near-term plan will address the following:

- Identification of the plan coordinator (a person)
- Definition of the reporting relationships and controls between the plan coordinator and the DP planning committee or other designated cognizant party (e.g., the Director of Data Processing)
- Definition of the formal structure of the data base implementation group (e.g., a staff committee, a formal project within the systems analysis and design function)
- Identification of the major milestones to be achieved within the scope of the near-term plan

- Definition of the budget elements of the plan, including
  - —Personnel requirements
  - —Other resource requirements (e.g., machine time, outside consultants)
  - —Cost allocations

INITIATING THE DATA BASE IMPLEMENTATION PLAN

The major consideration that must be addressed prior to initiating the data base implementation plan is the formal structure, or "status" of the implementation group within the organization. This formal structure of the implementation group within the organization typically takes one of three forms, characterized as follows:

- A formal line project within the DP organization's systems analysis and design function (or its equivalent)
- A staff committee reporting directly to the Director of Data Processing (or his equivalent)
- A formal line organization function apart from and on a level with the systems analysis, programming, and operations functions (or their equivalents) within the DP organization

The approach having the least impact within the DP organization is the line project structure within the systems analysis and design function. As the DP organization is already oriented toward the project as a vehicle for major systems implementation, the organization can really accommodate a data base implementation plan as another major project with few, if any, modifications to the structure or system of standards and procedures.

There are, however, potential disadvantages in this approach. Recognizing that a move toward a data-base-supported environment implies, if not *requires,* a major restatement of DP standards and procedures as well as intra-DP organization communication, the DP officials responsible for establishing and monitoring the data base implementation group must ensure that:

- *All* DP organization functions are equally represented.
- The project team has specific authorization in designated tasks to control and/or dictate the roles of personnel from other parts of the DP organization.
- The project team has eventual control over the definition and placement of the DBA function (the project team itself may indeed evolve into the DBA function).

- The project has eventual control over the initial definition of data base standards and procedures affecting all DP organizational functions. (Final and formal establishment of data base standards and procedures will fall within the DBA function.)

The potential disadvantage, then, of a project structure in executing the data base implementation plan is lack of effective communication between the project team (residing within the systems analysis and design function) and other DP organization functions (programming and operations, for example). As the data base implementation process is one demanding full cooperation within the DP organization, either the project team must be chartered with full authority over all DP functions in tasks or areas pertinent to the data base implementation plan, or other alternatives that imply such authority must be examined.

The two most effective alternatives that should be examined are the establishment of a *staff* function, reporting directly to the Director of Data Processing, or the creation of an additional line function, parallel to all other major DP line functions, to execute the data base implementation plan. Both have the advantages of supporting more effective communication within the DP organization and of having more defined lines of authorization over DP functions in areas directly related to the data base implementation plan. Furthermore, both are conducive to an orderly evolution into a formal DBA function.

Of the two alternatives, the *staff function* is the recommended approach, as it more closely parallels the preferred DBA organizational structure described in the Data Base Administration portfolio series.

ORGANIZING AND STAFFING THE PLAN IMPLEMENTATION GROUP

The organizing and staffing of the data base implementation group are not dissimilar to those of any major DP project. The major aspects of establishing the plan implementation group are:

- Selection of the project leader
- Selection of the project team members
- Identification and division of major responsibilities
- Establishment of the project team administrative structure
- Definition of reporting relationships and control mechanisms between the project team and the DP organization

Of these five considerations, the first two—selection of the project team leader and members—are perhaps the most crucial. As discussed earlier, the plan implementation group, or a subset of it, ideally would evolve into a formal DBA function once the data-base-supported environment has been implemented. Taking this view, the project leader should be selected on the basis that he either will become the DBA or have a major role in his selection.

Similar considerations must be given to the selection of the group staff members. Although the implementation group is generally larger in size than the eventual DBA function (5-10 persons versus 3-6 persons), it is nevertheless desirable to select key project team members on the basis that they will evolve into the formal DBA function when the data-base-supported environment achieves a production status.

Another major consideration in staffing the project team is the organizational representation of team members. Because of the broad impact resulting from the move into a data-base-supported environment, team members must represent a cross section of not only the DP function (systems analysis, programming, and operations) but also the end-user environment. The end-user interests may be represented either on a direct team membership basis or on a consulting/review basis, but in any case they must be represented.

The third consideration in organizing and staffing the DB implementation project is the identification and division of major areas of responsibilities. This aspect of establishing the DB implementation plan differs from normal DP-oriented implementation plans only in its orientation. The first efforts of the DB implementation team will be task identification (the elements of which were discussed earlier). It is recommended that the project leader divide the team functions into four major categories in order to facilitate the organization of the implementation plan. These four areas, which can be viewed as the four critical paths in the plan, are:

1. The DBA function—includes definition of authorities and responsibilities, as well as development of data base standards and procedures.

2. The DBMS evaluation and selection function—includes user-service analysis, identification of DBMS requirements, and the evaluation and selection of a DBMS package.

3. The Telecommunications Processor (TP) evaluation and selection—includes user-service analysis, identification of TP requirements, and the evaluation and selection of a TP package.

4. The Data Dictionary/Directory System selection or development function—includes identification of DD/DS requirements and the evaluation and selection (or design specifications) of a DD/DS facility.

Establishment of the project team administrative structure is the fourth step in setting the implementation plan into motion. Attention must be given to intrateam coordination and communications; reporting relationships, project control, and feedback mechanisms; and interfaces with the various functional areas within the DP and end-user organizations. These functions differ little from those of any major project; however, emphasis must be placed on *effective* structure and *thorough* planning because of the impact a data-base-supported environment will have on the entire organization.

The fifth, and final, step in establishing the data base implementation group is the definition of reporting relationships and control mechanisms between the project team and the DP organization. These relationships will be dependent upon the formal structure of the plan implementation group and, again, will be similar to the mechanisms appropriate for similar structures within the DP organization. The one critical consideration in formalizing the reporting relationships with the implementation is that of high-level review, especially in the event that the data implementation group is structured as a major project team within the systems analysis and design functions of the DP organization. Regardless of the group structure, it is recommended that the Director of Data Processing participate directly not only in establishing the initial framework of the plan but also in the reviews scheduled at major milestones during the execution of the implementation plan. The Director of Data Processing must monitor the implementation plan closely and devote extensive time to it in order to ensure its success.

SUMMARY

The success or failure of a data base implementation depends upon thorough and effective planning. An organization considering a move toward a data-base-supported environment must first become educated in the concepts of data base, conduct a preliminary feasibility study to ascertain the appropriateness and impact of a data base approach, and, if the decision is made to develop a data-base-supported environment, obtain a full management and user commitment to support the concept. Once these initial and mandatory steps are achieved, the data base implementation plan must be structured and executed. The following steps are recommended in establishing this plan and setting it into action:

1. Firmly commit resources to establish a long-range data base implementation plan.

2. Identify the major elements of the data base environment perceived to be appropriate for your organization.

3. Establish long-range and short-range objectives for your data-base-supported environment and integrate these into the overall data processing plan.

4. Define the data base implementation plan team structure and staff the team. Recognize that the team will ideally evolve into a formal DBA function and organize and staff it accordingly.

5. Identify the critical paths in the implementation and organize the team around these areas.

6. Set the plan into motion and monitor it at the highest level within the DP organization.

7. Never hesitate to admit that the data base concept and/or the approach being taken to implement such a concept is inappropriate for your organization—drop back and reconsider any major concerns before they become real problems.

chapter **2**

Management Issues in the Data Base Plan

INTRODUCTION

Managing data is a major challenge for today's manager. A rapidly changing environment and advancing technology have created an increased complexity of data interrelationships for the decision maker. These changes require the manager to employ (1) more quantitative techniques for preliminary analyses and (2) an organized approach for the handling, storage, and use of data (as a corporate resource). Data responsibilities traditionally have been line functions in which each manager took care of his own needs. Just as today's managers in large organizations no longer perform all facets of the work required for payroll, personnel, etc., tomorrow's managers will have many of their data needs serviced by a central unit. Due to its size, this unit will be in a better position to use the new computer technology. On the other hand, it will also require operating standards and procedures giving the outside image of bureaucracy. The establishment of this future organization is dependent on one important step—the creation of a data base environment. Having a well-planned strategy for the creation and implementation of the new data base environment forms the framework for a data base plan.

The Written DB Plan

Frequently the word "plan" is associated with a written document. Although this document serves as an important adjunct to the data base effort, it is more than just a schedule of events. It is a commitment to a course of action, and as such, the plan should represent the understanding of management. The management issues are associated more with the commitment than with the schedule of events. The written document usually discusses tasks involved in building data bases, writing standards, training personnel, acquiring software, developing applications, projecting costs, etc. Since the document focuses on the mechanics of data base work, such as the building of data bases, most people consider it the data base plan. The data base plan must, however, extend beyond these tasks. It must incorporate the organizational goals and needs with the development and integration of systems, data, and people.

The plan in its written and implied form becomes a statement of management's commitment to a new data base environment. Clearly, the entire management team must agree not only on "what to do" but "how to do it." The "how to" issues are imbued throughout both written and implied portions of the data base plan. The "how to" is the least discussed and least understood and yet the most pervasive component of a data base plan. The management issues in the written portion are concerned with topics such as economic justification and the establishment of ownership or custodianship of data. These issues are usually task- or decision-oriented and do not involve style or methods of execution. Frequently, technicians will develop a good direct plan discussing "what to do" and "when to do it." The plan must be augmented by the line manager to include "how to do it." This requires an unusual mix of top management perspective, technical skill, and knowledge of corporate operations. Management must understand how the individual implementing the plan will exercise his power, how he will resolve conflicts, how his leadership style will affect others, how the effectiveness of the plan will be measured, how control of the data will be achieved, and how commitment to the plan will be gained.

The Human Element

The thrust of this chapter is to provide managers with an understanding of the issues involved in the data base plan. These issues center around the effect the data base program has on people.

Significant to the manager are how to implement such a program, the impact of data base methodology on the various levels of management, the importance of giving data a corporate resource status, handling the change in working relationships for systems developers, the need for a development program for data base personnel, understanding the type of costs incurred in the program, and developing realistic expectations. These issues are addressed here.

HOW DATA BASE METHODOLOGY AFFECTS ORGANIZATIONAL BEHAVIOR

Managers view organizations from many different perspectives. While some managers are concerned with the orderly assignment of tasks, others dwell on human behavior. Still others have studied the flow of data through the formal and informal organization. They have concluded that individuals with knowledge of, or in control of, the information flow exert a great influence on organizational behavior. Since the data base approach can have drastic effects on the flow of information, it is not surprising to find resistance to such an effort by the line managers. If, for processing purposes, the data belong to a different community of users, the manager becomes dependent on another organization for a basic tool used in decision making. Further, a data base structure tends to subordinate individual interests to total efficiency.

The data base plan identifies three types of data bases:

- Two or three central data bases that contain much of the organization's data and are commonly used
- Several functional data bases that each contain data shared by a more limited set of programs
- A small amount of the organization's data that remains in dedicated data bases, each used by only a single application

The organization of data before and after implementation of the data base plan is shown in Figure 2-1.

Data Centralization

This centralization of data has a major effect upon the data processing organization. Individuals no longer "own" data; much redundant data is eliminated; and collection, updating and maintenance are centralized under the control of the Data Base Administrator (DBA). The central data bases are designed to serve

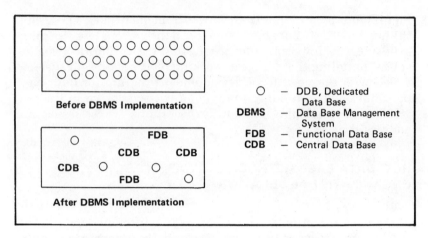

Figure 2-1. Management Issues in the Data Base Plan:
Effect of DBMS on Data Organization

all users in the organization. An occurrence of a data element which is used by many applications must be collected in time for the earliest use and maintained in the data base until the last application no longer needs it. With improved knowledge of data element usage, data flows can be changed and some eliminated. Individuals throughout the corporation who previously collected and maintained data for dedicated data bases find their work changed. The focus is now on the procedural logic of the application and on the selection of data from the central data bases to be used in the application. Expertise in the knowledge concerning data gradually shifts to the DBA, who maintains comprehensive documentation.

Opposition. Resistance to the implementation of the data base plan can be significant. People fear change. Individuals and groups see control over data functions being shifted. Confusion may arise among the roles of systems planning, systems programming, operations, applications, and data base administration. Many dislike the loss of control over the data. Many more resist attempts at scheduling the running of their programs and having the creative work of design and programming subjected to standards and procedures.

Others within the organization see the changes as an opportunity. Some wish to learn data base methodology to enhance their value in the marketplace. Some see the growing DBA function as an opportunity to garner individual power.

Management must critically observe the behavior of individuals in the organization and take positive steps to allay unfounded fears and discourage opportunism. The best approach is a thorough plan that satisfies the needs of all affected groups and is communicated via strong leadership.

Effects on Management

A data base plan affects all management levels. Top-management-level policies and strategic plans must be instituted to provide a new direction in the development of management systems. The shift to data base technology has not resulted in a change to the organizational structure at the top management level, although the methods and amount of top management involvement have been altered considerably. An exception to this situation has occurred in service corporations, where the service being provided is information. The management of data as a resource has become a line function to the chief executive officer of many information service companies. In these companies sooner and in others later, it is predictable that a corporate level (top management) executive will emerge with specific data responsibilities under such titles as Data Administrator, Director of Data Integrity/System Integration, Data Resource Manager, and the like. At the middle management level, firms are already creating positions, such as the Data Base Administrator, that develop data base programs and coordinate the data base activities. The occurrence of such positions is linked to the use of a DBMS, and, as a result, the leadership may suffer from an excessive software orientation and a lack of data resource understanding. At the operating management level, the most pronounced effects are seen in the organizational structure. Once clearly defined lines of authority and responsibility are now vague because of the splitting of work between the user, applications, DBA, and systems programming. The user can no longer dictate the development of his entire application because the data portions are part of a community data base. Figure 2-2 illustrates the change in responsibilities throughout the management structure.

Organizational Procedures

In order to effect a data base program, top management must commit itself to changing some of the basic processes of an organization. An overall program must be developed to ensure the data integrity for decision making. The decision to use data base methodology is a commitment to large changes at the operating

		Management Level	Type of Responsibility	Major Changes
Information System	Data Base Methodology	Top Management	Data Policies Strategic Planning	New Policies
		Middle Management	Data Program Development Data Coordination	Program Development Heavy Coordination
		Operating Management	Data Base Procedures, Protocols, Standards	New Procedures and Standards New Working Relationships

Figure 2-2. Organizational Responsibilities within the Data Base Environment

levels. The method of changing to a data base environment must be effective without intruding on the prerogatives of the other managers. Many operating mechanisms such as task forces, committees, joint efforts, staff assignments, and reorganizations have been devised to facilitate this change. Frequently, these techniques are used to bring together groups whose individual interests must be sacrificed for the sake of the whole. This type of "consensus-driven" management can result in inefficiencies, delays, and inferior decisions if the individuals are not committed to the process. However, the communications and motivational advantages of these management techniques, although difficult to quantify, should not be disregarded.

Technicians will often advocate a top-down approach to the creation of change. This management style may meet with passive resistance such as difficulty in scheduling meetings, doing only what is requested, etc. The principal problem for the corporate-level executive is "how to" implement the data base program for the entire management structure. A reasonable assumption is that the management group agrees in principle with the data base approach. Given that assumption, how do you reach a commitment level? It is easy to answer with cliches such as a situational, contingency, or systems approach. When you analyze these techniques you must find the style that works. There is no doubt that the individual makes it work!

Managerial Qualifications. The person leading the corporate data program must have a style compatible with senior management, must be able to plan and implement a method of gaining control over the data, and must have technical expertise to evaluate software and hardware considerations. This individual must provide strong and responsive leadership to his group so that communications at the operating level are consistent with senior management thinking. He must be able to exert influence without resorting to the use of top-management power. He must be assertive and yet be able to recognize the need for higher management involvement to resolve working issues.

Knowing "how to" is not learned from textbooks or case studies but rather through experience and common sense. Since changing the flow of data can be destructive to some of the existing relationships, the individual in the data base area must be politically wise. Frequently an outsider may fail, even though he is technically correct, because he or she failed to understand the chain of influence.

Strategy

The "how to" part of the data base plan can be developed using different strategies. For the sake of discussion, two of the strategies will be called "inductive" and "deductive."

Deductive Approach. The deductive approach involves much front-end selling before the program is actually started. Characteristics of this approach are presentations to executives, sending key personnel to training sessions, and using outside consultants. This type of data base strategy can be effective where centralized decision making exists. Implicit in this approach is strong leadership. Usually the decision to go to data bases is followed by some organizational changes such as setting up a DBA function. This deductive or top-down method requires a well-structured written plan for the line managers to use. In addition, the plan plays a major role as a communications device. An important preliminary step is the establishment of standards, procedures, and protocols. Consultants may be used to form a communications bridge between the various groups. Heavy top-management participation is a must for the deductive approach to succeed. All management levels should be aware of the following caveats:

1. Resistance is usually passive, resulting in a slowdown, not a stoppage
2. Progress is difficult to measure and monitor

3. A tendency exists to tackle problems that take a long time to correct

Inductive Approach. Creating a data base environment may require an inductive approach to the "how to" portion of the plan. The inductive approach is suggested when any one of the following conditions exists:

1. When decentralized decision making exists
2. When it is difficult to measure the relative effectiveness of the program, such as may occur in nonprofit, educational, or government operations
3. When the data are inherent in the user's work, such as in engineering and research

Since data base operations can result in a less efficient performance than a customized system for a given user, the top-down or deductive approach may be very difficult to market. Yet from a top-management perspective, the environment must be changed to ensure long-run efficiency and permit a modicum of systems integration. Knowing change must be brought about, management must find the proper "how to" in order to implement the data base environment.

The inductive approach is not discussed extensively in the data base literature, yet it is a way of introducing data base technology without creating large management issues. It is, by definition, a planned incremental program that defines a path to create a data base environment. Certain prerequisites must be satisfied before this approach can be used:

1. The user must accept the need to correct an existing data problem even though he may not be willing to underwrite the costs
2. The data items must be interrelated
3. The systems or data must be changing either for new development or maintenance

The inductive approach places most of the value of data base methods on the input side rather than on the retrievals. By use of generalized edits and data base techniques, the input processing could be made more efficient.

The DBA Function. Whether the inductive or deductive approach is used, there will be organizational changes at the mid and operating levels. The appearance of a DBA function is a natural outgrowth of a data base effort. Since the thrust of the data

base effort usually originates in data processing, the organizational impact of the data base program is largest in the data
processing area, specifically for the applications personnel. The
DBA function usually is placed on a par with the applications
developer, either as a staff position to the director or within the
systems programming group. The DBA function has a significant
impact on the behavior of the group because new working relationships must be established. Top management must be aware of
these new interfaces and be careful to prevent the development of
some hard-core resistance between the groups. Later, we will
discuss some ways of minimizing the possibilities of conflict.

DATA: AN IMPORTANT CORPORATE RESOURCE

Giving data the status of a corporate resource is important to the
successful implementation of a data base plan. In the past, data
has been considered inextricably a part of an applications system
and totally within the domain of individual line managers. Due
to these attitudes and rapidly expanding systems, technicians
have not been able to fully integrate systems and provide data
integrity. Inferior data, in turn, can be traced to the root of some
dangerous situations, e.g., a liquidity crisis occurring when procurement commitments exceed current cash inflow. Even more
significant is the status of data in a firm completely dependent on
data for business, e.g., a stock brokerage house. By providing
executive accountability and a separate corporate status for data,
the processing of data should improve in timeliness and quality.
The expectation of better decisions is reasonable. The need for an
accounting system for data is evident to indicate the value of the
asset and the associated costs. Further, procedures and standards
are essential for uniformity in company-wide use. The creation of
a data base can change many existing methods for the users and
systems developers. Management must be aware of the change
and create an environment that minimizes the trauma.

MAJOR CHANGES IN THE SYSTEM DEVELOPMENT
PROCESS—A MANAGEMENT CHALLENGE

The responsibilities of the applications analyst change when
data base methodology is employed in an organization. This
change is like the one that occurred with the development of operating system software and the advent of systems programmers.
The applications analyst "lost control" of his environment to

higher level language compilers, operating system data access methods, sort utilities, and the like. He had to depend upon another individual, the systems programmer, for assistance when he encountered problems with the software.

With a data base management system, the analyst must depend on a group for data base design and documentation as well as for protection and operation of the data base. The DBA staff must be involved during design and implementation of the application, helping to specify the correct data elements and to design efficient storage and input/output. For the applications analyst, this means that project schedules and product performance are affected by people outside of the organization.

Management Alternatives

For an organization that has not already done so for other reasons, the introduction of data base methodology can cause the need for management techniques to extend across existing organizational lines. Due to the interdependency of the software configuration, applications programs, and data base design, management has the choice of changing the organizational design or placing a heavy emphasis on improving the interpersonal competence of the individuals. Introducing a new organizational structure, such as matrix management, requires a major modification of the individual contributor's style. Strong leadership is required that may be lacking when a behavioral approach is taken. The importance of the project identity should be emphasized. The applications analyst's role as the major link to the user should be preserved. Teams under an applications manager should be formed for the duration of the project. A member from the data base area can be assigned full- or part-time. This individual must resolve the conflict between specific user demands and total configuration requirements.

Keys to Success

The keys to success in operating in this temporary organizational structure are

1. Having individuals committed to the data base method
2. Strong leadership
3. A give-and-take attitude among the team members
4. The ability to thrash out disagreements without lingering effects

Conflicts cannot be eliminated without these prerequisites. If management detects the absence of any of these qualities, it must take *direct* steps to instill them. In the past when top management in the aerospace industry saw a need for such conflict resolution capabilities, it saw fit to train the entire group. Although extensive training such as that in "T" groups is not advocated, management must remain acutely aware of the working relationships. Thus problems of organizational design are very complex, with one side wanting the behavioral advantages of a loose structure and the other side desiring clear, responsive direction concerning the many issues involved. Since the issues can be complex, a clear mandate on the length of time an issue may be discussed could serve to expedite conflict resolution.

In instituting this team approach, management should make it clear that the project leader is the technical supervisor of all people on the project and that the project leader is the one ultimately responsible for the success or failure of the project.

User Adaptation

The impact of data base methodology reaches beyond the data processing department of an organization. Users of data processing services must adapt to the changing environment, too. Successful implementation requires the understanding and cooperation of users. An advisory group of users can provide an organization-wide perspective on the implications of particular data base plans and recommend modifications to improve the end result. The give-and-take in a user group can also improve communications and dispel myths that arise in the organization about the DBA or the DBMS.

STANDARDS AND PROCEDURES: A MUST

Some organizations have a broad and well-enforced set of standards and procedures. Other organizations have few. For the latter organizations, the introduction or conversion to a data base environment is much more difficult. To achieve an integrated data base environment, extensive sharing of knowledge using standards and procedures is essential.

While the ultimate set of standards and procedures must be tailored for the needs of one organization, an initial step in the development can be to investigate existing standards of comparable firms or the industry as a whole. Many organizations are willing to share copies of their internal standards manual. Computer user groups, such as Guide and Cube, are good discussion forums for others with similar interests and problems.

Establishing standards and procedures must proceed in the following steps:

1. Determine the standards and procedures required
2. Establish a method with the user to specify the standards and procedures
3. Determine the order of work and move ahead
4. Develop and implement a mechanism to enforce the standards and procedures

Requirements. The objective in step 1 may be reached by a staff of technicians. An exhaustive list should be developed indicating the relationship of standards and procedures to the operation of software, applications development, user terminology, etc. It must be remembered that these changes can affect many basic work habits. Standards and procedures should *not* be introduced for the sake of standardization but must have recognizable value.

User Participation. The method of determining the standards, step 2, may be very easy or exceedingly difficult. In the case in which computer-knowledgeable users exist, it may be necessary to establish a cooperative group to review and approve standards. In other cases, the standards may be developed and published from within the data processing organization. The progress in developing standards can be used as a key indicator of the commitment of the managers to the data base environment.

Order and Implementation. Determining the order and implementing the standards, step 3, can be the most difficult step. One approach is to start with an area in which the lack of a standard or a consistent procedure has clearly caused problems. Another approach is to introduce a standard or procedure as an integral part of a new software capability (e.g., all users of source code librarian software must adhere to program-naming conventions). Caution must be exercised to ensure that the standards and procedures do not conflict with one another. Similarly, it is important that the standards be practical and do not unduly impede system development. Thus, staff with experience in systems development should design and implement the standards.

Enforcement. Keeping track of all the interdependent components in a data base environment is aided by standards and procedures, but the volume of clerical effort involved in enforcement can be staggering. The most effective approach to standards enforcement, step 4, is to make them an integral part of the normal work and to capture needed control information by software whenever possible.

Failure to enforce standards and procedures can result in anything from inconvenience or inefficiency to a system breakdown. In fact, a good test of the need for a particular standard is to ask what would happen without it. Enforcement can take two forms: monitoring and benign neglect. In the former case regular audits or a reporting system are in effect. In the latter case, discrepancies are identified and corrected when failure causes a breakdown. When the standards are well-conceived and the need for them understood by the organization, the monitoring approach is usually successful.

Many firms have used consultants for the development of standards and procedures. The consultant, having more objectivity, may be able to achieve results when other methods require an inordinate amount of coordinating.

PERSONNEL: THE KEY TO SUCCESS

A major concern for management is to recruit and retain personnel with the wide range of skills required for data base work. Even at the technical level, the staff must have a profile of skills that includes technical competence (even to the micro instruction level); interpersonal competence in dealing with fearful users, applications personnel, top management, and software programmers; top-management perspective for planning and corporate strategy; and good common sense. For one person to have all of these characteristics is practically impossible, so therefore a team must be built providing all of these components. Putting together such a team may involve taking personnel from existing organizations—once again a possible transgression into other corporate territories. Yet this action of giving up key personnel for a new and important corporate program is a good indication of commitment and provides other managers the opportunity to influence the direction of the program.

Since most of the skills required for the applications and data base personnel are the same, a complete list of attributes will not be provided. The main change in skill requirements from the pre-data base era is the ability to participate in and coordinate the solution of technical issues and development of managerial plans. The drive to have a territorial understanding of work assignments becomes difficult to overcome, and yet there is a definite need to differentiate between the applications and data base work. The major caveat for the applications programmer is to avoid over-involvement in software internal tasks such as the physical design of data bases. The project managers must constantly watch the balance between applications and data base work.

Personnel Availability

Hiring personnel with technical data base skills, especially those with specific DBMS knowledge, has been a major problem. With the growth of the data base software and the shift of former systems programmers into the area, the recruiting problem is not as acute as it once was. But hiring top managers remains difficult, especially managers with specific skills. The recommended source of managers has been individuals in line positions. This source offers the advantages of managerial creditability, knowledge of corporate operations, and good top-management perspective. On the other hand, line managers lack technical knowledge and must depend on their technical support for advice. Their bottom-up judgment may suffer from a poor overall perspective.

Hiring and maintaining data base technicians can be costly. Just as programmers could write their own tickets in the 1960s, the data base internals man enjoys a maximum of job mobility. This job mobility, coupled with the high cost of training data base personnel, makes hiring individuals from outside very risky. At this stage it is wise to train and develop internal personnel, thus instilling greater company loyalty. Once again, this type of thinking is only achieved if the program is viewed in the long term. Provided the corporate structure can support it, the training program for applications, user, and data base personnel needs to be defined as soon as possible. In-house and group training should be emphasized, as outside individual training is expensive. Communicating a well-defined career path for the individuals is a must.

UNDERSTANDING THE COST IMPLICATIONS

The cost structure of a data base program can be considerably different from other data processing costs. The payoff period from the data base program is longer than experienced from increasing the hardware configuration or adding programmers. Since data processing has grown so rapidly, the managers are accustomed to change, but the change has been, in the past, in direct response to a strong user demand. This is *not* the case in the data base environment. The manager must have a full appreciation of the cost behavior of the data base program and make a concerted effort to control costs. We will not discuss cost effectiveness and justification here.

Out-of-Pocket Costs. Since the out-of-pocket costs have an immediate impact on the operating budgets, the high cost of the data base effort is of great concern to the line manager. The high cost not only includes the price of software, hardware, and programmers but extends to the labor costs of developing standards and procedures and coordinating numerous requirements. In terms of out-of-pocket costs, managers must be careful to avoid spending monies too fast, too early. For example, a productivity aid or a data base software package may be acquired (or rented) before the data processing systems are ready. This early implementation would result in low utilization or even nonuse. The error of bringing in data base software before standards and procedures are established or before the data are of usable quality may occur in firms with aggressive and modern management teams. Firms, in their desire to have the latest technology, may also install a query language before enough data are in the data base to realize efficiencies. These types of mistakes only reinforce the need for phased implementation.

Misuse of DB Software. Another type of cost that firms may incur is that resulting from the misuse of the data base software. In order to compromise between going to a full-fledged data base and maintaining the user's custom system, nonstandard use of data base software may result. A situation results in which semi-integrated files are processed using data base software. This becomes a very costly compromise when expensive maintenance problems, poor system integration, and inefficient use of software result.

Hidden Costs. Managers making the commitment to data base technology must realize that many hidden costs exist. Since the data base can change the basic way systems work, many costs are not readily discernible until the actual change is made. Although managers cannot be relieved of responsibility for thoroughness, the following costs are not obvious:

1. Relationship between software and hardware when additional data base functions are added, since new software may mean more core or equipment
2. Software changes requiring unanticipated hardware upgrades to maintain or realize performance improvements
3. The users' need to commit large blocks of time to integrate previously independent systems (the delays could be very costly)
4. The cost of running parallel systems, especially for disc and labor
5. Having to keep up with the latest software releases to get benefits of enhancements or even maintenance support
6. The need for continuous specialized training to realize the benefits of the number of new capabilities or versions released
7. The need for more specific documentation and procedures to operate efficiently
8. An initial increase in applications design time due to the requirement for more coordination and the learning curve

Management Alternatives. The cost of alternative choices is an important concept for the data base manager. Even though building a data base environment is costly, the overall costs of not doing it could be greater due to loss of profits and sales, and poor decisions. Obviously, firms with fragile short-run positions may not be concerned with "opportunity costs" but must concentrate on "out-of-pocket" costs. Redundant data, poor data integrity, and inefficiencies can be tolerated only for short intervals. The managers looking to the future must ask: Can we afford to be in an inferior competitive posture relative to data for decisions? What is the cost of duplicative data systems? Can we continue to add more data without planned integration? Can poor data storage and retrieval lead to even more costly total computer configuration costs? Can we afford to have data coming from different locations support the same decision and not agree?

The "Data Resource Accounting System." Giving data the status of a corporate resource and being aware of the multitude of costs require management to take a new perspective on data. The existing management control and accounting systems do not provide a good mechanism for management to be aware of its data costs. The need for a "data resource accounting system" is evident. Most firms treat the cost of creating data or a data base as an expense and do not attempt to give the product an asset value. To many firms, data is a more important asset than the physical plant, and yet it does not show on the books of account. Data, as a resource and asset, has many attributes that should be captured in the accounting practice for tax purposes and should be used to reflect the true market value of the firm. For example, a firm with a good market data base would be in a better competitive position than a company without one, all other things being equal. Therefore, the former company is also a better investment. Management must find a method of placing an asset value on a data base, including a way to show the reduction in value as the data ages. Further, the "data resource accounting system" would improve managerial accountability for data and provide a better basis for performing cost/benefit analyses.

If you know your cost structure, you must estimate the return from your investment. Since the data base program is long-run, developing realistic expectations is difficult.

DEVELOPING REALISTIC EXPECTATIONS

From the top-management view, the data base program is a must to maintain a long-term competitive posture. Even with that attitude, a firm may be faced with immediate budget restraints preventing an all-out effort. Then the questions are: How much should we expend? How soon can we expect the benefits? For firms heavily dependent on their data for their basic business, e.g., a bank or an insurance company, the urgency of creating a data base environment may take on crisis proportions. The level of your firm's commitment could be greatly dependent on the actions of your competitors. Although it might be possible to develop one, we do not have a handy formula for you to use to determine the level of financial commitment needed.

Due to the nature of this program, the payoff will not start until a certain critical mass is attained. This critical mass can be identified by the amount of key data in the data base, the existence of a modicum of standards and procedures, the occurrence of several applications systems operating against the data base and supporting important decision processes, and a level of data quality. You must define the critical mass in those terms as one of your first steps. Then a phased schedule of events must be established. Measuring against this timetable can be a way to evaluate the reasonableness of the results that you are getting. Unfortunately, the schedule may never be met, while more money and time are expended each year. Top management must be able to detect when a situation like this one is occurring.

Signs of Trouble. Since information is filtered going up, it could be very late before managerial actions are taken. Top management frequently attempts to watch the situation by personally reviewing with key personnel. Given an astute top-management team, this is probably the best approach. Two signs that indicate a slowed rate of progress are

1. The need for a multitude of meetings when a decision is apparent to an outsider
2. The lack of dynamic planning under which adjustments can readily be made.

Item 1 usually indicates a lack of commitment by the mid-level managers, resulting in a constant effort to compromise or to keep everyone happy. Item 2 can be indicative of a very serious situation. Since a new data base program is constantly running into unanticipated situations, the lack of changes can mean no planning or that the technicians are making ad hoc adjustments without looking at the whole program. Management must create the environment in which the entire data base plan (as previously defined) is reviewed and changed regularly.

SUMMARY

The key part of a data base plan is the "how to" portion that management understands and has made a commitment to. The "people" part of the plan has been the major obstacle to the successful implementation of data base programs. The technology exists but has not been exploited. The program leadership requires the style, perspective, and values of top management while still having a full appreciation of sophisticated technical problems. Most data base plans and programs have been originated by data processing technicians and suffer the deficiencies of bottom-up management thinking. Once again the appeal for top-management awareness and participation is made.

Many new concepts are being introduced by the data base program. Data is a corporate resource and must be given that status. A top-level executive must be selected to develop and control that resource. An accounting system must be implemented to provide a means of placing a value on data, to offer a better mechanism to do cost/benefit analyses, and to establish the executive accountability for data. Thought on data program costs must be oriented to the future and to possible penalties incurred for *not* taking the correct alternative. Even beyond appointing a corporate executive to the data program, an organization must be established with specific data and data base responsibilities. Forming the organization out of existing structures can be beneficial, as it is definitely a sign of commitment. Although some advocate the setting up of an organization outside of data processing, the DBA has typically been formed within the data processing function reporting to the director. Some larger corporations have elevated the data management information system and corporate planning responsibilities to the top-management group with the DBA remaining in data processing. This concept has become popular, as it gives top management visibility and provides an excellent vehicle for corporate integration.

The data base program provides a challenge for the manager and technician. A new career path to top management is emerging; individuals in software programming, applications development, corporate operations (business-knowledgeable), and planning can compete equally. These programs must succeed if the firm is to maintain its competitive status.

chapter 3

System Development Life Cycle for Data Base Development

INTRODUCTION

The data base approach in supporting the information processing requirements of an organization has a dramatic impact on both the user and the data processing environment. Successful *implementation* of a data-base-supported environment requires a thorough, well-managed plan. Successful *operation* of a data-base-supported environment depends on a sound system development structure. Many aspects of the traditional system development cycle will not be affected. However, there are crucial areas that must be modified as an organization moves from implementation of a data-base-supported environment into production mode of that environment.

SYSTEM PLANNING

An essential element of any effective data processing organization is an established system planning framework. Without an adequate system planning function, a data processing organization cannot achieve any significant degree of responsiveness to the needs of its end users; for without effective planning, one cannot expect effective implementation.

The system planning framework will vary from organization to organization; however, three essential elements will always be present in a responsive, well-managed system planning function. These elements, or cycles are:

- A long-range system planning cycle
- A system prioritizing cycle
- A system development cycle

The Long-Range System Planning Cycle

The long-range system planning cycle addresses the general information processing requirements of an organization over a five- to seven-year period. Emphasis in this phase of system planning is on *functional* needs, rather than specific, isolated system requirements. For example, a bank may identify a long-range requirement for a customer information and service system but not identify the specific components of the system (e.g., an on-line demand deposit system, an on-line customer inquiry system, or an integrated monthly statement system). In addition, no attempt is made to establish priorities, other than those implied by inter-system dependencies (e.g., implementation of an automated inventory control system would generally precede development of an on-line order entry system). More detailed statements of system components and assignments of system priorities are addressed in the system prioritizing cycle.

The System Prioritizing Cycle

The major objectives of the system prioritizing cycle are the refinement of system requirements and the assignment of system implementation priorities. During this phase of the system planning cycle, general statements of information processing requirements are reduced to specific system requirements. The end users are consulted to determine detailed service needs and desired time frames. With these service specifications and time frame requirements, the planning group can weigh requirements against resources and establish a moderate term (generally two to three years) implementation plan taking into consideration user priorities, system resources, and staff availability.

The System Development Cycle

Formal assignments of staff, hardware resources, and budgets to specific systems, according to priorities established during the system prioritizing cycle, is the initial task of the system development cycle. The system development cycle typically corresponds to one fiscal or budget cycle (generally one year). Specific system projects are identified, staffed, and initiated during this cycle. The cycle may be further segmented into smaller periods (e.g., quarters) for budget and review purposes.

Although a given system development project initiated during one system development effort may extend into a subsequent cycle, the completion of a system development cycle initiates a reiteration of all *three* cycles. Thus, the system development cycle functions as a review point. Project overruns, changing priorities, and evolving user needs are therefore fully accounted for on a periodic basis, forming the basis for an effective system planning and development environment.

Many organizations today practice sound planning and development methods. Use of these techniques will become mandatory as an organization embarks on a data base system implementation plan and eventually shifts to a production mode data base environment.

SYSTEM DEVELOPMENT LIFE CYCLE (SDLC)

Within the overall system planning framework, user needs are identified, refined to a general statement of requirements, prioritized, refined to more detailed levels of specification, scheduled for implementation, and eventually initiated as system development projects.

Among the three elements or cycles of the system planning framework, it is within the system development project life cycle that a data base approach will have the greatest impact. To contrast the differences between system development in traditional data processing environments and data-base-supported environments, the major elements of a system development cycle must be identified. As with system planning in general, system development procedures vary from organization to organization, but the key elements of a system development methodology can almost always be identified within any specific approach. These key elements are as follows:

- Definition of system requirements

- Generation of detailed system specifications
- Coding of system elements
- Integration and testing of system elements
- Acceptance of the system
- Documentation of the system
- Training of system user and support personnel
- Cutover of system to production environment

These elements, or tasks, generally progress in the sequence presented above, though some may overlap (e.g., system documentation efforts could well commence during final testing of the system).

This "model" of a system development project is applicable, at the level shown, for both conventional and data-base-supported environments. When these major tasks are further refined, however, significant differences arise. To appreciate the full impact of a data base approach, we first consider the project life cycle in a conventional (non-data-base-supported) environment.

System Development in a Non-Data-Base-Supported Environment

At the outset of a conventional system development project, responsibility for the entire system implementation typically lies within the project itself. Exceptions may include final system documentation (performed by technical writers) or user/support personnel training (performed by a training staff), however, cognizant authority may still rest with the project team. Figure 3-1 represents a typical system development project life cycle in a conventional data processing environment. The eight major elements of a system development project are identified with an asterisk. Key subtasks within the major project elements are represented in Figure 3-1 as subsequent or following events.

The one major characteristic of the conventional system development project that will be impacted the most by a transition to a data-base-supported environment is its "self-contained" approach to system implementation. All tasks identified in Figure 3-1 remain entirely within the bounds of the project team (typically structured within the system analysis and programming function of a data processing organization). In an environment where several projects may be in progress concurrently, this characteristic may, and generally does, create several problems.

These problems have given rise to key justifications for a data-base-supported information systems environment. The

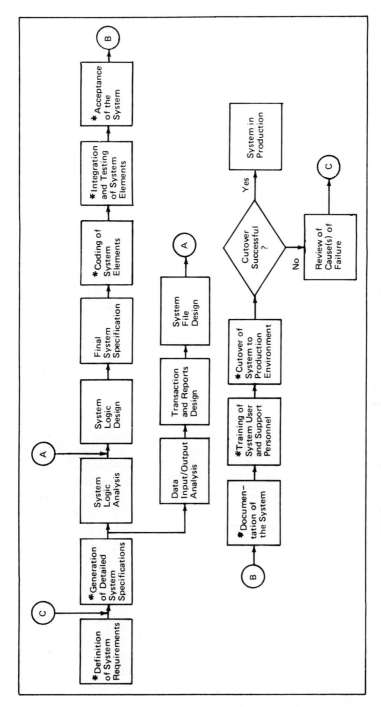

Figure 3-1. System Development Life Cycle in a Non-Data-Base Environment

57

primary justification for developing a DB environment has been presented in an earlier chapter. These justifications, or areas of potential benefit, are as follows:

- An information system structure that "models" the natural flow of information and its use in an organization's environment
- An information system environment that provides many economic benefits from more effective utilization of people and hardware resources
- An information system that is more responsive to the requirements of the end user

To realize these benefits, certain fundamental concepts in the data processing environment must change. Key among these concepts is the method of handling data. In the conventional approach to system development, data is identified, defined, and structured within the confines of the system development project. In an organization that, over time, develops many systems, the result will be a heavily fragmented information system environment characterized by a high degree of data and software redundancy and a correspondingly high degree of data inconsistency and inaccuracy.

Although a certain level of data and software redundancy is known and necessary due to the lack of data independence in conventional data storage and access methodologies, much is the result of a fragmented, uncoordinated approach to systems development.

In adopting a data base philosophy, an organization must recognize data as a *corporate resource* and establish a framework of standards and procedures for the definition, collection, storage, maintenance, and dissemination of data in a manner consistent with the requirements of the end user. In applying these standards and procedures, major changes in the systems development process will be required.

System Development in a Data-Base-Supported Environment

The major procedural change in the system development process as an organization moves to a data-base-supported environment is the separation of the data definition and data file (or data base) design function from the application design function. The system development project team will, however, continue to be responsible for analysis of user requirements, system specification, coding, testing, and implementation. Included in the project team's responsibilities is the identification of *data requirements*. In a conventional system development project, the project team would proceed with a transaction, reports, and file design process specific to the system under development. However, in a data-base-supported environment, the project team will submit a *request for data* to a central data base design group, a group reporting directly to, or contained within, the data base administration function.

The separation of the actual data base design function from the system development project is necessary to ensure that the standards and procedures for data definition, collection, storage, maintenance, and dissemination are observed. Concerns of the data base design group include:

- Minimization of unnecessary or "blind" data redundancy and inconsistency
- Minimization of processing redundancies and inconsistencies
- Minimization of data collection redundancies and inconsistencies

The specific responsibilities of the data base design function include:

- Analysis of data requests to determine key identifying characteristics
- Search of the Data Dictionary to determine whether the requested data already exists in the data base
- Determination of standard definition, naming, storage, maintenance, and dissemination procedures (if the requested data does not presently exist in the data base)
- Construction of a data base description (schema) enumerating the data and its relationships, storage structure, and access method, and a determination of data capture/conversion procedures and device residency characteristics
- Construction of subsets of the data description (subschemas) to be referenced by the system development project team in accessing the data

The project team and the data base design group will maintain a close dialogue throughout the data base design process to ensure complete understanding and agreement as to data characteristics. It is the responsibility of the project team to communicate data format requirements, editing and validation rules, and processing/response characteristics to the data base design team. The data base administrator establishes the procedures necessary to ensure that this communication takes place and to monitor the communication process.

Communication and Supporting Documentation

Effective communication between the data base design team and the various system development project teams requires the use of adequate documentation tools. Likewise, the effectiveness of coordination and control by the data base administrator is dependent on well-defined communications lines and supporting documentation tools.

The support documents and documentation aids utilized during data base and system design fall into three general categories:

- Documents initiated by the project team in support of requests for data
- Documents initiated by the data base design team in support of responses to requests for data
- Documents generated by the data base design team and utilized by both the data base design and project teams in the course of data base and system development

In the first category, documents initiated by the project team, the major document is the data request form. This is the project team's formal request for access to data required by the system under development. It will include a detailed description of each data item required as input to, output from, and permanent or temporary storage for the system under development.

Documents initiated by the data base design team in response to requests from the project team include:

- Approved data item/data record descriptions, definitions, names, and detailed attributes
- Supporting subschema(s) for use by the system implementors in accessing required data in the data base
- Environment-related documents and procedures (e.g., JCL, system parameters)

The data base design team will also generate any data base schemas or schema modifications necessary to support the requirements of the system. These "documents," however, are typically *not* communicated to the project team, as they deal with the universe of data and its physical characteristics rather than the *logical* view of data *specific* to the system being developed by the project team.

Documents generated by the data base design team and utilized by both the data base design and the system project teams focus on areas of shared, or joint, responsibility during the course of data base and system development. The primary document in this category is the system and data base test specifications. Although joint participation in the generation of a test specification is typical (and probably required), the final responsibility for producing the test specification, as it relates to data access and manipulation, rests with the data base design team. It is within the data base administration function that all test data-related standards and procedures are ultimately approved. As the data base design team is defined as a major element within the data base administration function, the task of assuring adherence to test data-related standards and procedures during system implementation is best placed within the data base design function.

The test specifications will address the following major areas:

- Data naming
- Data/record relationships
- Data edit/validation
- Data access authorization
- Data access response time
- Data base integrity

In addition to producing the system test specifications, the data base design team will also produce a test data base for use by the system project team during system coding, integration, and initial testing. This test data base should adequately represent the key data attributes and relationships necessary to perform basic system logic and data flow checks. Volume-related and more thorough logic and data flow tests will be performed in the latter stages of system integration, testing, and acceptance against live or pseudo-live data bases.

A related responsibility of the data base design team is the production of *data conversion* specifications for projects engaged in converting existing, non-data-base-supported systems to a data-base-supported environment. As in the case of test specifications generation, both the system project and the data base design teams would participate in producing the data conversion specification, but final approval of the specification would lie within the data base administration function, represented by the data base design team. The actual task of data conversion may be delegated to the data base design team, the system project team, or to a dedicated, and distinct, data conversion project team, depending upon the standard procedures adopted by an organization.

SYSTEM DESIGN FLOW IN A DATA-BASE-SUPPORTED ENVIRONMENT

A major commitment to a data-base-supported environment will require, as has been discussed, a significant change in the conventional approach to system development. This change relates to the manner in which data-related specifications are generated and approved. The impact on a system development cycle will, of course, depend on the degree to which data-related development processes are currently structured in an organization. Those organizations having highly "self-contained" system development procedures will feel the most impact, while those supporting some degree of centralized or coordinated data file design functions will see less impact. The organizational structure of the data base administration function can also influence the ease of transition to a data-base-oriented system development procedure. A general "model" of a systems design cycle, however, can be constructed to illustrate the major differences between the non-data-base and data-base-oriented system design flow. Figures 3-2 through 3-4 present general level diagrams of major system development tasks, their interrelationships, and the divisions of responsibility between the system development and data base design functions.

Figure 3-2 illustrates the major tasks performed by the system development project team. These tasks relate to the *logical* problem and specifically address interpretation of the user requirements and the implementation of a system responsive to these requirements. The system development team focuses its concern on solving a stated problem utilizing high-level procedural languages (e.g. COBOL, PL/1) and high-level data definition/manipulation techniques. In the conventional systems development process, the project team must turn its attention from the user requirements and become involved in the task of "creating" a data repository sensitive to the identified requirements of the system under development, *highly* sensitive to hardware/device characteristics, and insensitive to the integrated data requirements of and the availability of data within the overall corporate environment.

The placement of the data base design responsibility into a high-level, centralized function (the data base design team) does *not* relieve the system development project team of the responsibility of identifying data *requirements* specific to the system under development. Note in Figure 3-2 the tasks of analyzing data input/output and data residency (data that must be retained or "stored" over time by the system for to respond to a given input with a given output) requirements and of defining logical (i.e.,

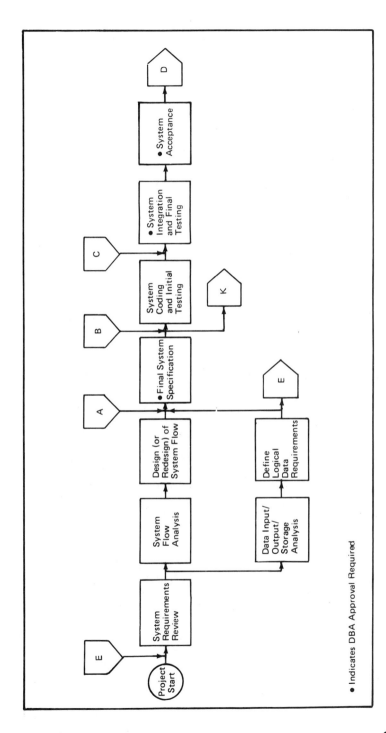

Figure 3-2. System Development Project Tasks

• Indicates DBA Approval Required

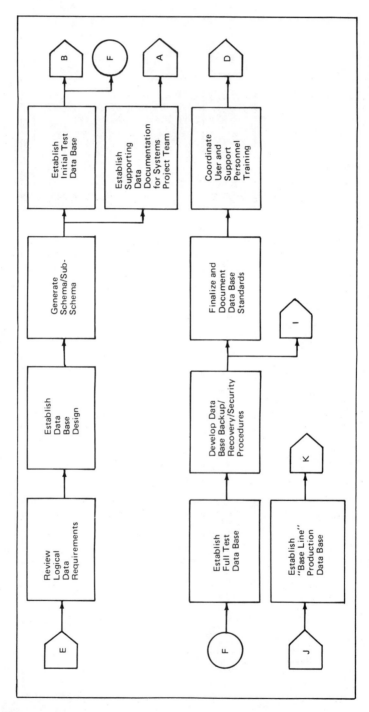

Figure 3-3. Data Base Design Project Tasks
(Note: DBA approval is implied for all major tasks)

64

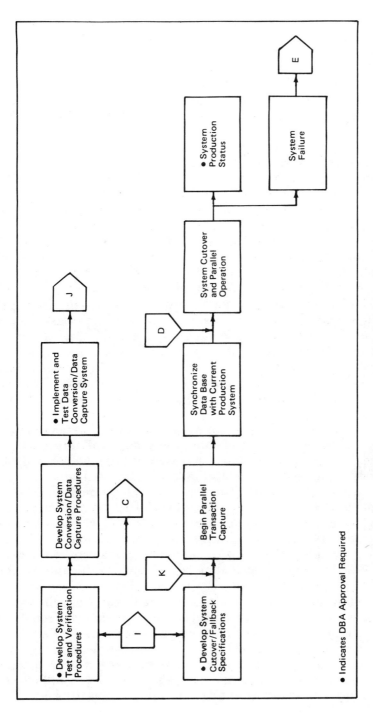

Figure 3-4. Joint Systems Development and Data Base Design Project Tasks

65

nonhardware/device dependent attributes) data requirements. However, responsibility for providing necessary data residency support and *approving* data capture/reporting standards rests with the data base design team (Figure 3-3).

After the system development project team has completed its analysis of system flow and logical data requirements and the data base design team has approved the data request from the project team, a formal system specification is generated. The data base administrator will review the system specification at this point to ensure that all applicable data, system, and environmental standards have been adhered to. The data base administrator must also endorse the final system integration and testing procedure as well as the system acceptance process, again to ensure compliance with all applicable standards and procedures (e.g., test procedures, system conventions, documentation).

The data base design function receives input from the system development project team in the form of a data requirements document. The team reviews these requirements and, after dialogue with the system project team to verify its own understanding of the system data requirements, establishes a data base design optionally responsive to the *integrated* data requirements of all systems/users accessing the data. The data base design is next translated into a data base schema (if the data currently does not exist in the data base) or into a data base schema modification (if some or all of the data currently exists in the data base but not in a form responsive to the requirements of the new system). In those instances in which the data requested by the systems project team currently exists in the data base and is available in a form responsive to the defined system requirements, there would, obviously, be no need to translate the data base design into a schema or schema modification. This point is brought out, however, to reemphasize one of the prime advantages of a data-base-supported environment—as the data base expands in a well-coordinated and administered environment, a growing percentage of data requests will be satisfied with data already resident in the data base—an economy of scale that will produce significant savings in both people and machine costs through increased productivity.

Following generation of any required data base schemas or schema modification, the data base design team will construct the subschema(s) necessary to provide access to the data base and communicate these to the system project team along with supporting documentation. Data derived during system processing, data delivered as output, and data received as input will also be identified with standards and procedures relative to its use documented and communicated to the system project team by the data base design group.[1]

Having communicated the required data base subschema(s) and supporting data documentation to the system project team, the data base design team must then construct test data bases for use by the system project team during actual coding and implementation of the various system software components. Generally, the test data base(s) will consist of at least two "levels," or iterations, of scope and complexity. The first level test data base(s) are constructed for access during the initial phases of system coding and testing. They are designed to test system logic and thus address the data content, interrecord relationships (structure) and data base access characteristics of the system. During latter stages of system testing and integration, additional "levels" of the data base are constructed in which data base size, more comprehensive data content and structural characteristics, and various "boundary" conditions are considered to more accurately reflect the real environment in which the system will operate.

The data base design group will also bear responsibility for establishing data backup/recovery and security procedures and for final documentation of all data-base-related standards and procedures. As the system nears formal cutover and production status, the data base design group will have the major task of establishing the "base line" production data base[2] and will begin coordinating the formal education of system user and support personnel.

Several tasks of overall system development effort generally require extensive joint participation on the part of the system development project team and the data base design group (see Figure 3-4). These tasks typically include the following:

- Development of system test and verification procedures, where close coordination of system processing and data access testing is mandatory

---

[1]Documentation of data attributes is generally supported by a formal Data Dictionary/Directory System. Responsibility for entering data documentation into the DD/DS rests with the data base administration function and may be delegated to the data base design group.

[2]The "base line" production data base is the data base created from the current production system at a designated point in time. Transactions from the current production system will be accumulated from this point in time and applied to the "base line" data base until it is synchronized with the current production system at some time + n, at which point parallel operation can commence.

- Development and implementation of data capture or data conversion (e.g., from existing automated files) systems, where close communication relative to current and proposed data attributes and standards is required
- Establishment of system cutover and fallback procedures, where close coordination of system processing and data access standards is necessary
- Actual execution of system cutover procedures and final sign-off on system production, where system processing and data access standards require close coordination

As in the previous system development task flows, the data base administrator has final approval authority at major milestones in the joint system project and data base design tasks. The data base administrator's most critical decision is the determination of the system's status at the completion of the parallel operation (or acceptance period, if the system is a new implementation as opposed to a conversion of an existing system). At this point, the system must be declared as acceptable for full production status, in which case operation of the "old" system is terminated, or as nonacceptable. If deemed nonacceptable for production status, a fallback procedure must be initiated, providing for a return to the existing system for interim production while the cause of failure of the data-base-supported system is isolated, analyzed, and corrected.

Any system failure at this point in the development cycle must receive thorough evaluation, even if the perceived cause/effect appears minor. In a well-planned and coordinated development cycle, there is rarely cause for system failure at this advanced stage; therefore any failure must be considered major. To minimize the impact on the user environment, it is *mandatory* that a comprehensive fallback procedure be developed. The data base administrator must also take all steps to ensure that the next cutover attempt will be successful. This will require that the project be literally restarted at the first major systems development task—system requirements review—and progress through *every* development task as though the project were a new development effort. Casual modifications to system logic or data base design without first progressing through each prior task and review point will in all probability aggravate the original problem or result in system failure or major problems well into production operation.

SYSTEM MAINTENANCE IN THE DATA BASE ENVIRONMENT

As in the case of system failure during final cutover and parallel operation, any and all modifications of a maintenance nature should be initiated as if it were a complete system development project. Included in the category of maintenance is system logic modification and data content, structure, or access method modification in response to either changing user requirements or changing environmental factors (e.g., hardware changes, DBMS enhancements, programming language enhancements).

SUMMARY

As an organization moves into a data-base-supported production environment, the impact on the conventional system development life cycle has been shown to be significant. With all data-related standards and procedures centralized under the function of data base administration, separation of the responsibility of system design and data base design is mandatory if the general objectives of a data-base-supported environment are to be achieved. Data processing management must establish a thorough plan of implementing an effective, well-administered system and data base design methodology. The major considerations management must address in establishing this plan include the following:

- Recognize that the centralization of data-related standards and procedures under the auspices of data base administration *requires* removal of data base design responsibility from the system development project team.
- Establish a system/data base development procedure that recognizes the three major task flows—system development, data base design, and coordinated system development/data base design. Isolation of these major development paths will enhance administration and coordination of the entire project.
- *Always* include a comprehensive fallback procedure to be initiated if the system fails in advanced stages of system cutover/parallel operation.
- Do not hesitate to initiate the fallback procedure if any question of production suitability of a new system cannot be satisfactorily resolved.

- Treat any system failure or system maintenance process as a *complete* project cycle—casual repairs/modifications will invariably aggravate any problems or subject the system to a high risk of future problems or major failures.

PART II

Data Base Environment Components

Data base management systems are now more economical and more available, providing an excellent means of optimizing the management of an organization's data base. Most enlightened management groups understand the value of data as a corporate resource, a resource that must be organized and regulated as any other asset.

To justify the investment of time and money, the data base must be more than the domain of one department alone. Its reservoir of steadily proliferating information must be made accessible to myriad users in myriad ways. Data independence must be maintained as well, in order to protect programs against unauthorized change, to allow optimization of the physical organization, to minimize application development, and to centralize and control data resources.

chapter 4

The Data Base Management System

INTRODUCTION

The purpose of this chapter is to present the concepts of Data Base Management Systems (DBMSs) in terms understandable to management not directly involved in, but nevertheless responsible for, the implementation of data processing systems. The areas covered answer basic questions currently being raised by managers involved in making decisions relative to the implementation of this new but proven technology.

Many managers faced with proposals for the installation of a DBMS are asking some very simple questions but are not getting understandable answers. Among these questions are:

- *What* is this "thing" called a DBMS?
- *Why* the sudden interest in this software package?
- *How* does this piece of software fit into my DP environment?

WHAT, WHY, AND HOW

The answers to these three basic questions lie in understanding the basic definition of data base management systems, the application of the definition in terms of implementation alternatives, and an enumeration of the objectives of the DBMS.

DEFINITION OF A DBMS

As data base technology is currently implemented in commercially available packages, a DBMS is a piece of software. Moreover, it is generalized software that is application independent and thus can be employed by any user requiring data-related services. The services it performs are generally aimed at the *organization*, *access*, and *control* of data.

Prior to presenting a concise definition of a DBMS, we should first define the meaning of the term "data base" and distinguish it from the widely used term, "data file":

- **Data Base**—a collection of data logically organized to meet the information and time requirements of a universe of users.
- **Data File**—a collection of like records.

Thus, the important distinction between a data base and a data file is the shared nature of data usage in a data base, and the logical organization of data designed to support this type of usage. Whereas a data file is a collection of like records designed to produce information, a data base is a collection of files integrated in a manner to serve the diverse requirements of a universe of users.

Now that we have defined a data base, it is appropriate to move on and define a DBMS. (We will use the term "data base" as a reference point.)

- **Data Base Management System**—a generalized software system designed to manage the data base, providing facilities for *organization*, *access*, and *control*.

It is worthwhile to analyze the key elements of this definition to achieve a better conception of the types of facilities provided by a DBMS.

- **Organization Facilities.** Organization facilities provided by DBMS software packages are aimed at representing the users' view of data in such a way that it can be produced efficiently from a single storage implementation.

- **Access Facilities.** Access facilities of DBMS software packages provide the mechanisms required for storage, retrieval, and dissemination of data to and from the data base.
- **Control Facilities.** Control facilities included in DBMS software packages strive to maintain the data base with a high degree of integrity. Such facilities are usually provided in the form of auxiliary data services.

Figure 4-1 provides examples of these three types of facilities as they are found in commercially available DBMS packages.

Our brief description of DBMS facilities would not be complete without mentioning the capabilities provided by DBMSs that enhance and/or contribute to greater degrees of program/data independence. This phenomenon is manifested in the ability to alter data descriptions without adversely affecting the programs that process the underlying data. DBMSs provide varying degrees of program/data independence based upon different combinations of organization, access, and control facilities. Some proponents of data base technology feel that the benefits afforded by program/data independence are the most important selling point of the data base approach.

Central to the theme of providing data base management services to a defined universe of users on a shared basis is the concept of a generalized, multi-purpose software system. The age-old debate of generality versus "tailor-made" software is applicable. Rather than engage in the debate, suffice it to say that the commercially available DBMS is a generalized software system and that its applicability in specific situations is both constrained and enhanced by this characteristic. It is constrained by the levels of indirection employed in its implementation; and it is enhanced by the wide range of applicability of the technology.

FACILITY TYPE	FACILITY
Organization	Physical Sequential Indexed Sequential Inverted Index Embedded Linkages Compaction
Access	Sequential Access Methods Directory Based Access Methods Conditional Retrieval
Control	Security Recovery/Restart Edit/Validate

Figure 4-1. Data Base Management System Facilities

IMPLEMENTATION ALTERNATIVES

The best way to understand how the DBMS is being used is to survey its historical development and to trace the evolution of implementation alternatives.

The early implementations of commercial DBMSs were motivated by requirements for support of complex data structures and the need for sophisticated access methods. These requirements were usually bounded by and limited to the scope of a particular application. The field of data base was widely viewed as a technical issue, to be addressed by the systems programmers assigned to the project.

Many DBMS implementations are very much project-oriented. More recently, however, DP management and systems planners have recognized that the DBMS can serve as an important tool in support of a data resource management environment. This approach treats data as a corporate resource and strives for company-wide administration and control of the data resource. With this type of implementation strategy, the emphasis is on integration of systems and the sharing of data resources. The DBMS provides the mechanism whereby a set of integrated data bases can be designed and maintained for a universe of diverse users, i.e., provide multiple user views of data from a single physical representation.

From a management viewpoint the distinction between implementation strategies is extremely important. With the access method approach to the use of the DBMS, management involvement is minimal, since the issue remains technical and the scope is confined to the project. However, when the DBMS is considered within the context of a program for data resource management, the involvement and commitment of senior management becomes an important ingredient for success. Figure 4-2 illustrates the nature of the management commitment required in the early stages of data base implementation.

OBJECTIVES OF A DBMS

In order to fully answer the question of how the DBMS fits into the DP environment, we need to explore the objectives of a DBMS implementation.

- **Flexible Data Structure Support.** In implementing the DBMS it will be necessary, during the course of data base design, to support a variety of user views of data and data interrelationships. This is done through the use of data structures. The data structure of the DBMS should be flexible enough to support a wide variety of these user views.

- **Variety of Access Methods.** At the technical level, the DBMS controls the physical access of data. In order to accomplish data access in the most efficient manner possible, the DBMS should provide maximum flexibility for the data base designer in choosing the appropriate access method for a particular design problem.

- **Central Control Over Physical Storage.** This objective is implicit in the design of the DBMS and is true to the extent that the principle of data resource management is applied.

- **Hierarchical Storage Device Support.** With a larger proportion of an organization's data being stored in the data base environment, it would be cost effective to take advantage of cheaper storage media when response time and frequency of use so indicate.

- **Data Independence.** This objective refers, primarily, to program/data independence. It is desirable to separate programs from the data they process in order that changes in the data, as perceived or stored, will have minimum impact on the programs that process the data.

- **Data Integrity.** With the data resources of an organization being managed by the DBMS, facilities should be provided to protect these resources, i.e., the content of the data base. Examples of data base integrity support are recovery/restart, security, and access control.

- **Flexible and Responsive User Interfaces.** The DBMS is not an end in itself. It is a tool to provide users with information. Its effectiveness can only be realized through flexible and responsive interfaces. These interfaces should include *ad hoc* user languages, programming interfaces, and on-line multiuser access.

DBMS packages currently available meet the foregoing objectives in varying degrees; no single DBMS meets all of the objectives satisfactorily. Because of this, prospective DBMS user organizations go through extensive evaluation and selection procedures.

WHAT SHOULD MANAGEMENT DO?

Use of the data base concept, as represented in a data resource management environment, is the next logical development in the continuing evolution of computerized information systems. It encompasses the specialization of DP functions; it allows information users genuine flexibility in satisfying their needs; and it encourages viewing data as a tangible resource to be managed in a positive fashion.

A Note of Caution

Recent experience has shown that caution and patience are advisable in pursuing the DBMS. Many installations have enthusiastically undertaken data base efforts only to be extremely disappointed in the progress they have achieved. There are numerous reasons for these failures, many of which have no connection at all with data base issues. Nevertheless, it may be helpful to point up some of the more common difficulties encountered.

- The issues and concerns associated with encouraging people to work within the confines of the discipline required by a data resource management environment have caused problems. Apprehension about change and a more structured environment, combined with the political implications that can result from the centralization and shared use of data bases, has had a detrimental effect on data base efforts.
- The requirements for the DBMS are significantly different from those the vendors have supplied to date. This has caused considerable difficulty in such areas as integrity, reliability, and performance.
- Most installations that have attempted to develop (i.e., "make") a DBMS in-house have encountered almost insurmountable problems. Software reliability and performance have been disappointing, and the eventual development price often far exceeds original estimates.
- The administration and control of the data base is usually underbudgeted and understaffed. This has caused difficulties

in maintaining the required control over the data resource management environment.

- The DBMS selected has sometimes proved to be ill-chosen because of a lack of understanding of future requirements. This has "locked in" the installation with the data bases and programs developed. A lack of flexibility in the DBMS can cause difficulty in almost every facet of the data base environment.
- Senior management in many cases has not been fully apprised of the commitment required on its part.
- Finally, many managers and computer professionals do not yet have a good understanding of the full implications of the data base concepts.

The preceding list of potential difficulties should not discourage the prospective DBMS implementor. It should, however, create enough skepticism to cause management to approach these issues with a degree of caution.

SUMMARY

In order to avoid potential difficulties, it is recommended that management take the following steps in preparing for a data base environment. (The common thread in this course of action is the necessity for commitment and involvement on the part of senior management. See Figure 4-2.)

1. Become reasonably familiar with the concepts and issues involved. This chapter is a first step in that direction. Selections from the following list of references can reinforce these concepts and provide additional detail as appropriate. A couple of days should be invested by the senior DP official at a well-chosen data base concepts seminar specifically designed for management. This provides not only interaction with other senior managers in similar situations, but also an intensive period of exposure to the pertinent issues at hand.

2. Commit resources for an exploratory study to ascertain the position of your corporation with respect to the data base concepts discussed here and to determine the goal at which the data base effort should be aimed. This is the initial step in the planning stages for data base environment—it is extremely important that the study be performed by com-

petent individuals. In some situations, you may need to seek
assistance in the form of new personnel or outside counsel.

3. Elicit a commitment from senior management to the data
base concept. From the very beginning of the data base
effort, senior management should be kept abreast of its
development, and they should use their influence to ensure
maximum cooperation from all concerned.

4. Spend the time and effort to carefully plan, on a long-range
basis and a short-range basis, the development and implementation of the data base concept.

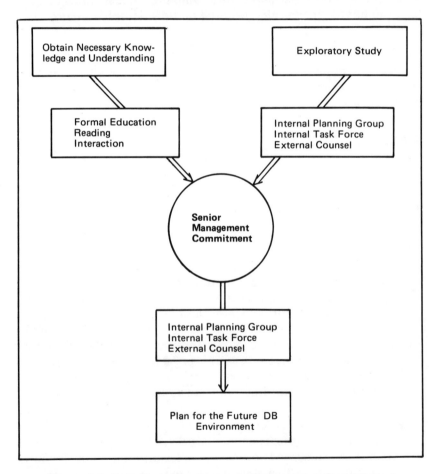

Figure 4-2. Data Base Management: Management Commitment

chapter 5

Data Dictionary/ Directory System: A Tool for Data Administration and Control

INTRODUCTION

Commercial business applications have evolved from simple repetitive accounting procedures to extremely complex information systems, and have been characterized by decentralized control of data. Most corporations began their automation efforts by computerizing the repetitive tasks associated with daily operations. With the advent of second- and third-generation computer systems these applications were broadened in scope but remained separate with respect to their processing of data. Each of these application systems was developed independently of all other applications. The data was computerized, but it was fragmented. Each application system was developed with its own data files, creating and maintaining data collections on an "as-needed basis."

The advent of the information system, emphasizing the relationships among business operations, underscored the need for the development of integrated application systems. Attempts at developing such systems were complicated by intricate data structures. From these attempts came the first application of data base technology in the form of Data Base Management Systems. This early use of the DBMS was confined for the most part, to a specific application area. These early efforts, moreover, used the DBMS as a sophisticated access method to solve the data organization problems inherent in the application development process. The issue of integrating the data underlying the applications was largely ignored.

These developments caused a number of problems in the administration and control of data in the organization.

Data Redundancy. As each application system evolved, it created and maintained its own data files. To cite an example in the banking industry: If the Deposit system and the Loan system were dealing with the same customer, typically the customer's identification data (e.g., name, address, and social security number) were stored redundantly in each system. Furthermore, if the bank were supporting a Central Customer Information File, all of the data would usually be stored again. This is but one type of redundancy. Data is actually needed in more than one place, and the current technological trade-offs dictate redundancy. However, the problem has been compounded in large organizations where communication among staff has failed, and inadvertent redundancies have been introduced in data systems.

Inconsistency/Incompatibility of Data. As data files were created and maintained by each application system, large corporations found themselves in a position where each system was dealing with data that was either inconsistent or incompatible with the data of other systems. At one high-level meeting of a large computer manufacturer, attendees brought what were purported to be comparable financial reports from their respective operating divisions, only to realize that the reports were unrelatable. Definitions of terms, and therefore the data collection in the various systems, were so diverse as to render the comparison of information useless.

Application Software Data Dependence. As each system was designed and implemented utilizing its own data files, the supporting software became bound to the data that it manipulated. This, in turn, created high maintenance costs when the dynamic aspects of data manifested themselves, causing large reprogramming and recompiling efforts. A common example of this phenomenon is the situation in many financial systems when economic inflation causes the expansion of monetary fields.

DATA BASE ENVIRONMENT

These major problems and others not mentioned have one thing in common: they all stem from decentralized control over data, i.e., from allowing each application to "own" and control the data that it manipulates. One potential solution to these problems is the implementation of the concept of a data base environment. This involves treating data as a corporate resource, just like machines and money. Furthermore, the data resource ought to be considered as multi-faceted, inasmuch as all other resources can only be managed effectively with adequate data about them.

The data base environment can be formally defined as:

- The consideration of the collection, storage, and dissemination of data as a logical, centrally controlled, and standardized utility function.

The Data Dictionary/Directory System plays an important role in realizing the objectives of data base environment. As the central repository of all information about the organization's data, the DD/DS functions as the primary tool of the Data Base Administrator in maintaining administrative and operational control over the utilization of the data resource.

THE DATA DICTIONARY/DIRECTORY SYSTEM

This section will present the basic definitions widely used for the DD/DS, the objectives of user organizations in implementing DD/DSs, and alternative system architectures for DD/DS implementation.

Definitions

The following is a working definition for the DD/DS:

- The DD/DS is the repository for all definitive information about data in the organization, such as identifying characteristics, relationships, and authorities.

The name DD/DS contains both the terms "dictionary" and "directory." While these terms seem redundant, they actually have distinctive meanings with respect to the functions of the DD/DS. The DD/DS can realistically be viewed as bifunctional.

The *dictionary* function answers the question, "What data is available/contained in the organization's data bases?" The *directory* function replies to: "Where is the data stored?" Another way of perceiving this difference is recognition that *dictionary* users of the DD/DS are humans, while *directory* users are (for the most part) systems components, i.e., hardware and software.

Carrying this distinction further, the contents of the DD/DS can be identified and classified in terms of dictionary versus directory data. Figure 5-1 illustrates this point and the fact that dictionary and directory data are *not* mutually exclusive.

Before continuing with the implementation objectives for a DD/DS, one additional definition is offered:

- *Metadata*—the contents of the DD/DS, i.e., data about data.

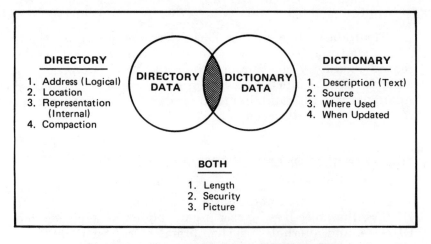

Figure 5-1. Types of Dictionary/Directory Data

DD/DS Implementation Objectives

The DD/DS is a tool that carries out the activities of data base development (data collection and analysis and reduction) and that serves as the central control mechanism (data standardization and documentation) in the data base environment.

Data Collection. The data collection process is predicated on the clear and concise definition of current and future information needs. The DD/DS will serve as the central control point for data description and specification throughout the entire data base development effort.

Data Analysis and Reduction. The DD/DS will provide analysts and designers with a mechanism to detect inconsistent and/or redundant data entities.

Data Documentation. The DD/DS will provide for certain documentation and procedural aspects of data definition. Thus, the DD/DS will be the repository for information relative to all data attributes. Among these attributes are the sources, users, location, and availability of data collections, and the documentation of security and access limitations for data entities. Documentation of the use of these data entities is equally important in order to ensure against unintentional deletion from the data base. For example, since it is expected that many data entities will be shared by many different users, it will be necessary for the DBA to ensure that there is no further need among *any* users of a particular data collection prior to making a decision to delete.

Another aspect of data documentation is the requirements inherent in the systems development process. For each application system designed and implemented, it will be necessary to document the manner in which the data is used and manipulated in that application, i.e., to deal with the data specification aspects of systems documentation. The DD/DS will provide documentation support in all these areas.

Data Standardization. The need for establishing and enforcing standards for data usage and responsibility is accentuated in a data base environment, where extensive sharing of data is expected. Standardization will be required for formats, the meaning of terminology, and use of codes, among other things.

One important aspect of data standards relates to data editing and validation standards. It is imperative to establish stringent edit and validation requirements to ensure maximum integrity of the data base content. If these edit and validation rules are not uniformly applied to all data base input, the consistency of the content will suffer. The DD/DS can be used to record and control these standards for editing and validating input.

Another aspect of data standardization is employment of the DD/DS to ensure consistent usage of redundant data entities. Redundancy may be tolerated because of certain technological trade-offs. However, it is necessary that the use of duplicated data entities be consistent. This can be accomplished by employing the DD/DS's cross-referencing and/or version designation facilities.

DD/DS System Architecture

A very important aspect of the DD/DS implementation strategy is the selection of a systems architecture as a framework in which the DD/DS will function. Broadly speaking, there are two alternative strategies in this regard: a *passive* DD/DS and an *active* DD/DS (within these two strategies there are many variations).

Passive DD/DS. The passive DD/DS records metadata (data descriptions used in programs, the DBMS, and other activities) on an after-the-fact basis. If they are entered into the DD/DS prior to use in the programs or DBMS, the data descriptions must be reentered. In fact, this type of DD/DS is actually more of a data dictionary than a data directory.

This type of DD/DS implementation strategy evolved because every DBMS contains a data directory. The necessity for a data dictionary facility was not associated with, or integrated into, the data directory within the DBMS. Whatever association was established was effected on an after-the-fact documentation basis.

Active DD/DS. The active DD/DS records metadata and is also the source for all metadata usage within the system. In this type of architecture the DD/DS has the potential for functioning as a controlling mechanism for all metadata usage in the data base environment.

The first implementations of this concept were accomplished with DD/DSs that were implemented separately from the DBMS. The DD/DSs, however, had special interfaces to generate the data descriptions required by the DDL pre-processor to generate the internal directories of the DBMS. Similarly, these DD/DSs were equipped with interfaces that could generate the data divisions for COBOL programs. One of these early DD/DSs contained special software to generate edit-and-validate programs to be executed on incoming transactions. The general approach in these systems was to provide a single source for all data descriptions required.

Developments in active DD/DSs include an effort on the part of some DBMS vendors to share the information in the "metadata base" between the DD/DS and the DBMS. Cullinane Corporation has implemented its Integrated Data Dictionary as an extension of the internal IDMS data base.

Further possibilities in the active DD/DS may include active control by the DD/DS of the method by which programs process data. This could be accomplished through tight DD/DS control over subschema specification and subschema/program binding.

It should be noted that whether the DD/DS is passive or active, it can still be decided if the DD/DS data base (the metadata base) will be dependent on or independent of any particular DBMS. The decision to be made is how to manage the DD/DS data base from an access/retrieval viewpoint. One obvious choice is to use DBMS software for this chore; the result is a dependent DD/DS. Alternatively, the metadata base could be organized and managed by independent access methods and file organization techniques; such a DD/DS is termed independent.

Figure 5-2 summarizes the architectural placement of the DD/DS within the data base environment. Note the interfaces between the DD/DS and each major component in the environment and the addition of the metadata data base.

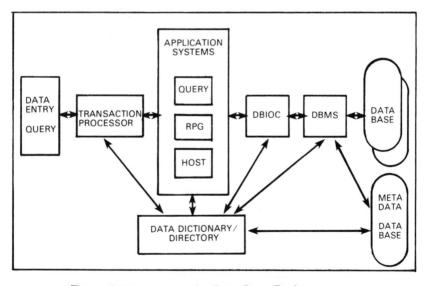

Figure 5-2. Elements of a Data Base Environment

FUNCTIONAL REQUIREMENTS FOR THE DD/DS

There are nine common functions that DD/DSs are designed to support.

1. *Clear specification of data.* Most data processing installations are engaged in the continuing activity of creating
systems to support the development of integrated information systems. In order to design the appropriate information flows for future management support, the systems
designers must be able to analyze existing data and data
flows precisely. Designers want to specify and describe data
so that any interested user can see exactly how to utilize
the data elements. A DD/DS designed to maintain clear
specifications of data will provide this necessary support.

2. *Simple, selective retrieval.* The users of the data should be
able to select precisely the items of metadata that are of
interest to them and review the specifications only of those
individual items. This requirement implies the ability to
access metadata on the basis of standard labels (keys) as
well as by associative searching.

3. *Inconsistent/redundant data analysis capability.* Identical
or very similar items of data occurring in data files in different parts of the business, indicate potential areas for concern.
Detection of such cases must be possible so that each may
be studied in detail. Those responsible for the data involved
(the DBA in general and the user in particular) must have a
tool to enable them to determine if inconsistency/redundancy
does actually exist. In general there are two types of redundancy. Technical redundancy is knowingly built into a
system because of existing technological trade-offs. Periodically these trade-offs should be reevaluated, and if it is
decided that redundancy should be tolerated, consistency
between duplicated items must be maintained. The second
type of redundancy, the inadvertent type, should *never* be
tolerated, and where possible should always be eliminated
when detected. Unless one has precise specifications of
data and can readily compare these specifications, it is
very difficult to detect cases of possible inconsistency and/
or redundancy.

4. *Knowledge of the location of data.* When a systems analyst
requiring certain data for a particular application does not
know of the existence of relevant data, redundancy may
occur. To avoid this, the DD/DS must include not only a
clear specification of the data but also a statement of where
it exists and, when appropriate, how it can be retrieved.

5. *Determination of data users.* It is possible that an individual
in one functional area has been an unofficial user of data

generated in a second functional area. When the users in the functional area that generated and maintained this data no longer need it, they will delete the data items, unaware of the impact on the other users. To avoid undesirable deletion and/or change in such circumstances, the DD/DS must include means for registering all users of each data item, both in terms of programs and end-users.

6. *Assignment of responsibility for data integrity and specification.* In general, the DBA carries the ultimate responsibility for ensuring the correctness and completeness of the data itself and the specification data. He or she must, however, delegate responsibility to users of data. When, for example, data is transmitted from a remote location to a central point and modified there, confusion may arise over who is responsible for specifying the data that is processed centrally, and who is responsible for the correctness and completeness of the data *per se.* The DD/DS must clearly delineate both of these responsibilities.

7. *Support of the DBMS.* All of the DBMS on the market today include directory modules containing descriptive data that the Data Base Management software needs to execute requests. The DD/DS should contain this information and be able to supply it (via an appropriate interface) to the DBMS upon request. This will preclude storing such data twice and ensure the integrity of the DD/DS to the extent of the information transferred to the DBMS for use in executing requests. (This functional requirement ensures an active DD/DS.)

8. *Support of data validation.* Most corporations with highly transaction-oriented businesses (e.g., public utilities) require elaborate data validation procedures. The DD/DS should provide the facility to detail the validation requirements for each data item specified and be able to pass parameters to appropriate software modules (which may or may not be part of the DBMS); these modules then actually perform the validation and produce error reports. By centralizing validation procedures in this manner, greater control over input can be realized as well as a savings in terms of software development, since each application will no longer be required to develop its own validation routines.

9. *Support of evolving technology.* The design of the DD/DS must be such that it allows for graceful expansion to satisfy new and varied requirements of data users and DBMS. The

new and evolving nature of data base technology dictates that any element of the data base environment that is to remain useful for any period of time, must be designed so that it can adapt to changing needs. For example, should the need arise to support a second DBMS, there should be no problem of compatibility. The open-endedness of design will ensure against any such problem. To cite a different example: Should the need arise to include a new type of specification for data (e.g., including data element names for a new programming language), the DD/DS should be able to accommodate the specifications for it.

SUMMARY

The DD/DS should be the cornerstone of the data base environment. The implementation of an active DD/DS can provide the DBA with an important and indispensable tool for administration and control. Figure 5-3 summarizes the points made in this chapter in terms of justifying a DD/DS implementation in a DBMS-sup-

```
JUSTIFICATIONS FOR DD/DS

IN A DB ENVIRONMENT

• COORDINATION & CONTROL IN SYSTEMS
  DEVELOPMENT

    — DATA COLLECTION & ANALYSIS
    — DESIGN OF SHARED DATA BASES
    — MAINTENANCE OF SHARED DATA BASES

• IDENTIFICATION & REDUCTION OF DATA
  REDUNDANCY

    — ELIMINATE INADVERTENT (UNPLANNED)
      REDUNDANCY
    — CONTROL OF TECHNICAL (PLANNED)
      REDUNDANCY

• ADMINISTRATIVE TOOL (DBA TOOL)

    — STANDARDS DEVELOPMENT
    — META-DATA CONTROL
    — DATA INTEGRITY
    — DBMS CONTROL
```

Figure 5-3. Justifications for DD/DS

ported data base environment. A DD/DS implementation may be justified prior to DBMS implementation on the basis of the arguments listed in Figure 5-4, a subset of the justifications for a DD/ DS with a DBMS that are listed in Figure 5-3. If a company is considering the use of the data base technology, it is strongly recommended that the firm consider a Data Dictionary/Directory System.

JUSTIFICATIONS FOR DD/DS

WITHOUT A DBMS IMPLEMENTATION

- REDUCE RISK OF INADVERTENT REDUNDANCY

- INCREASE ABILITY TO TRANSFER DATA BETWEEN CONVENTIONALLY DESIGNED SYSTEMS

- FACILITATE SEARCH FOR RELEVANT DATA ELEMENTS DURING NEW SYSTEMS DESIGN AND MAINTENANCE

- DOCUMENTATION SUPPORT

- CONVENTIONAL DATA DEFINITION SUPPORT (E.G., COPYLIB)

LONG-RANGE CONSIDERATIONS

- DD/DS INTEGRATION WITH DBMS

- EVENTUAL IMPLEMENTATION OF A DBMS

- ORGANIZATION-WIDE IMPACT OF A PROGRAM OF DATA RESOURCE MANAGEMENT

Figure 5-4. Subset of Justifications for DD/DS

chapter 6

The Function of Data Base Administration and Control

INTRODUCTION

It is generally agreed that the most basic responsibility of a manager is to formulate and achieve objectives. Many different resources are applied to this end, for example, equipment, material, finances, and, of course, people. Recently, however, management has begun to recognize that the effective use of these resources and the long-term survival of an organization increasingly depend on that most varied and illusory of all resources — information. Information, therefore, has a dual nature: it is itself a resource, and it is also required to control and direct the use of all other resources.

New approaches are currently being developed to meet the challenge of providing and managing required information. One of these is embodied in the concept of data resource management. There are three areas in which administration and control of the data base can effectively demonstrate the benefits of data resource management.

Reduction in the Cost of Application Systems Development and Maintenance. Reducing the dependencies between the application programs and data (*data independence*) provides greater flexibility in application systems development and maintenance. In addition, data nonredundancy and increased data relatability result in improved data integrity or reliability. To ensure that these concepts are implemented for the good of all users, there must be a person or functional group charged with the management of the data in the organization's data base(s). Certainly, data base management systems provide an environment in which application systems development and maintenance are facilitated and are less costly. Many application programmer tasks can be performed by a DBMS, thus enhancing productivity.

Increased Responsiveness to Users of the Data Base. The services provided by DBMS software allow programmers to deal with logical interfaces, thus eliminating concern for physical input/output operations. A program can be produced quickly because application programmers are free to concentrate on the logic of the application and can give less consideration to the complex trade-offs of data management. If the interfaces that invoke these services are standardized and controlled, the benefits can be more readily achieved. Responsiveness can also be enhanced because the data is usually current and in a form conducive to handling requests for data.

Provide a Base from which an Integrated Information System Structure Rather than Traditional DP Systems Can Be Constructed. Many functions that have been application-system-dependent and embedded in the application programs can now be interpreted as data base management functions. Such functions as data security, data integrity, restart/recovery, and some data validation can be provided by the DBMS. Characteristically, the multi-application environment associated with an information system structure requires that these functions be centrally controlled. Controlling parameters should be defined by a central group entrusted with custody of the data base. This group must ensure that all processes against the data are performed in a manner consistent with the rules governing the overall operation of the data base environment.

The common denominator of these three areas is the notion of coordination and control. This chapter presents a detailed discussion of guidelines and procedures for the functional responsibilities required to ensure adequate coordination and control of a data base.

THE FUNCTION OF DATA BASE ADMINISTRATION AND CONTROL

The function of administration and control of the data base environment has been defined as responsibility for the coordination of all data-related activities. An expanded definition specifying the areas of functional responsibility is responsibility for the definition, organization, protection, and efficiency of the data base(s) in a data resource management environment, including responsibility for defining the rules by which data is to be accessed and stored.

The Dual Function

Experience has taught us that there are two aspects to the administration and control of data bases, which should be considered separately:

- The functional definition of *what* should be in the organization's data bases
- The implementation definition of *how* to effect the realization of the organization's data bases

There are two practical reasons for making the distinction between these two types of administration activity:

- *Skill requirements*—The two types of administrative activities require remarkably different skills. The definition of what should be in the data base requires nontechnical analytic and administrative skills. The definition of how to implement largely depends on knowledge and skills directly related to the DBMS being used.
- *Development life-cycle requirements*—The need for both technical and nontechnical administrative support varies, depending on the point relative to the development life cycle of a given application system. The early part of the development life cycle is largely devoted to the specification of functional requirements. At this point, it is appropriate to describe what will be in the data base. As the life cycle progresses, it is increasingly necessary to define how the data base will be implemented.

The terminology used to refer to these administration and control functions has evolved to the point where specific nomenclature is used to differentiate between the two types of administrative responsibilities — data administration (DA) is differentiated from data base administration (DBA).

Data administration refers to the nontechnical activities of planning for the data base environment as well as to the conceptual details of design that are not related to specific DBMS use. The data administration function is end-user oriented and is concerned with functional requirements relative to the data base environment.

Data base administration refers to the decisions and activities that directly lead to or have an immediate impact on operational data bases. Data base administration is involved with the technical design and implementation issues inherent in the particular DBMS being used.

FUNCTIONAL RESPONSIBILITIES

Table 6-1 shows 10 areas of functional responsibility for the DA/DBA. Each is discussed as follows.

Data Definition

The DA is responsible for data definition within the context of the data base environment. This responsibility has applicability in a number of related areas of activity, including:

Data Collection. During the initial phase, when data relative to information handling is being gathered, the DA is responsible for developing uniform procedures for defining and describing the data attributes of the data entities under scrutiny.

Systems Development. Defining and describing new data entities and relationships is clearly a part of systems development. The DA is responsible for uniform data definition procedures.

Table 6-1.   Areas of DA/DBA Responsibility

• Data Definition
• Data Base Design and Implementation
• Data Base Access
• Data Base Standards Control
• Documentation
• Operations
• Monitoring
• Data Base Management System Enhancements
• Education
• Vendor Enhancements

Data Dictionary. One of the DA/DBA's most essential tools is the dictionary, which also depends on uniform data definition procedures.

Data Base Design and Implementation

DA/DBA data base design and implementation responsibilities revolve around the definition and organization of the data base. The DA/DBA must be involved in the following areas.

Developing an Understanding of User Requirements. The relationship between the DA/DBA and the user community (those users in DP as well as end users) can be a problem, especially if a particular user must or thinks he must expend more effort or accept a lower level of service than he would outside the data base environment. A good relationship is required to establish a meaningful dialogue and an understanding of the full range of user requirements.

The DA/DBA must have the full confidence of the people to whom he provides support. The users should feel that they are dealing with an impartial and unbiased authority whose decisions enhance the welfare and support the policies of the organization as a whole. If any user must be given a negative response to a request for service, the DA/DBA should cite the reasons for the decision.

Schedule and accuracy requirements must be explicitly agreed upon by users and the DA/DBA and then adhered to. In order to appreciate variations in time and expense, users must be educated in the differences between access to specific existing data, references to external data, information dynamically derived from existing data, and the extension of the data base to include new types of data entities.

The understanding of user requirements has both strategic (long-range) and tactical (short-range) implications. The DA/DBA must be aware of both corporate long-range plans and long-range user needs. For example, two functional user groups might be developing plans for data bases with interrelated data. The DA/DBA must be able to provide for shared use and common access for both users. The understanding of short-range user plans and needs pertains to specific application systems needs. For instance, a user might require data from an existing automated data collection; this could cause conflicts with the interests of current users. Such differences must be reconciled. Both strategic and tactical understanding are necessary in order to allow the DA/DBA to perform the data-related coordination function within the corporation. The DA/DBA is thus explicitly representing corporate management in ensuring that the data base environment is an effective and efficient tool for all users.

Understanding and interpreting end-user requirements are, for the most part, data-administration oriented because dealing with end-user needs is a function of what should be in the data base.

Establishing Data Availability. It is the DA's responsibility to assist users in their search for data to satisfy their information and other reporting requirements. A data dictionary can be used as the initial source for information regarding data availability. If some data entities (for example, referenced data) are not available within the confines of the data base under the direct control of the DA/DBA, he should assist the user in making arrangements to expeditiously interface with the necessary data sources in order to satisfy the requirement. Note that the cost of satisfying these user requests must be within the constraints that the organization has placed on the user and the DA/DBA.

Additional factors to be included in the consideration of data availability are:

- Present form and location of data
- Access techniques to be used
- Intended use of the data in relation to its present accuracy, completeness, and timeliness
- Need for modification of data
- Authorizing agent for use of data
- Cost of providing the data

Data Base Organization. The formulation and definition of data relationships for the purpose of defining logical data structures is a vital function of the DA. Users making requests generally indicate their logical data needs by stating retrieval content. The DA should respond with explicitly defined proposals for data structures that reflect his knowledge of foreseeable developments and the needs of other users. This function has two major aspects: defining and organizing existing data, and adding new data. Note that the addition of new data to the data base can mean anything from a simple modification to a complete restructuring involving entirely new relationships.

The physical (i.e., storage) structure of the data base must be designed to effectively meet user needs for multiple logical data structures. Efficient physical structuring requires that the DBA have technical expertise in translating and effecting global logical relationships. In the establishment and organization process, the DBA must weigh the advantages of a given set of linkages or indices against its cost in terms of the additional space required and in terms of the degradation of data base access performance. A variety of parameters must be taken into consideration, including:

- Data structure (logical data formats and relationships)
- Storage structure (physical data formats and relationships)
- Access methods
- Frequency of access
- Physical storage media requirements
- Timing considerations
- Search strategies

Sophisticated user information needs might require complex data structures involving many interrelationships. These, in turn, might demand complex access strategies, resulting in long processing times. It should be recognized that using current technology, it may not be possible to meet all needs economically within a single data base. Redundant data or multiple data bases containing the same data may be required for the sake of maximizing performance.

Given all these parameters, achieving an optimal solution should be an iterative process. The DBA can use formal analytical tools (e.g., simulation) for complex data bases. In this crucial area, the DBA acquires valuable technical expertise through participation in the generation of diverse kinds of data bases for users. This is where the DBA functions best in his role as data base expert and consultant. The reasoning behind DBA solutions should be carefully recorded in order to facilitate understanding and to justify subsequent change.

Determining Physical Storage Requirements. Following the design and specification of the logical and the physical data structures, the DBA is responsible for assisting in the determination of physical storage requirements. This involves establishing, by type, the amount of storage space required for each data set within a data base. The following parameters are considered in the computation of space allocations:

- Volume of data
- Data relationships (data structure)
- Size of records

- Anticipated growth
- Additions and deletions of records
- Blocking factors
- Data representation
- Access methods
- Compression methods

The DBA should have explicit guidelines for evaluating the trade-offs between minimizing storage media and processing costs while maximizing service (speed). These trade-offs, summarized in Table 6-2, are based on the hierarchy of physical storage devices.

Table 6-2.   Data Base Management Physical Storage Hierarchy
—Trade-offs

Storage Type	Speed	Cost	Volume
Core	Very high	Very high	Low
Drum	High	High	Moderate
Disk	Moderate	Moderate	Moderately high
Tape	Low	Very Low	Unlimited

Generation of the Data Base Description. The final responsibility of the DBA in the design and implementation of the data base is to formally describe the data base using the data dictionary.

Data Base Access and Manipulation

The DA/DBA should have administrative control over access (reading) and manipulation (writing) of the data base. Without this, little meaningful control or protection can be exercised over the data base environment. The lack of such control can result in serious security and integrity problems. The following guidelines can strengthen the DA/DBA's administrative control over data base access and manipulation.

Corporate Data Base Policy. Publication of corporate policy statements regarding the data base environment is essential. These statements must reflect data base use among the various operating units within the organization. Such policy statements can do much to enhance the DA/DBA's administrative control and help promote a clear understanding with user and DP operating personnel regarding the data base.

Access Authorization. The authority over each data entity must be established. It must be decided who has the right and/or the need to know the content of the data as well as its existence. Those allowed to (1) read data from the data base, (2) add new occurrences of data into the data base, (3) update or change existing values of data, and (4) delete data from the data base should also be determined. Once such authority has been established, proper controls must be set up to prevent authority violations of the data base.

Data Base Security Procedures. Certain data entities in a given data base may be confidential (e.g., sensitive personnel data or competitive market statistics). Consideration should be given to the required data security in the following areas.

Software Protection. The DBMS can be implemented in a manner that will enforce data security. Passwords, for example, can be used to restrict or control access to the data base. Data access based on terminal location can be controlled by software. In addition, scrambling data into some unrecognizable format can protect the contents against unauthorized or accidental access, thus maintaining the confidentiality and security of the data.

Physical Protection. Numerous types of physical protections are also possible. One concept gaining popularity is the communications room, a controlled central facility with appropriate hardware and software for access to and manipulation of the data base. The main ingredient is the positive human control. Other types of physical protection include the physical separation of data entities, placing terminals in secured areas, the use of lockable terminals, taking terminals off-line when not in use, using dedicated leased lines rather than dial-up lines, and limiting the publication of information about data to the appropriate data base users.

Data Base Standards Control

If considerable sharing of data is expected, an important DA/DBA function is to formulate, establish, and maintain a consistent set of data base standards. Specific areas that the DA/DBA must consider for standards development include the following.

Data Definition. It is essential that all those involved in describing data entities use a uniform methodology and standard procedures for data definition. The DA must establish company-wide standards for the data entity hierarchy and data attributes as well as detailed procedures for the process of data definition. Much of this responsibility overlaps the task of establishing the data dictionary as a tool for data definition.

Data Use. The DA is responsible for standards relative to the use and/or interpretation of specific data entities. For certain widely used data entities, it is essential that the DA establish commonly agreed-upon definitions for all users concerned. For example, standards for data entities describing modes of transportation or types of freight would be useful in correlating surveys and reports in the transportation industry. Other common data entities that are candidates for standardization are date and commonly used codes. In this regard, it is the DA's responsibility to keep abreast of developments of the American National Standards Institute (ANSI) and the International Standards Organization (ISO).

Data Access and Manipulation. The DBA is responsible for standards relative to the manner in which the data base is accessed and manipulated. Without such standards, the data integrity relative to a DBMS cannot be ensured. For instance, if allowed to be used indiscriminately, certain DBMS commands can lead to inadvertent errors in the data base. The updating of values of an access key, for example, should be limited. Simple standard procedures for coding requests from the data base can reduce the number of errors and increase DBMS use.

Data Edit and Validation. The DA is also responsible for the standards relative to the editing and validation of data base input. In addition to ensuring that minimum criteria for data quality are met, the DA must see to it that the quality of input is uniform so that the data base remains as consistent as is practicable. The data dictionary can serve as a tool in recording these editing and validation rules. The DBA, however, must establish procedures to ensure compliance and maintain consistent quality in the data base. From a software viewpoint, this can be accomplished through the use of common edit and validation procedures, which can be called as subroutines by application programs.

Computer Operations. The DBA has the responsibility of ensuring that standard procedures are used by computer operations personnel when they are dealing with data bases. This includes standard backup procedures, restart, and recovery procedures, and other operations-related activities.

The formulation, establishment, and maintenance of data base environment standards is a thankless task. There are always those who resist acceptance of a uniform approach in deference to the old way of doing things. Areas of standardization should be carefully selected, and consideration should be given to the *status* of the standard. The DBA can issue a *proposed* standard, in which case compliance would be optional and the DBA would record deviations. Subsequently, the DBA can decide to upgrade the status to *approved,* in which case compliance would be mandatory and deviations would not be allowed. In general, a new standard requires negotiation, arbitration, and compromise before it is accepted by all parties concerned.

Data Base Documentation

Among the DA/DBA's purely administrative responsibilities are the tedious but essential tasks relating to documentation of the data base environment. This important responsibility includes the recording of the procedures, standards, guidelines, and data base descriptions necessary for the proper, efficient, and continuing use of the data base environment.

The various recipients of data base documentation include:

- End users
- The DA/DBA
- The computer operations staff
- The applications development staff

The DA/DBA is responsible for providing and maintaining adequate documentation of various types including, but not limited to, the following.

Description of Data Sources. The data dictionary is the primary tool for determining potential sources of information.

Description of the Data Base
- Data structures (logical)
- Storage structures (physical)
- Data attributes

Standards
- Approved standards
- Proposed standards and approved deviations

Data Access and Manipulation Procedures
- Constraints on use of DBMS commands
- CALL procedures
- Maintenance and update procedures

Passwords and User Identification
- Assignment procedures
- Actual ID assignments
- Terminal and data access procedures

DBMS Performance and Measurement
- Resources used, including frequency
- Users serviced
- Effectiveness with respect to response time and cost
- Procedures for monitoring frequency of DBMS use
- Procedures for DBMS performance management

Backup Procedures
- Identification of data to be backed up
- Volume of data to be backed up
- Backup facilities to be used
- Backup schedule

Restart and Recovery Procedures
- Restart procedures for the DBMS
- Recovery procedures
- Priority and sequence of restoration

Data Base Testing
- Test data base creation procedures
- Test completeness criteria
- Program acceptance criteria

Training and Education
- User training documentation
- Training criteria and curriculum

Table 6-3 shows suggested guidelines for the distribution of this documentation. Note that the majority of the documentation requirements for the data base environment can be supported by the data dictionary. With an automated dictionary, the manual labor devoted to producing data base documentation can be reduced.

Table 6-3.   Guidelines for the Distribution of Documentation

| | | Recipients | | |
Types of Documentation	End Users	DA/DBA	Computer Operations	Applications Development
Description of Data Sources	O	M		O
Description of the Data Base	M	M	O	M
Standards	M	M	M	M
Data Access and Manipulation Procedures	O	M		M
DBMS Performance and Measurement		M		O
Backup Procedures		M	M	O
Restart and Recovery Procedures		M	M	M
Data Base Testing		M	M	M
Password and User Identification	M	M		M
Training and Education	M	M	M	M

Legend:
M = Mandatory
O = Optional
Blank = Not applicable

Computer Operations

The DBA is responsible for ensuring that the computer operations staff performs its data-base-related duties properly. In this capacity, the DBA assists in establishing data-base-related operating procedures, restart and recovery procedures, special data base utilities, and schedules for computer time for data-base-related work.

Operating Procedures. The DBA is responsible for working with computer operations personnel to develop formal and documented procedures for data-base-related jobs on the computer. The areas that should be considered are:

• Loading a new data base
• Running special data base utilities
• Dictionary maintenance
• Data base maintenance
• Backup procedures

Restart and Recovery Procedures. The DBA must take steps to ensure that the data base can be restored to its proper state in the event of destruction or damage. The DBA must develop restart and recovery standards, procedures, and rules to provide such capability. Those involved in systems analysis, design, programming, computer operations, and data base administration must be educated in and adhere to these standards and procedures in order to ensure that restart and recovery of the data base can be accomplished. The DBA must enforce the standards, procedures, and rules.

Restart and recovery should be planned for and designed in conjunction with DBMS implementation rather than added as an afterthought.

Data Base Utilities. The DBA has the responsibility for the development or acquisition of utilities in order to facilitate certain functions involving the data base. One important utility function is to create test data bases of suitable size that reflect all the features of real-life data bases. Some other utility functions are:

- To dump and restore individual data sets or the entire data base
- To provide automated reports reflecting the integrity of the data in the data base
- To provide automatic reporting of security violations
- To provide facilities for restricting incompatible access to any or all data sets during restart and recovery
- To provide statistical information on data set load factors and the need for reorganization

Scheduling Computer Time. Although direct control over the computer schedule should reside with computer operations personnel, it is advisable to allow the DBA some control over computer scheduling as it relates to data base processing. This facilitates scheduling around problems and providing for priority use of the data base. Problems involving concurrency of update can be avoided in this way, and response times during relatively infrequent peak load times can be satisfied without undue effort.

Monitoring the Data Base Environment

The DBA must monitor the data base environment on a continuous basis in order to ensure an efficient level of service while maintaining data base integrity. This responsibility takes the form of a variety of activities and procedures, including the following.

Performance Management. The DBA is responsible for establishing a positive program of action to determine and ensure the continued stable performance of the data base software and hardware configuration. This involves an organized approach to continued monitoring of the following areas:

- Hardware configuration
- Software configuration (DBMS and operating systems)
- Data base design
- Application systems design
- Application programs
- Bottlenecks (contention for resources)

To perform the monitoring function in these areas, the DBA can use specialized measurement tools, including:

- Benchmark jobstreams
- Simulation models
- Synthetic programs
- Hardware/software monitors

Applied selectively, a combination of these tools can provide the DBA with enough information to manage the performance of the data base environment.

Data Base Controls. The DBA should establish appropriate data base controls and monitor them to assist him in ensuring data base integrity. Computer-generated control totals can be checked and cross-footed between computer processing runs or generated reports. Batch responses (e.g., inquiries calling for classes of things) can include such information as the exact run time, search parameters, the time of the last update of the data, and the primary parameter controls. This increases the confidence level and helps ensure the integrity of the data base.

Data Base Audit Trails. The DBA can protect the data base and help ensure data integrity by having a complete audit trail of activity against the data base. Such an audit trail usually consists of identification of the input transaction or message, a copy of the data base record before the update, and a copy of the data base record after the update. When data base problems occur, this type of audit trail is useful in determining what happened and in reconstructing the data.

In addition, the audit function is a means by which the DBA can detect missing data, late transaction reporting, and untimely error correction. This is important because problems must be detected and corrected before they have a serious impact on the operational capability to provide information upon request.

Another important capability that is derived from auditing the data base is prevention of a gradual erosion of the data base, which can be caused by various undetected problems (e.g., subtle bugs in application programs and obscure I/O errors). Such errors can go unnoticed for long periods of time. An audit tool that can aid the DBA in achieving a high level of data integrity is a data base diagnostic program, which can check data entities for reasonableness, forward and backward pointers, directory entries, and disk storage allocation tables.

Error Follow-up. To ensure common procedures in error handling and thus improve data base integrity, the DBA should consider having a common data error follow-up system. Data detected as erroneous should not be allowed to alter any part of the data base until the data is corrected. Data errors should be noted and returned to the party responsible for correction and then resubmitted for data base update. The error follow-up system should keep track of all errors, as well as those people responsible for correcting the errors. A positive error correction action would remove the error from the follow-up system. This type of follow-up system can also provide such statistical information as the percentages of errors being submitted, types of errors, sources of errors, and speed of error correction.

Violations of Standards and Guidelines. In administering the monitoring and control of the data base environment, it is necessary to know when violations of standards and guidelines occur. Whenever a violation occurs, the DA/DBA should take the following actions:

- *Identify the Violator.* It is important to determine who is committing the violations or causing the problems so that the situation can be rectified.
- *Report the Violation.* The appropriate organizational unit or individual must be informed so that the situation can be corrected.
- *Follow-up.* Follow-up by the DBA can ensure that all problems and violations are satisfactorily resolved. Should repeat violations or failure to correct a problem occur, the DBA must bring these incidents to the attention of appropriate management for review and resolution.

DBMS Improvement

Monitoring, auditing, and operations activities tend to uncover potential areas for DBMS improvement. The DBA is responsible for evaluating possible improvements and initiating improvement activities.

Education and Training

The DA/DBA is responsible for the education and training of all personnel in data base concepts and the procedures and techniques involved in operating in the data base environment. He is responsible for the training curriculum and the content of the training materials to be used. DP personnel training must include data base environment implementation, maintenance, and operation. Non-DP users must be trained in concepts, data availability, data entry, report generation, and query facilities.

Vendor Interfaces

The DA/DBA is the primary interface between the company and the vendors of data base products. He must maintain communications with the vendors in order to maintain state-of-the-art knowledge of software and hardware developments and DBMS capabilities. Because the DBA plays a significant part in the installation and subsequent enhancement of the DBMS and because a viable data base is dependent on communication and teamwork between the vendors and the DP department, the DBA can help determine the roots of problems leading to equipment and operating system failures.

SUMMARY

DA/DBA functional responsibility is presented in this chapter as a somewhat abstract ideal of what the DA/DBA should accomplish. In reality, the DA/DBA function must evolve gradually. It also requires extensive interface with other parts of the corporation, both inside and outside the DP area. In addition, the organizational implications of introducing the DA/DBA function are complex and require considerable attention.

chapter 7

User/System Interfaces in a Data Base Environment

INTRODUCTION

The long-sought-after goal of an integrated management information system has yet to be achieved. A major cause of this failure has been the lack of software to organize, access, and control corporate data. As a consequence, there has been a flurry of activity toward developing constructs, requirements, and specifications for Data Base Management Systems.

Numerous DBMSs have been introduced in past years and new ones are in various stages of development and implementation. DBMSs alone, however, cannot create an integrated information system that will help the user to solve problems. The user also needs a clearly defined method for approaching the data that is required to solve problems. To this end, interfaces are established between the user and the data. These interfaces are known collectively as User/System Interfaces.

This chapter will treat two distinct levels of interfaces:

- **User Level USIs**—these interfaces are aimed directly at the user and enable the user to structure data into usable information, thus providing fuller utilization of system resources.

- **System Level USIs**—these are specially designed interfaces within the system that increase control, generalization, and/or flexibility. These interfaces generally allow more users to interface with the data base, increase the DBA's control over the data base environment, and provide for greater independence of the components of the data base environment.

USER INTERFACES

The following aspects of user interfaces will be discussed:

- Support of the decision process
- User language interfaces
- USI augmentation tools
- USI commercial products

Support of the Decision Process

The decision process has been analyzed by numerous researchers. Barkin and Lasky[1] have synthesized much of this work and have established a sequential decision process that consists of three analytical phases:

1. *Intelligence phase*—identification of the problem
2. *Design phase*—generation of alternative solutions
3. *Choice phase*—evaluation of alternatives and selection of the final solution

By applying Miller's research on the decision process,[2] these phases can be expanded:

1. *Intelligence phase*
   - *Status inquiry*—equivalent to simple inquiry, this operation involves retrieval or update by a unique identifier and/or attribute of interest.
   - *Briefing*—this is a request for information about what is being accomplished or what has been accomplished; briefing is usually done according to a set of categories that relate to subject matter or responsibility of the specific user.
   - *Exception detection*—this involves comparing briefing information (what is) with planning information (what should be) and then interpreting any deviations. An exception exists if the user decides to take action, even if that action is further inquiry.

- *Diagnosis*—this involves posing test questions in such a manner that the source of the gross symptoms is discovered by a logical process of exclusion.

2. *Design phase*
   - *Construction*—this involves building new systems based on selected alternatives. The supporting system does two basic chores. It applies the rules and constraints to each design action taken, and it remembers the work already done by the user.
   - *Evaluation/Optimization*—in this operation the problem solver uses a graphic language to construct a model that will simulate the problem set.

3. *Choice phase*
   - *Planning/Choosing*—this involves matching requirements with resources; it is, in effect, multiple-category statistics matching.
   - *Discovery*—this involves such operations as selective browsing through references or examination of different quantitative data in order to form a "hunch" about the control variables that might explain diverse phenomena.

The USI must support the decision process in order to facilitate the user's problem-solving needs. Individual modules of the USI will provide specific support to some or all of the activities in the decision process. Languages, for example, will provide support across the entire process, while simulation tools can assist in the design and choice phases.

The decision process is also affected by the types of decisions that need to be made and by the types of data that are available to the user.

For our purposes, decisions can be classified as those that can be anticipated (or preformulated) and those that cannot (see Figure 7-1). The former class comprises decisions that tend to be repetitive. Thus, they are more adaptable to preestablished computer logic and consume fewer system resources. Decisions in the latter class, however, tend to be unique, less adaptable to computer logic, and more expensive in terms of system resources.

Data, too, can be assigned to two broad categories: quantitative and nonquantitative. Quantitative data can be further partitioned into "soft" data (e.g., GNP estimates or the Consumer Price Index) and "hard" data (e.g., units of production in a manufacturing facility); both are easily manipulated by the computer (see Figure 7-1). Nonquantitative data, such as employee morale or the mood of stockholders, can also be stored and retrieved by the computer, but they do not lend themselves to algorithmic manipulation. While it is possible to quantify such data, the user

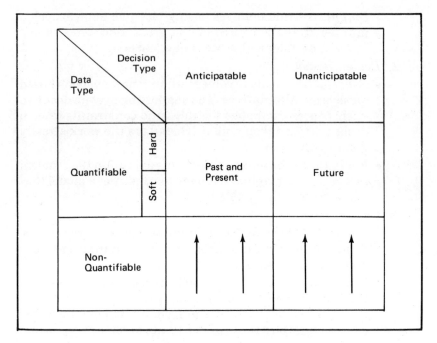

Figure 7-1. Decision Model

must realize that the resulting "numbers" are subjective in nature and must be analyzed with different statistical techniques than either the "hard" or "soft" quantitative data. Figure 7-1 depicts the decision model that results from these considerations.

User Language Interfaces

Each type of user has a different view of the data base and generally accesses the data base with a characteristically unique subset of his native language. Following Senko's lead, users can be divided into three classes for the purposes of surveying user language interfaces:

- Structurally independent
- Structurally parametric
- Structurally dependent

The *structurally independent* user is generally unconcerned about the storage structure. Rather, this user is interested in specific data values and, sometimes, in specific attributes of items of metadata (data about data, e.g., frequency of update, source). Typical of this class of user is the manager who in all probability has an information model in mind. It is for this type of user that the work on natural language recognition and programming is being conducted. The goal of this research is to provide the user with the capability to express a request for information in natural language and have the system interpret the request, search the data bank, select the necessary data, structure and/or associate the data, and return the information.

The *structurally parametric* user is concerned only with a finite subset of the data bank and generally requires only a limited number of ways to structure or associate this data. This user requires a specific logical view, not a physical one. Thus, the parametric user will typically invoke one of an array of preestablished transactions that vary only in the values supplied at the time of retrieval. For example, someone in the purchasing department might request the part numbers of all the parts produced in Plant 3 that are used in assembly A and have an inventory lower than four weeks production.

The *structurally dependent* user is concerned with the physical, or storage, structure of data and their characteristics and attributes; this user has only a minimal interest in specific data values. The primary objective of this user is to optimize repetitive, procedural manipulation of data and not to interpret or use the results. The data base administration function would fall into this class, as would the programmer and analyst in facilities where there is no data base administration function.

It is important that each of these types of users be provided with the facilities to operate on the same data with their individual language subsets. In addition, it is important that the language facilities support multiple classes of users in order to satisfy query, parametric, and metadata requests.

User/System Augmentation Tools

Perhaps because they are more tangible and thus easier to define, operands have been the focus of a significant amount of research. Three types of operands are noteworthy: arithmetic, graphical, and modeling.

Arithmetic operands are by far the most simplistic—their origins can be traced to the principles of the digital computer. Basic arithmetic operations are continuously performed on data under the preestablished logic approach. When dealing with decisions that cannot be anticipated, however, the time frame cannot accommodate the development of this logic. Thus, the logic must be established on an ad hoc basis or supplied before-hand or, possibly, both.

Establishing procedural logic on an ad hoc basis is much more difficult than attempting to anticipate needs and supply the requisite tools in advance; the latter approach, therefore, is more desirable. (Work on establishing procedural logic on an ad hoc basis—natural language programming—is being done, but substantive results are not expected for quite some time. A first step in this process is selecting pieces of preestablished procedural logic from a catalog and structuring them into a program. The goal, however, is for this process to occur automatically on the basis of a problem statement expressed in natural language.)

Examples of arithmetic operands range from the basic, such as addition, subtraction, division, multiplication, to the more sophisticated, such as confidence limits and standard deviations. All of these operands would be callable via macros and capable of accepting as input the subset of data that the user has selected and retrieved from the data bank.

The second type of operand—the graphical operand—fulfills the almost universal human need for graphical representation of large amounts of complex data. Computers can perform these graphical operations much more efficiently than humans. All that the machine requires is to be supplied with a catalog of graphs —curves, histograms, pie charts, scatter diagrams—and with the capability to contract or expand the axis and to store, retrieve, overlay, and combine such graphs.

The modeling operand fulfills another human need in the decision process—the need to successively rearrange the crucial variables in a specific decision-making process. For example, when confronted with the relatively simple decision of purchasing a number of different items that are available only at specific locations, a simple transportation model might be constructed that takes into account such variables as current locations, available conveyance, one-way streets, and hours of business. Presumably, an optimal route can be plotted from the model.

Interactive, computer-aided modeling is a necessary adjunct to arithmetic and graphical operands. Modeling allows users to perform simulations with extracted data, identify and isolate key relationships, and identify and discard meaningless or insignificant variables.

Unfortunately, interactive modeling operands are not currently available nor will they be in the near future. Currently available modeling and simulation tools are not interactive and are not accessible through the available query languages.

USI Commercial Products

Commercial endeavors in the area of User/System Interfaces are as old as the software industry itself. Generally, USI commercial offerings have been restricted to language and software that are supported for information retrieval. Two categories of software have emerged:

- Report Generators (RPG)—Report Generator products consist of a usually sophisticated user-oriented language for the specification of user reports, code-generation modules, and/or executable code to generate the reports.
- Query Processors (QP)—Query processor products also consist of a usually sophisticated user-oriented language for the specification of information requirements, interpretive modules, and/or executable code.

Figure 7-2 illustrates the major difference between RPGs and QPs. The RPG package is typically used for precoding anticipatable requests for quantifiable data. In contrast, the QP packages are used for requests that cannot be anticipated for quantified data. The fact that these requests cannot be anticipated precludes precoding them. Thus, the QP is used to increase turnaround by interpreting the user-specified request "on the fly."

It should be noted that some commercial products (e.g., Mark IV) can be used as an RPG and/or a QP.

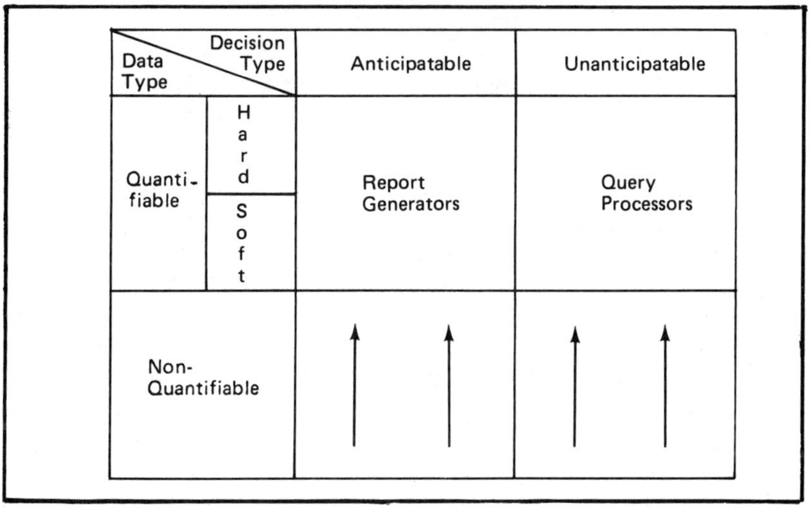

Data Type \ Decision Type		Anticipatable	Unanticipatable
Quanti- fiable	H a r d S o f t	Report Generators	Query Processors
Non- Quantifiable		↑ ↑	↑ ↑

Figure 7-2. The Use of USI Commercial Products

SYSTEM INTERFACES

The concept of User/System Interfaces can be extended to include the provision of generalized and flexible interfaces for other system components. The need for such interfaces must be weighed against their overhead and the additional level(s) of indirection that they introduce. Two such system interfaces are typical examples of low-level USIs: the Transaction Controller and the Data Base Input/Output Controller (DBIOC). Figure 7-3 illustrates the relationship between these two low-level USIs and other elements of the data base environment.

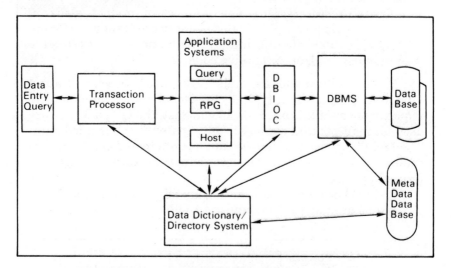

Figure 7-3. Elements of a Data Base Environment

Transaction Controller

The Transaction Controller, which is located between the Data Entry/Query Facilities and Application Systems, has two general functions:

- It handles transactions entering the data base environment and distributes messages/responses flowing from the environment.
- It schedules and monitors application systems and subsystems within the environment.

Within the first category of transaction handling, the Transaction Controller may perform a wide variety of functions. Among these are:

- Basic edit/validation (size/range check)
- Terminal and user password verification
- Transaction logging
- Message and/or query checkpointing

As a low-level USI, the Transaction Controller performs these functions as a generalized software utility, providing services that would otherwise have to be coded within application systems as dedicated codes.

Data Base I/O Controller (DBIOC)

The DBIOC is an optional USI element of the data base environment. Functionally, the DBIOC acts as an intermediate process between application programs or processes (host, query or report writer languages, i.e., other higher-level USIs) and the DBMS. As shown in Figure 7-3 the DBIOC would accept all "calls" or service requests from an application program. The DBIOC would further process the request, pass the request to the DBMS, and return all responses (both status and data) from the DBMS to the requesting application program.

Use of this low-level USI helps to provide greater flexibility and control over the data base environment. Greater flexibility can be achieved, for example, by allowing for non-DBMS access methods to be utilized with effective transparency to application programs. Similarly, more than one DBMS could be accommodated while still maintaining a uniform programming interface (i.e., DML). This concept is called DBMS independence. Additional control over the data base environment could be achieved by including modules in the DBIOC that handle specific functions uniformly according to installation standards. These might include:

- Additional data security
- Edit/validate functions
- Error handling
- Status control

DBIOC products are generally offered by the DBMS vendors themselves. Independent software houses have not as yet entered this field. Thus, the DBIOC products currently available are oriented towards additional control facilities and are not intended to allow for DBMS package independence.

SUMMARY

The concept of USIs focuses attention on the need to emphasize the usability of information. Data base supported information systems are made useful at the user interface level. The benefits of data base technology (e.g., DBMSs) can only be realized with appropriate USIs facilitating and supporting the use of system and data resources.

Management, in considering the implementation of data base supported information systems, should allow for significant emphasis on the user-oriented aspects of the interfaces. In particular, emphasis should be placed on the ability of the system to support identifiable decision processes and user language requirements.

Notes

---

1   S. R. Barkin and J. A. Lasky, *The Analysis and Design of Man-Machine Decision Systems: A Behavioral Perspective.* Working Paper Series, Management Information Systems Research Center. University of Minnesota.

2   R. B. Miller, *Archetypes in Man-Computer Problem Solving.* (TR 00.1909, IBM Corporation, Systems Development Division. Poughkeepsie, New York, August 1969).

chapter **8**

Data Independence in Data Base Management Systems

INTRODUCTION

The fact that users of data (often programmers) do not have to be aware of the format in which data is physically stored is called data independence.

Transparent record buffering is a simple form of data independence offered by almost all operating systems. While coding, the programmer need not be aware of the file blocking factor to be used; the factor can be selected at a later time in order to make optimal use of the assigned storage device.

Another form of data independence is offered in some commercially available data base management systems (DBMSs). This allows the addition of a field to a file without affecting existing programs. In some cases it can even be done without reloading the file. This can drastically reduce the time necessary for DP department response to new user requirements.

This chapter addresses data independence in the context of DBMSs and other components of the data base environment. The chapter begins with a discussion of costs and benefits. An example illustrating levels of data independence is introduced followed by detailed discussion of specific categories of data independence in a data base environment. Implementation considerations are addressed in terms of software components and the design approach.

COSTS AND BENEFITS

The costs and benefits of data independence are related to the amount of change in the DP installation. Achieving data independence involves definite costs for an organization, and few (if any) benefits can be realized in the operation of existing systems. However, when new applications are developed or old ones are modified, significant savings can be realized.

The Benefits of Data Independence

Protection of Your Investment in Existing Systems. Most systems are subject to changing functional requirements and operating environments. These changes may require modification in the application's use of the data—for instance, addition of a new field or index to a file. Changes may require reorganization of the physical storage of data (such as combining two files into one or separating one file into on-line and off-line parts). If applications can continue to operate through a data-independent interface, these modifications can be achieved with relatively low cost. Frequently, the ability to effect such changes without reprogramming can make the difference between cost-justification and cancellation of a new project.

More Rapid Development of New Systems. The ability to access a data base in a new way without affecting existing applications can mean the difference between continuing and cancelling a project. Analysis and programming are simplified by systems that allow each user to view the data as if it were tailored to the current problem(s). Effective user access to a data base requires that the data be described in a logical fashion; there is no reason for the user to be aware of the details of the physical storage or even the file structure. A DBMS with sufficient data independence should provide for easy and rapid definitions of new logical views, thus facilitating faster development of new systems.

Control of Sharing the Data Resource. In a large organization that has committed itself to viewing its data resource as a significant asset, administration and control of the sharing of the data is a major task. If the data base administrator can understand, define, and manage the data at the logical level, this task is greatly simplified. Optimizing the storage of data for the best possible performance in the environment, however, should be recognized as a separate task requiring different technical expertise. Data independence in this sense need not involve software at all but instead requires a discipline and vocabulary for discussing information at the logical (conceptual) level.

Costs of Data Independence

Machine Resources. Data independence is implemented through interfaces, each of which costs something in machine resources. The overall installation of a system must be evaluated in terms of the capital as opposed to the labor costs of implementing a high level of data independence. Note that the costs in machine resources are primarily expended in implementing levels of "indirection" between the user and the DBMS.

Cost of Introducing a New Approach. Introducing any new approach involves the cost of retraining personnel. Data independence implemented at a high level may involve new concepts that are not readily understood. For instance, instead of data being information in a file on tape that is moved into an area in working storage, it is fluid. This change in concept can be a bigger hurdle for personnel to jump than learning the details of the software. Note that the available software varies greatly in terms of ease of use.

Cost of Centralization. Data independence implemented through a high-level central dictionary with created user views (subschemas) requires centralized coordination among DBAs, programmers, analysts, and management. This centralization should benefit the organization, but it will also consume personnel resources. The cost of new forms, meetings, and procedures should be considered carefully.

AN EXAMPLE OF DATA INDEPENDENCE

A system that incorporates most of the levels of data independence discussed here is the LADDER system developed at SRI International for the U.S. Navy. This self-contained query system accepts questions framed using an English-like vocabulary (much more like English than is acceptable for most commercial user query languages) and extracts answers from a data base that can be distributed over a number of files in a number of computers. The user can be completely unaware of the structure of the files in the data base and/or their physical location. As long as the user asks an intelligent question in terms of the data base content, the LADDER system can provide an answer.

The significance of different levels of data independence is shown in Table 8-1. The corresponding LADDER components are listed in Table 8-2. An explanation of the implementation of these components follows:

- The natural language interpretation is performed by a module called INLAND, which uses a system called LIFER to interpret user questions and reduce them to a simple standard format. This format uses standard field names but does not require file identification. In a data base containing data on presidents and elections, the inquiry "Who was the last president from California?" would be reformulated to something like:

$$\text{(? ELECTION-YEAR)(*MAX ELECTION-YEAR)}$$
$$\text{(HOME-STATE EQ "CALIFORNIA")}$$

which can be read as: Give me the largest election year for presidents whose home state is California.

- The Intelligent Data Access (IDA) module receives the inquiry and determines which files it must access and the logical relationships among them. In this case, it discovers that it must access two files—an ELECTIONS file that contains the presidents and the year(s) in which they won an election and a PRESIDENTS file that supplies the presidents and their home states. An internal query is formulated based on the logical link between the two files:
  - —In the PRESIDENTS file, find all the presidents whose home state is California.
  - —For each president found, find his election year (or years) in the ELECTION file and return the maximum value found.

- This internal query is passed to the File Access Manager (FAM) module, which determines where the files are located on the ARPANET (an extensive network of computers of various types). FAM establishes a communications link with the DBMSs on the computer(s) housing the pertinent files. Note that it is conceivable that the two files would be on two separate machines running two different DBMSs.

- In this example, the operating interface is with the *Datacomputer*, a computer on the network dedicated to data base management. The *Datacomputer* accepts the file query, determines if there is an index built on the fields specified, transfers the data from one of several levels of storage into memory, translates the data into a form compatible with the receiving CPU, and returns the requested data. If the PRESIDENTS file has an index on the homestate field, it will be used; if not, the file will be scanned for the value "CALIFORNIA." The *president* identifier will be formulated into a character string readable by the LADDER computer. If the data resides on a mass storage device, it will be transferred to a high-speed device. The *president* value is returned, and IDA uses it to formulate the second part of the inquiry, which may go to a different computer and/or DBMS.

Table 8-1.   Levels of Data Independence

Level of Data Independence	What the User Does Not Have to Know
File Contents	Which elements are in which file.
File Linkage	How the files are related to each other.
Element Order	What the order of the data elements in a record is.
Element Equivalence	What elements identify the record.
Element Characteristics	How a data item is derived, used, or edited.
Element Format	What the internal format of the data item is.
File Access Path	Which data elements are keys. What the relationships in the data base are.
File Access Method	How the file is physically organized.
Device Type	On what type of device the data is stored.

Table 8-2.   Levels of Data Independence in the LADDER System

Level	LADDER Component
File Contents	IDA (Intelligent Data Access)
File Linkage	IDA
Element Order	The *Datacomputer*
Element Equivalence	INLAND (Natural Language Interface)
Element Characteristics	IDA
Element Format	The *Datacomputer*
File Access Path	The *Datacomputer*
File Location	FAM (File Access Manager)
File Access Method	First Operating System for *Datacomputer*
Device Type	*Datacomputer* Operating System

This example illustrates what can be done with a data-independent set-up in a management information system. The transparency from the physical device to the user is apparent. As would be expected, given the amount of machine and line activity involved, answers to queries are not instantaneous; but, to quote one user, "I don't mind waiting 10 minutes for the tube to come back when I know it would take two weeks for the DP department to process my request."

TYPES OF DATA INDEPENDENCE

Once the concept of data independence is understood many categorizations are possible. The breakdown given here and summarized in Table 8-1 starts at a low level with storage devices and becomes increasingly more abstract as it covers types of independence oriented toward the end user instead of the programmer.

Physical Device Independence

Physical device transparency is offered in many DBMSs. With this feature, the programmer need not know whether he or she is writing to a disk, tape, printer, or the newest in mass storage devices. With the rapid development of memory technology (data storage in the broader sense), device transparency is as important to hardware vendors marketing new equipment as it is to the user. In fact, many mass storage devices have been designed to resemble disks.

A discussion of the three types of physical device transparency follows.

Operating Systems. Each operating system offers a different level of device transparency, particularly at the command language (job control) level. Systems programmers moving from a DEC-10 to an IBM operating system, for instance, find themselves specifying all sorts of parameters for data sets that the first operating system was perfectly able to determine. A good modern operating system requires, at most, a general indication of the size of a file before creating it and is able to optimize the blocking factor for the device used. This is not trivial transparency because command language conversion is often one of the major factors preventing an installation from changing to a different machine.

One successful approach has been to design operating systems with the idea that all I/O appear in the same format to the system. Device drivers are used for this purpose. It is interesting that this approach has been forced on the designers of teleprocessing monitors through sheer necessity. In the MULTICS system developed for MIT, for example, there is no difference between a disk file, a tape, a segment of memory (which is, in fact, virtual), or a teletype. File positioning commands do not, of course, work with sequential devices; nevertheless, transferring data to and from tape, disk, and memory is transparent to the user. IBM's TSO approaches this but with only partial success.

DBMSs. Various commercial DBMSs offer physical device transparency in one form or another. Most of them run on all common random access devices; IMS even supports tapes for certain access methods. The evaluator of a DBMS should consider the ease with which one can add or change to a new device. Note that a change of this type should have minimum effect on programs.

Storage management in many packages is based on the paging system of the supporting operating system. This should be transparent to the user and device-independent. In such systems as MULTICS, a DBMS can build directly on the operating system's storage management.

The user of a very large data base should investigate the ability of a DBMS to transfer data in a hierarchy of storage devices. The questions, "Can the data base be run partly on-line and partly off-line?" and "Must users be interrupted in order to bring parts of the data base on-line?" are directly related to the ability of the DBMS to support physical device independence.

Associative Memories and Intelligent Data Storage Devices.
There are definite indications that associative memory will be used in commercially available devices in the near future. This is memory that is content-addressable. A key is provided that retrieves the data without a sequential or index search. This has

obvious application in data base management (particularly in index implementation), but it could create problems in terms of device transparency. The question of using this type of memory with existing data base management software is part of the broader question of intelligent data storage devices. If parts of the software are converted into "firmware" on new data devices, will this give an overwhelming advantage to the DBMSs from the hardware vendors? There are no easy answers to this type of question. In the perspective of this chapter, the software/firmware transparency question is not a practical issue.

Access Methods

Many modern operating systems and DBMSs offer a level of access method transparency to the programmer. Most systems allow sequential access to files that have different internal structures; this is, in fact, the purpose of ISAM (although COBOL requires specifications of an ISAM file even when it is to be accessed sequentially). IBM, in encouraging a switch from ISAM to VSAM, has provided a transparency interface. Physical record formats are usually transparent in that there is no need to know whether a record is fixed- or variable-length.

Indexing and space management allow a wide variety of algorithms for different uses. VSAM, for example, is a major change from ISAM both in terms of indexing algorithms and space management.

DBMSs also vary in access method transparency. IBM's IMS is the undisputed champion in its offering of access methods. Two levels of access methods transparency, with four logical access methods, are available; each access method is based on one or more of four physical access methods, depending on the operating system being used. This kind of choice in access method offers considerable flexibility to the DBA in tuning data base physical storage to a particular application. In IMS, however, the access methods are only partially transparent. A program designed for one access method at the logical level may not operate if this access method is changed. A data base tuned for one application may not perform well for a second application that accesses the data in a different manner.

One of the major choices in indexing is between physical indexing (as used by VSAM and various "inverted" DBMSs) and randomized indexing (hashing or CALC in CODASYL). These methods should be functionally equivalent for the programmer, but many DBMSs require specification of the accesssing method in the access language as well as the data definition. This difference is inherent in DBMSs like TOTAL or those that are CODASYL based. They draw a distinction between files with unique keys and those that are chained to them through a nonunique key. ADABAS, on the other hand, now supports a hashed index for a file, which is entirely transparent to the programmer.

In summary, conceptually, only a few different things can be done with files. They can be read sequentially, positioned at a given point, or read at random; a record can be written, updated, or deleted. Transparency of access method implies that the programmer or user need not know specifics about the physical implementation of a file in order to perform these functions.

Access Path Independence

An *access path* is a way of getting at data. An index is one obvious example. In a completely data-independent system, the physical access paths are transparent to the user. In the LADDER system and in various implementations of "relational" systems, the user requests the information he wants by specifying the search criteria, and the system chooses the best one from its catalog of access paths. As such, the user does not have to be aware of how the access path is implemented.

At a more basic level is the question of whether a DBMS or access method can supply secondary indexes. If so, can they be created without disturbing existing applications or reloading the data base? Many "inverted" DBMSs (e.g., SYSTEM 2000 and ADABAS) offer this facility, which is an inherent benefit derived from their separation of data and indexing information. In fact, this multiple-index capability is one of the main attractions of this type of DBMS. It should be noted that VSAM and IMS now offer a secondary indexing capability and that various CODASYL packages (e.g., IDMS) have added this facility. This is not surprising because direct access to a record from a variety of viewpoints is one of the principal reasons for having a data base.

The same kind of questions should be asked of systems based on chained records. In a CODASYL data base, for instance, how easy is it to add a new *set*? In some implementations, this requires a reload of the file in order to make room for the new pointers. In others, the pointers and data are stored separately, and a measure of independence is thereby attained.

An important aspect of data independence in a DBMS is the impact of storage reorganization on access paths. Access paths involve pointers, from an index to data or from one record to the next. If a data record is moved from one place to another, either as part of a reorganization or because it has been expanded, how many sets of physical pointers must be changed? In any DBMS, for example, it may be desirable to place records in a particular physical sequential order (transparent to the program code) to achieve optimal access times. In some systems, this involves unloading and reloading not only the file's data but also all of its indexes and all other files that contain pointers to it. This can be very time consuming. Other systems, by separating physical addressing from logical addressing, offer a significant degree of internal transparency.

This example raises another point. Access paths may be transparent to the programmer, but they are not transparent in terms of processing efficiency. The application that accesses records in the order in which they are stored in the physical blocks will be far more efficient than one that requires disk arm movement for almost every access. This is the reason that one of the CODASYL specifications requires some records to be stored "near" others. As applications change, however, the major application may be one that accesses records in a sequence or pointer chain that was not planned for. In this situation, the ease with which the physical arrangement of records can be changed becomes important. And if it *can* be done, it is important to know whether it will be transparent to existing applications.

Finally, we return to the first point, Does the user have to be aware of indexes or pointers at all? SYSTEM 2000 accepts any specification of selection criteria, determines which ones are supported by indexes, and scans the records to select those satisfying criteria that are not based on indexed fields. This ability is a prerequisite for any true relational DBMS, and the experimental systems, such as System R and INGRES, contain algorithms for similar determination of the optimum processing strategy for finding a requested set of records. Some systems will dynamically create indexes if this is found to be more efficient than repeated sequential scans. This level of transparency may not be significant for large high-volume applications in which analysis predetermines the best physical access paths, but it is of great importance in the implementation of effective end-user interfaces.

Data Element Independence

Format-Related Independence. In distinguishing between information and its representation, the most basic distinction is between an item of information and its form of storage. A tem-

perature is a real, physical fact. It may be stated in degrees—
Kelvin, Celsius, or Fahrenheit. The number of degrees may be
stored in computer memory as a fixed-point binary integer, a
floating-point number, a decimal number, or a character string.
These representations have different uses but convey the same
information.

A number of DBMSs (e.g., SYSTEM 2000 and ADABAS) allow
the user or programmer to specify an input or output format for a
data item. This allows the conversion of a number from any standard format to any other, and sometimes allows conversion from a
number to a character string and vice versa. It also allows for
retrieval of data items into a field of a specified length. (This is a
corollary of the fact that the internal format of data in a data base
is usually the most compact format possible.)

SYSTEM 2000 has a special data type for dates. It can store
dates in a format requiring minimum space, and the user can
access the dates in any of several formats. This feature is greatly
appreciated by programmers bored with converting YYMMDD
dates to DDMMYY or MMDDYY for display.

Characteristics and Qualification. Date is an example of the
idea of the *domain* of a variable. An employee's birthday is a fact,
and its domain is "date." Furthermore, if it is the birthday of a
living person, its domain is "date within the past 100 years." A
variable in a data base possesses not only a format but characteristics; it has a domain that defines all of its possible values and
the way(s) in which it can be used. If this information can be stored
centrally, it gives a new level of data transparency (i.e., the logic
involved in using the variable can be changed without affecting
existing programs).

Some CODASYL implementations offer an approach to this
facility through the *data base procedure*. A similar nonCODASYL
type of data independence is available through the use of the
derived data element. Such virtual fields are available in a number
of systems. When fields or records are accessed, code is automatically invoked to perform certain user-specified functions. In the
case of a virtual field, this function is the actual calculation of the
field from other fields in the data base; the prgrammer (or user) is
not aware that the field does not physically exist. The calculation
for creating the field can be changed, and the programmer need
never change any code.

When this kind of facility is extended to field editing, it becomes possible for a DBA to maintain tight control of the integrity
of the data base. All updated fields are subjected to a single well-

controlled edit that cannot be bypassed. The edit can be altered any time to reflect changing criteria for validity, and the editing logic is transparent to the programmer and the user. This kind of facility is essential if user-oriented languages are to be extended to cover update as well as inquiry applications.

This type of generalized field validation is not widely available in today's commercial DBMSs. It is often argued that it cannot be accomplished efficiently. Careful implementation, however, should result in merely moving processing functions from application programs (where they may be coded many times) to the DBMS (where they need only be coded once).

Equivalence of Data Items

In dealing with information instead of data, it becomes evident that many data items are logically equivalent to others. Thus, an employee number may simply be a more convenient identifier for DP purposes than the person's name; in fact, either item could be used to make inquiries. It is possible to conceive of a DBMS that would keep track of this kind of equivalence and would support data access retrieval using any of the equivalent specifications. The LADDER system approaches this; it knows in a query where a specification for "ship" should occur, and any sort of identification of a ship or ships can be correctly interpreted.

Data Structure Independence

Data structure independence refers to the various forms of data independence relating to the grouping of data entities on storage devices. Programmers and analysts are accustomed to working with well-defined records containing a fixed set of elements in a fixed order. The first deviation with this simple structure was the variable-length record with groups of elements occurring a variable number of times (as in the OCCURS DEPENDING ON feature in COBOL). This type of data independence falls into three categories based on element order within a record, logical structure independence, and the transparency of actual record content (in which elements can migrate from one record type to another without affecting the application programs).

Element Order. This type of facility has been present for many years through the FORTRAN format statement, which can be specified at run time. Many DBMSs offer this facility (frequently along with element format independence) through some type of format specification that lists the elements required by an application and the order in which they should be accessed. This is also one of the purposes of the Subschema Facility in the CODASYL standard, although some implementations allow subschema definition only to the record level. IMS until very recently only allowed logical view definition to the segment level.

The importance of accessing only the desired elements from a record type lies not so much in user convenience but in the transparency of the addition of an element to a record type. If an application accesses a specified set of elements from a record, the addition of a new element should not affect the application; if the application accesses complete records, any change in one of the record types will at least force a recompilation of the application.

Evaluators of DBMSs should note the ease with which an element can be added or elements can be reordered within a data base. In some cases, the addition of an element can force a recompilation of the entire data base definition or subschema definitions. This type of change can be accomplished with or without physical file reorganization. In ADABAS, for example, a field can be added to the end of a record type without requiring physical reorganization, but any change to the order of elements requires redefinition and reorganization of the file.

Logical Design Independence. Logical design independence is the independence of access from the actual organization of data into record types and record structures. An example may help to clarify the concept.

Figure 8-1 shows a common data structure for an educational institution. Students enroll in a number of classes, teachers teach a number of classes, and each class may have a number of teachers teaching it. This description suggests two many-to-many relation-

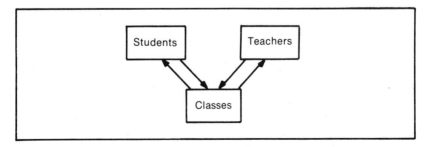

Figure 8-1. Data Structure for an Educational Institution

ships linked through the classes. Many questions can be asked of this data base:

- Who are a student's teachers?
- Who are a teacher's students?
- Who are the students in a class?
- What is a student's schedule?

The ways in which this data structure can be physically organized are also numerous; a few are shown in Figure 8-2.

A hierarchical or network-structured DBMS will choose one of these designs as the physical implementation. Many implementations based on traditional files may also want to do so, depending on the known importance of a single application in the installation. For example, if students' class schedules are known to be the principal processing task of the data base, the system

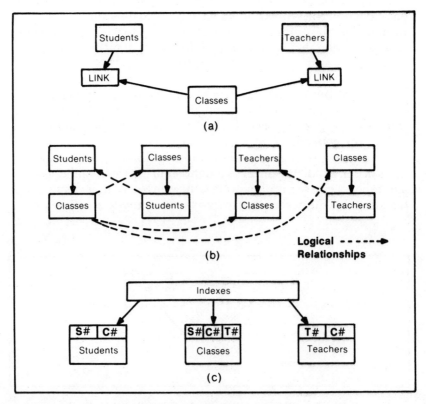

Figure 8-2. Physical Implementation Alternatives for the Educational Institution Data Structure

can be implemented using the design shown in Figure 8-2(a). Note, however, that this particular implementation is not inherent in the data.

Data independence means that any application can view the data in the way most convenient to it (a user view) without actual knowledge of the structure of the records in the data base. In the educational institution example, if it is discovered that the generation of class lists is consuming five times the resources of the student-scheduling application, it may be best to move the student numbers into the class file, instead of having the class numbers in the student file, as in the design shown in Figure 8-2(b). But, can this be done without changing the existing applications?

IMS allows a definition of logical hierarchies that can solve this problem to some extent. Maintaining the information in separate files as shown in Figure 8-2(c), using only logical connections between common fields, offers the best possibility of application independence.

The reader may wish to consider the problems of updating the data base in other file configurations. We know that the configuration that exhibits the fewest problems is the one with the simplest files. In this case, it is the file structure that most closely corresponds to the relational model of data; this means that simple files with simple characteristics have been used. Whether an installation can actually use files organized this way depends on the applications. The point here is that the user should not be required to know what the physical files look like or how they are physically related.

Records can be logically linked by containing some common data elements. We can read one record, obtain a data value, and use it as a key for another record (assuming an access path using that element is present in the second record). Linkage can be accomplished physically by the use of pointers (as it is in most owner/member implementations) or through physical contiguity (one record next to another, as it is in a sequential file implementation of a hierarchical data structure using record types). The logical linkage can always be reversed, while a physical linkage may or may not be reversible. The data base designer should remember that any relationship goes two ways and that users may wish to see the information from the bottom of a hierarchy instead of the top.

Record Content Independence. Strictly speaking, a record is only a convenient way of organizing a set of data elements that may be related. It has been suggested that the actual data definition need not be in terms of records at all. This view of information is the one presented to the user of LADDER. An intelligent user is assumed to be able to ask questions in the realm of interest of the data base without concern about files and linkages. The system designer defines to LADDER all the files and implicit linkages, which are software uses in the most efficient way based on LADDER's optimization algorithm to answer queries.

This level of record structure transparency is not generally available, even in user-oriented query languages; it is, however, available in the prototype System R, developed by IBM Research Labs, San Jose, California. With such facilities, a user accessing one field in a file can implicitly (through a user exit) access other files. In a restructuring of record content, this facility could be used to make structure changes in the data base that are transparent to the programs. For example, RAMIS has a virtual record facility that essentially creates a user view out of several files, making them look like one file. Few commercially available data base management or data dictionary/directory systems seem to have a general user-view facility like those built into some of the experimental relational DBMSs. This may well reflect a lack of need (or perceived need) on the part of the DP community.

Other Types of Data Independence

Some types of data independence do not fit into the categories discussed above. Others are just beginning to become important.

Data Location Independence. In a distributed system, it is important that an application does not have to know the actual location of a file in the computer network; this was discussed in the earlier example of data independence in the LADDER system. Most distributed data base systems maintain their data at one central site, although portions of the data may be copied at remote locations. This is probably because of the dearth of experience with distributed data bases. The problems inherent in controlling updates in a distributed data base are greater than in a centralized system; much exchange of coordinating messages is required. Nevertheless, it is to be expected that data base will be distributed in the next few years, and it is important that the user is not faced with the task of keeping track of the data he requires. This capability will be accomplished with the Network Data Directory.

Production/Test Independence. The testing of systems prior to their implementation is sometimes more difficult in the data base environment. The method of systems testing depends on the physical handling of data by the DBMS and (with a given DBMS) may vary from installation to installation. In planning for a DBMS, it is important to ensure that applications can be tested and moved into production in a transparent fashion without, for example, changing source code to set different file identifiers. It should be possible to run tests and be assured that they are running against test files or the test data base. This may seem obvious, but in DBMSs that run in a "central" mode (i.e., those accepting commands from different regions), the problem of getting to the test data base in a region different from the production data base may be important.

Time Independence. Much data is time dependent. A data base can be viewed as a picture of an enterprise at a particular moment. As updates occur, this picture changes. Quantity-on-hand decreases or increases, for instance. Furthermore, shipments are scheduled, and the expected quantity-on-hand can be predicted for a given future date. Budgets are known, as are past and future planned expenditures. It is conceivable that a DBMS could be designed to deliver the state of the data base for a time in the past and be able to predict the state for a time in the future. In fact, much programming effort is devoted to preserving past states of data for auditors and predicting future states for managers. It is possible in this regard that a DBMS could be cost-justified in which an element could be specified as time dependent, all past values could be kept in the data base with a time stamp, and an inquiry could be made with a time or a date attached.

PRODUCTS AND STANDARDS SHOWING INCREASED DATA INDEPENDENCE

One of the stated objectives of most data base management systems (DBMSs) is to increase data independence. To accomplish this objective, the DBMSs should make system changes and additions easier to accomplish than they were before implementation of the DBMS. Many early DBMSs have not had this effect. In some cases the effect has been quite the opposite—many users have been concerned about conversion to another system should support for the current product end or be decreased. Complex file structures with varying access methods that depend on specific physical storage organization make changes to the data base or applications very expensive.

DP is frequently referred to as a labor-intensive industry. Therefore, one objective of DP managers should be to reduce personnel costs. Since data independence contributes to the possibility of such a reduction, it was predictable that it would be a feature of many specification and product announcements. The following are examples of recent developments and their relevant features.

The CODASYL 1978 Standards. Recent changes to the CODA-SYL proposals for data base definition and manipulation are specifically designed to answer criticisms of the previous proposal's lack of data independence. The following changes are particularly noteworthy:

- *The data definition language (DDL)* has been separated into two parts—the DDL and the *data storage description language (DSDL)*. This creates a clear separation between the logical specification of the data base (DDL) and its physical implementation (DSDL).
- *Data base keys,* defined in the 1973 specification as "unique and permanent" record identifiers, have been eliminated from the 1978 specification. Because record keys identified specific addresses, they led to transparency problems in data base reorganization.
- *New validation criteria,* which allow automatic checking of certain structural constraints, can be defined in the DDL.
- *Ordinary indexing* has finally been added to the network data model on which the specification is based. This will allow more flexible data access and structuring, which will lead to simpler, more data-independent models. Other changes have been made; unfortunately, they are mainly additions to an already complex specification that come at a time when the trend is toward simplification of data description and access.

Distributed Data. A number of systems now allow access to files on remote systems without requiring users to be aware of their locations:

- *CICS,* IBM's teleprocessing monitor, now requires the use of the Advanced Communications Function for VTAM users. This allows the CICS user to access transaction programs or files that are located on a nonlocal 370 system.
- *Tandem Computers* has extended its minicomputer multiprocessor architecture to access processing units over remote lines. The result is a system that accesses remote files and programs, with transparency at the operating system and hardware levels.

Recent and Expected IBM Announcements. A number of new IBM hardware and software products have been announced, and other announcements are expected in the near future. Because IBM products can be expected to result in competitive offerings from other vendors, aspects of data independence in IBM systems are of particular interest:

- *The 8100 Distributed Processing System.* This interfaces directly to IBM's Systems Network Architecture (SNA). User interfaces that allow end users with little DP experience or knowledge of physical aspects to build their own systems are emphasized.

- *The System/38.* This small computer from the General Systems Division has such interesting features as a transparent storage hierarchy with disk storage that appears to be an extension of main memory. No traditional files exist as such; rather, the user is constrained to use a relational data management system that accesses logical files of flat records. These files can be created with multiple indexes, and indexed and sequential access times are comparable. Many system functions, including indexing, are microcoded.

- *Query-by-Example (QBE).* This end-user-oriented file access language allows a user to display and select data in an easy-to-understand tabular format. QBE was originally developed as an end-user interface to System R but has been released by IBM as a product running under the virtual machine operating system.

- *System R.* This has been IBM's premier data base research project for a number of years. There was speculation that it might be announced in 1979 or 1980 as a program product operating under the MVS operating system, but this did not occur. System R offers a relational file structure, dynamic creation of relations and user views (including user views defined from other user views), an access language (SEQUEL) that can be used either by the end user or from within a program, and a sophisticated security authorization system. An independent vendor, RSI, has announced a relational package called ORACLE.

This range of products suggests that IBM might be moving away from the complex system interfaces necessitated by current operating systems and such products as CICS and IMS. The relational model is used by all the new data base products; this use could be a deciding factor in the controversy about data models (if such a controversy is meaningful at all). The emphasis on the end user, with transparency of storage modes, file structures, indexing, and so on, implies an order of data transparency that, together with new application development systems, could mean a major change in the way DP is performed.

IMPLEMENTATION OF DATA INDEPENDENCE ON THE COMPUTER SYSTEM

Once data is defined at appropriate levels of abstraction and the mappings between the levels are defined to the system, the actual movement from one level to another will use standard software and hardware techniques. This section describes the levels at which some kinds of data transparency have been implemented. Even these levels can disappear, however, when different types of computer systems are employed. The LADDER system described in this chapter, for example, is implemented in LISP. Ordinarily, this would mean that it is a compiled program, but LISP is a different type of language; a function implemented in LISP is actually somewhat of an extension of the LISP language itself. Add to this the development of a LISP machine that executes LISP code directly, and we would conclude that the LADDER system is implemented in machine code.

Hardware. True associative memory is implemented in hardware—that is, it depends on circuitry specifically designed for the task. This is the most straightforward implementation of access-path independence in that data is content-addressable and indexes are not necessary.

Firmware. Microcode is the internal programming of the CPU that executes the instruction set of the computer. Additional microcoding extends this instruction set, resulting in fast execution of commonly used low-level functions. As noted previously, this is a good way to implement indexing algorithms. Most of the associative processors that have been described use microcode actions from an instruction set on it. Devices of this kind will probably be the basis of the *data base machines* that are expected to be available in the next few years.

Operating System. The operating system itself is now being microcoded or separated into independent pieces to a greater extent than before so that distinctions at this level become fuzzy. (Access methods should probably also be included here.) The operating system represents the fixed environment on which the programmer expects to base programs. Many types of data independence are taken for granted in the modern operating system's catalog and file management activities. Some mainframe manufacturers (e.g., SPERRY UNIVAC) supply DBMSs that are considered a component of the operating system after installation.

Data Base Management System. The DBMS generally sits logically between the application program and the operating system. Data independence is offered statically or dynamically by the DBMS in the translation from program request to file access.

Data Base Input/Output Controller (DBIOC)—A DBMS Front End. If a desirable level of data independence is not offered by a DBMS, either that vendor or another software vendor may offer a package that operates between the application program and the DBMS. IBM, for example, offers an application development facility as an interface between the programmer and IMS. This simplifies programmer calls and offers element-level independence (which may not exist in IMS) as well as a number of other facilities. Independent data dictionary packages (active or passive) act logically at this level.

Compiler. The CODASYL proposals are designed to be implemented by the COBOL compiler at the data manipulation language (DML) level. Manufacturers with control of both the compiler and the DBMS can do this kind of implementation, actually using the declared subschema to optimize code. Languages specifically designed for data base access can be either compiled or interpretive. SEQUEL offers an interesting combination. SEQUEL access modules are compiled when first submitted to System R and are executed from the library. If it is found that an authorized change has taken place in a data base that has been accessed since the module was compiled, the module is dynamically recompiled.

Precompiler. When a software company or user has no control over the compiler, using a precompiler is the best way to implement a DML. Extensions to the language are implemented using a macroprocessor programmed to recognize keywords or structures. Appropriate control blocks, assignments, and CALL statements are generated. Types of data independence other than subschemas can be implemented using this technique. Various forms of element independence can be accomplished using a combination of a preprocessor and a data dictionary.

In general, the larger the portion of a function that can be implemented through hardware, the more efficient will be its execution. Note, however, that the basic determinant of efficiency is the algorithm used; no amount of microcoding will make an algorithm that takes n^2 iterations perform as well as one that takes n, when n reaches any reasonable value.

Implementations that are efficient and useful for one class of user may be of no use to another. For example, if data independence is implemented with a precompiler, it is of little use to the end user who is asking ad hoc questions and who cannot write programs. Data independence will have to be implemented differently for this user, while if it is implemented at a lower level initially, it might serve all of the users.

DATA-INDEPENDENT INFORMATION

As stated previously, the most difficult problem in implementing data independence is not in developing the hardware and software but in defining the data base. This breaks down into three problems of definition:

- Choosing the most useful levels of abstraction
- Defining the information resource at each level of abstraction
- Defining the mapping from one level to the next

In moving from the level of the physical device to the level of system data set names, for example, we have defined two levels of abstraction: that of sets of tracks on disk tape and that of a "data set" containing a logical contiguous set of records not associated with any particular device type. The lower level is not very abstract, while the second level offers an important form of data independence. At each level, we must be able to define the data. At the physical device level, we have information on the extents occupied, the physical record lengths, and so forth. At the data set level, we have information on the data set name, logical record length, data set of organization, and so forth. The system catalog tells us how to map from a data set name to physical device extents.

Levels of Abstraction

The lowest levels of abstraction in the system, which are determined by the physical device characteristics, are usually not very abstract. As hardware and software design are more closely integrated, however, less is determined, even at the lowest level. It may be difficult to differentiate between a software product and a hardware device. The selection of a clean, effective interface to the "black box" will be very important.

The choice of the highest level of abstraction is perhaps the most difficult. The CODASYL specification stipulates as its highest level of abstraction a programmer-oriented schema based on a data model of sets that consists of owner and member records. The LADDER system's highest level is an end-user-oriented collection of things and their attributes. The only structure imposed is by the semantic characteristics of the questions that the data base designer thinks are likely to be asked.

Each data management product available to the DP organization has a user interface and a system interface. These may represent clear, consistent levels of abstraction, or they may be hopelessly confused. Data independence is virtually impossible in situations where software forces the mixture of several levels at the same time. A higher level of abstraction at the user interface will make ad hoc queries easier. It will also reduce the amount of programming necessary for a given requirement. Clear levels of abstraction in the data base internal definitions simplify the task of the data base administrator. The extent to which the DBMS uses operating system access methods and services and the extent to which it can surpass the operating system in efficiency and the promotion of data independence should be determined.

The Three-Level Structure

The following description of a skeleton design for the levels of abstraction suggests that there are three basic ways in which data should be viewed to facilitate data independence and ease administrative tasks. The mappings between the three definitions serve as the bridge from the user to the physical data.

This proposal (or model or specification) was developed by ANSI/SPARC, the committee created by the American National Standards Institute to determine whether any areas of data base management were ready for standardization. The committee determined that the interfaces between the components of a DBMS could be standardized. The final report was issued, the committee was disbanded, and a new committee (with the same purpose) has been formed. The report of the original committee caused much discussion and some frustration: the committee attempted a fairly thorough analysis of the data base management process and, in considering just part of the total function, identified 38 interfaces that could probably be standardized.

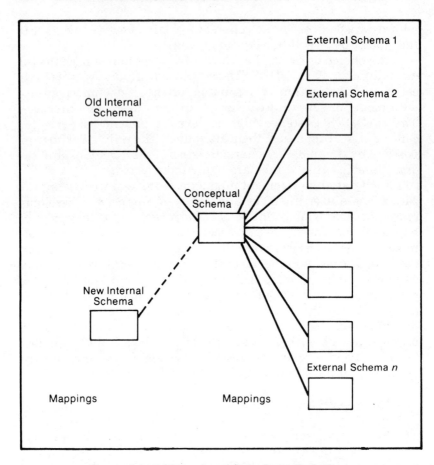

Figure 8-3. A Three-Level Data Base Definition

It is not the purpose of this chapter to comment on the necessity or desirability of standardization or on the readiness of data base management for standards. What is of interest is the three-level model that was developed and its implications for data independence.

The three parts of the data base definition (see Figure 8-3) are:

- *The Conceptual Schema*—which defines the entire information resource of the organization at an abstract level. The conceptual schema can describe information that is not even contained in the DP files.
- *The External (User) Schemas*—which correspond to the users or groups of users who access data base information.

These user views are subsets of the conceptual schema, described and formatted according to user needs.

- *The Internal (Physical) Schema*—which is the physical data base definition, recording the disposition of data in files or other structures. This type of schema would include the directory of a DBMS.

The importance of the proposal is in the introduction of the conceptual level of data base definition, which has precedence over the internal schema and the external schemas. The idea of a logical design for a data base is frequently mentioned. The conceptual schema is not actually a design, but rather is the best possible description of the information resources of an organization, including data, relationships among the data, and the rules and controls pertinent to data use. The internal and external schemas must be consistent with the conceptual schema. Data requested by a user is mapped first to the conceptual schema (which is precise and machine-readable) and from there to the internal schema. There are several implications of this model for data independence:

- Most DBMSs use a two-level model, mapping from a user view directly to a physical data base (see Figure 8-4). When the physical data base is reconfigured (as it inevitably will be), the two-level model requires modification of many or all of the mappings between the user views and data base. In the three-level model (as shown in Figure 8-3), only the mapping between the conceptual schema and the physical (internal) schema need be changed. The saving involved in this transparency could be considerable when either a change in the DBMS or a large number of user views are involved.
- The conceptual description of the data resource offers a useful and accessible view of information to non-DP management. Whether a data base is designed and used by a single researcher or consolidates the management information of a large corporation, a conceptual schema will clarify the essential nature of the information, its interrelationships, and the gaps that may be present in existing data bases. A conceptual schema provides a data-independent description of the data base that requires no technical knowledge of the means of access and offers common ground for discussion.
- Since the conceptual schema forms a point of central control of the data resource, it is the place to record security and integrity rules. Many of the levels of data independence can

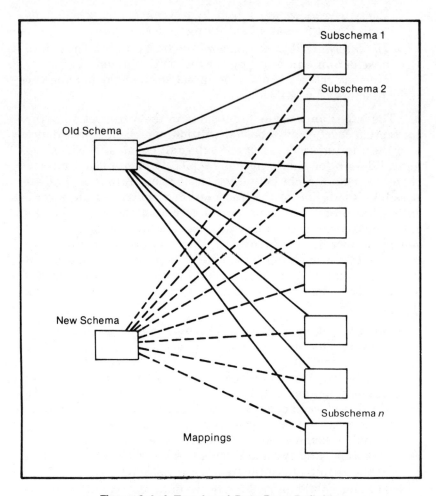

Figure 8-4. A Two-Level Data Base Definition

be implemented through proper central recording of data relationships. For example, a field that is the total of several others will be described as such in the conceptual schema; the physical data base may or may not actually contain the value of the field. In this case, the value can be calculated in the process of mapping from the internal to the conceptual schema. If the total is also in the physical data base, the integrity of the field will be checked against the individual fields that comprise the total. The same record of an obligatory data relationship can thus serve as either a virtual field calculation rule or a validation rule. Security authorization rules will also be recorded in the conceptual schema. Since all accesses pass through this schema, security cannot be bypassed.

The advantages of this three-level design for data independence are considerable. Its disadvantages are also apparent:

- An extra level of mapping and definition is necessary, which may lead to unacceptable performance.
- Not every organization is interested in making a complete assessment of its data resources in order to build a finished conceptual schema.
- No one has been able to develop a widely accepted way of recording the conceptual schema.

Current DBMSs that provide any clear levels of abstraction generally conform to the two-level model. IMS and others offer methods for creating user views, and the new CODASYL specification offers three levels: the DSDL corresponds to the internal schema, the subschema corresponds to the user view, and the DDL-described data base stands between them. Whether the DDL schema satisfies the requirements for a conceptual schema is arguable. System R, for example, allows specification of very flexible integrity and security rules that can be applied to either user views of relations, but it lacks any central data base definition.

It is not clear whether any DBMS will ever satisfy the intent of the ANSI/SPARC data base requirement, but the idea of a central, independent definition of information is of major importance in the implementation of data independence.

THE DESCRIPTION OF DATA

In its final report, the ANSI/SPARC committee stated that it hoped it had finally ended the data model controversy and that hierarchies, networks, and relations would be able to coexist and without problem. The actual effect of the report, however, was to move the controversy to a discussion of the best data model for describing the conceptual schema. This remains a major problem, but the report has at least demonstrated that different models may be appropriate for different levels of abstraction or different users and that all of these models might refer to the same data base.

Data Models

Data models provide methods of describing data independent of the way it is to be used.

The Hierarchical Model. Although a hierarchy is appropriate for certain kinds of data, it is distinctly limited in its ability to model the range of data structures found in the real world. Note, however, that the vast majority of reporting requirements depend on hierarchical user views.

The Network Model. The network model does not encompass the commonly accepted idea of a network, as does a teleprocessing network. It is, rather, based on the idea of a set, not as defined mathematically, but as a special type of hierarchy, with owner and member records. One important feature of the network model is that several hierarchies can be overlapped through a concept of linkages. In addition, this model is said to have considerable generality and to be especially well designed for DP problem-solving, although it is not easily applied to the type of many-to-many relationship described in Part I.

The Relational Model. The relational model is named for the mathematical techniques used in analyzing it. Its origins, however, lie in the simple idea of tables. The results of the mathematical analysis—the *normal forms*—are important in theory; they are even useful in practice, at times. They tend, however, to obscure the basic simplicity of the model; and this simplicity is its chief attraction. Any data structure can be represented by using simple flat tables. Relationships between two tables are represented by equal values in columns of the different relations. Relationships between the tables are implicit, and apparent relationships may have no real meaning. The major criticism of this model is that not enough is said.

The Entity-Relationship Model. This term refers to a group of models that describe information in terms of entities, meaningful relationships between the entities, and sometimes the attributes of the entities. All relationships are bidirectional (correcting the assumption that because a relationship is one-to-many, the single entity has some special status). The problem with the entity-relationship model is in deciding which information constitutes an entity and its attributes and what information is embodied in relationships. A change in perspective or processing needs can change an attribute (e.g., order-date) into an entity (e.g., the goods ordered on June 30). Furthermore, a relationship is also a kind of attribute, which can become an entity with attributes itself (e.g., a marriage of 20 years). One subset of the entity-relationship model drops the idea of attributes completely, leaving only "atomic" entities and the binary relationships between them. This eliminates the arbitrary breaking down of data into records (or relations). Note that the circles and arrows involved in depicting this kind of data base graphically can become overwhelming.

No particular model solves all the problems of describing high-level information. The data administrator should therefore have some knowledge of all these data models in order to decide which model is most appropriate. The whole area of data description is very active, with new ideas being generated constantly (for example, the idea of a hierarchical structuring of *types* of entities has been suggested).

The key to data base analysis and description should be to keep it simple and comprehensible. Many data base designers are now using a simple entity-relationship model augmented with integrity rules and processing information.

Mappings Between Levels of Abstraction

On the basis of the three-level model, it seems probable that the data resource described at the conceptual level will have the simplest structure. The user views may have more complex structures (often hierarchical), and the internal schema will correspond to the DBMS requirements and the need for processing efficiency. Entities in the conceptual data base can map to one or several records. Their attributes can be physically represented or dynamically calculated, and relationships can be implemented in a variety of ways. For example, one-to-many relationships can be implemented using header and trailer records, repeating groups, implicit keys, pointer chains, duplication of data, and so forth. The following points consider the impact of various mappings on data independence:

- A straightforward mapping of entities to records presents the fewest problems when new applications that use the data base are implemented.
- Representation of relationships implicitly through equal keys in different records presents few problems when applications are added or modified but may give poor performance because multiple index searches are necessary.
- Entities in a many-to-one relationship with another entity

(which is always referred to through this relationship) can be safely represented in the form of repeating groups.

- Attempts to reduce redundant data or to speed access by substituting a pointer for a natural key will destroy the bidirectional nature of a relationship and introduce all the problems of pointers.
- Integrity constraints may or may not be automatically enforced by the DBMS. For example, a network structure guarantees that a master record exists when a member record is added. To ensure data independence, it is important to declare rules independently and to include validation logic in editing routines.
- Relational analysis of the logical and physical data base designs can be helpful. Much the same effect can be achieved, however, by imagining the processing logic necessary to update all the fields in the data base. If the update requires changes only to a single entity or record, the data base is well structured. If it requires changing a large set of records not related in the purpose of the update, the structure should be reconsidered.

The design of a physical data base depends on the hardware and software of an individual installation. The design should not result in too many obstacles to changing applications. In any event, the mapping (correspondence) between the logical data that has been identified and the actual data base in the system files should be explicitly recorded. In this way, the implications of any change in the physical data base will be immediately apparent.

Data Translation

The data translation process involved in mapping can be performed in two ways. The levels of the data base definitions may be recorded in tables, possibly with pointers to processing routines that require executable logic. The aim of the mapping process is to get from the user view to the physical data and back again. The mappings themselves can be either precompiled or dynamically interpreted when the data is requested. A precompiled translation routine provides the possibility of generating an access module tailored to user needs, moving directly from the user program to the physical data. Unfortunately, this approach loses the advantages of the three-level model. Any change in the physical data base requires changes in a whole set of user view modules.

This approach is also of no value to the end user.

Dynamic interpretation of user requests offers greater flexibility and data independence, but run efficiency suffers as a result. Several compromises are possible. One such compromise is that of System R, in which dynamic recompilation occurs whenever a change is detected. Another choice is to compile the conceptual-to-internal-schema mapping, which can be closely controlled, and dynamically interpret the mapping from the user view to the conceptual data base.

User View Independence. Full independence of user views from the physical data base structure is dependent on software or hardware. It is desirable that the translation be made in two stages (preferably at run time): from the user view to the logical definition and from the logical definition to the physical data base. A sophisticated system will examine a user request and optimize the access paths used, minimizing record accesses.

With less sophisticated systems, an installation can implement user views by making all data accesses through called subroutines. Many installations already use standard file access routines, especially with complex file structures. A user view can extend this. If an application program needs a hierarchical view of data, a multiple-file READ can be programmed as a single-access module that handles the logic of detecting breakpoints. If an application needs two related file records, the user view can deliver what appears to be a single record.

The installation can extend this by creating its own data manipulation language. Few things can actually be done to data; it can be read, written, added, changed, and deleted. Data modification routines can incorporate data validation logic or call-independent data validation routines, thus incorporating this level of data independence and ensuring the integrity of the data base.

All user views and their users should, of course, be recorded. An effectively indexed data dictionary can then immediately make apparent the effects of any change on the rest of the system. Such changes should have minimal impact.

THE DATA DICTIONARY/DIRECTORY SYSTEM

In a data base system that possesses a high level of data independence, the data dictionary/directory system becomes more than a documentation aid. It is the place where information on the definition of data at each level of abstraction and the mappings between levels are recorded. The DD/DS becomes an active part of a system in which data is constantly being translated from one form to another to achieve data independence. It supplies information on the location of data, its format, its validation rules, its relation to other data, and a variety of other things.

As such, desirable characteristics of a DD/DS are:

- It should be active. The DBMS software should use the information in the data dictionary.
- It should clearly differentiate between definitions of data at the various levels of abstraction.
- It should provide for the specification of logical integrity constraints of some degree of complexity and the definition of virtual fields.
- It should provide the means for defining the mappings between physical data bases, logical definitions of data, and user views.
- It should not unduly limit the choice of data models.

A DD/DS is not necessarily implemented as a single piece of software. It may, however, be advantageous to record all information about the data base in a single place.

ACHIEVING DATA INDEPENDENCE

While new hardware and software products are in the offing, their features alone will not achieve the control of the cost of change that is the aim of data independence. The fundamental idea of data independence—separating the user of data from its physical characteristics—can be achieved by any installation with the personnel and tools at hand. Some suggestions on the practical implementation of some of the foregoing ideas follow.

The Data-Independent Description of Information

While the DP department may find it difficult to make a full inventory of the information resources of the organization, it can make a useful start with a few of its systems. The definition should record:

- *Business entities and their attributes.* Existing record formats should not determine which data items are defined as entities and their attributes. An entity should be an object, place, person, or concept that is easily recognizable as necessary to describe the normal course of business operations. Its attributes are the things that the organization must know about it and that are directly related to it alone (not related to it in conjunction with some other thing).

- *Relationships between entities* are things that are known about two or more entities in conjunction with each other. Sometimes a relationship is important enough to be named an entity in and of itself. A sale, for example, is a sort of relationship between a seller, a buyer, and an item. Often, however, it is of such importance that it should also be defined as an entity with its own attributes (e.g., date of the sale, the quantity, the items sold, etc.).

- *Validation and authorization rules* may be the most difficult part of the effort because the analyst may conclude that he or she is rewriting the program specifications. In fact, this is so, but this effort should provide clarification on which parts of the system are fundamental and which are merely results of the manner in which the current system is implemented.

- *Activities and events* are not strictly part of data base definition, but the data is of little use unless there is an understanding of the way in which it can be used and modified. This information should be defined at the same level of abstraction as the other data; that is, not in terms of data processing but in terms of the fundamental business functions of the organization.

When this definition has been completed, the DP installation should have:

- Separated fundamental characteristics of data from particular processing requirements
- Shown dependencies between existing applications
- Created a basis for system design at a data-independent level
- Created a common terminology with which users can state their requirements, analysts can design, and programmers can access data

It would be desirable to record this information in a form that can be computer processed, but few existing data dictionary products are suitable for the task. Some of the system design languages available may be more helpful.

SUMMARY

This chapter has outlined levels of data independence, including those types of transparency close to the physical device level and those that are more abstract and end-user oriented. Many of these levels of independence are provided in commercially available operating systems and DBMSs; others are operating in research environments; a few are only ideas. Most of these levels of independence can occur independently, although the lower levels are usually necessary for achieving the higher levels.

In the process of selecting and implementing a DBMS, the costs and benefits of the various forms of data independence should be assessed because it is difficult to transcend the physical data dependencies of the DBMS that is chosen. The selection should be justified on the costs and benefits not only for a single application but for the entire DP organization. It is important to remember that it is the costs of change that are profoundly affected by the level of data independence in a DBMS.

The implementation of data independence and the minimization of the costs of change are not completely dependent on particular software or hardware. Rather, they are accomplished through a process of analysis, definition, and design aimed at separating the fundamental data structures of the organization from the details of particular system implementations. This process includes:

- Defining the information resource in a data-independent manner, using a straightforward descriptive technique that is comfortable for the installation and its users.

- Designing the data base to be as flexible a structure as possible, while still meeting the processing requirements. Note that the correspondence between physical files and the logical data base should be explicitly recorded.

- Having both programmers and end users access the data base in terms of its logical rather than its physical definition. User views can be implemented in the form of independently compiled access subroutines and a simple data manipulation language.

- Recording all of the above in a DD/DS that is as easy to use as possible, while still effectively exhibiting the effects of any changes on the system.

PART III

Evaluation and Selection of Software

Control within the data base frequently depends on selecting the proper software product. Many software products are commercially available, each having a host of characteristics and capabilities. Establishing a uniform set of criteria for evaluating the various offerings on the market is essential. If selection is imprudent, the complex, time-consuming, and often frustrating task of selecting a data base management system will result in massive expenditures of time and money. The ultimate frustration will be user dissatisfaction.

To satisfy the user, the structure and composition of the underlying data must represent the user's logical view. In addition, data definitions must be accurate, comprehensible, and accessible. Toward this end, the most important software tool is the Data Dictionary/Directory System (DD/DS). Proper selection and implementation of an active DD/DS can help ensure user satisfaction.

chapter 9

Criteria for the Selection of a Data Dictionary/ Directory System

INTRODUCTION

The DD/DS can be viewed as an application whose primary users are systems and organization personnel involved in the shared use of data. The advent of data base management systems has allowed users to share a single physical representation of a data base without undue sacrifice in operating efficiencies. The DBMS accomplishes this at a technical level by separating the physical representation of data from the logical (i.e., user's) view of the data.

However, the DBMS alone cannot coordinate and control the shared use of data resources. To accomplish this, it is necessary to support data resources as other corporate resources are managed. The data base administrator, like other corporate managers, needs an automated system to aid in the inventory and control of the resources for which he or she is responsible. A DD/DS provides automated support for data inventory and control.

For many years, there were few commercial systems available. As a consequence, users were compelled to develop their own systems. Such an effort typically took 9 to 12 months to complete and cost between \$40,000 and \$100,000. In contrast, there are many commercial packages available whose costs range between \$15,000 and \$40,000. Applying the logic of the "Make vs Buy" analysis (Figure 9-1), most organizations considering a DD/DS are shopping among the commercial systems.

This chapter discusses how to compare, evaluate, and select a commercial DD/DS to ensure a "best fit" in a particular data base environment. The recommended approach for DD/DS package selection is to establish a selection methodology that minimizes the subjectivity and bias of those involved in the selection process. The steps in this methodology are outlined in Figure 9-2 and presented in greater detail in the remainder of this chapter.

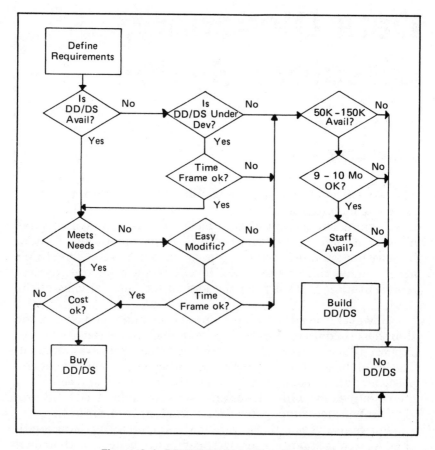

Figure 9-1. DD/DS Make or Buy Decision

DD/DS SELECTION METHODOLOGY

The initial activities in evaluating and selecting a DD/DS package deal with planning (see Figure 9-2). The steps in the selection methodology need to be enumerated, and the time required for the completion of tasks needs to be estimated. Personnel to perform these tasks should be chosen on the basis of each person's value to the selection effort.

A typical selection team might include five persons representing the following areas within the organization:

- Data base administration (chairperson)
- Technical services
- Applications programming
- Systems design
- Operations

With wide representation, the selection team is less likely to be swayed by the bias of any one viewpoint.

In conjunction with establishing the selection methodology, the selection team must establish an education and training program. The purpose of the program is twofold: to provide DP management with information on the major considerations involved in the selection process; and to provide team members with the information needed to make an evaluation.

For the most part, information will be derived from the literature. In addition, there are seminars offered that can provide a good foundation for the selection team.

1. Establish Selection Methodology
   - Enumerate steps
   - Select evaluation team
   - Acquire training and education

2. Identify and Describe Selection Criteria
   - Enumerate criteria
   - Describe criteria
   - Classify criteria: mandatory/desirable, eliminating packages failing mandatory criteria

3. Assign Weights to Selection Criteria

4. Evaluate Packages for Each Selection Criterion

5. Calculate Scores and Select DD/DS Package

Figure 9-2. DD/DS Selection Methodology

1. **Data Description Facilities** — includes consideration of entity descriptions allowed, types of data structures supported, range of options left to user discretion, and host language supported.

   1.1   Type of Input (keyword vs. preformatted)
   1.2   Entity Structure Definition Support
   1.3   Mandatory/Optional Definitions
   1.4   Default Functions
   1.5   Reference Definition
   1.6   Generation of DD/DS Input from Host Language Code

2. **Data Documentation Support** — covers the range of attributes provided to describe DD/DS entities and the ease of extracting documentation information.

   2.1   Identification Attributes
   2.2   Source Attributes
   2.3   Type of Data Attributes (generic classifications)
   2.4   Usage/User Attributes
   2.5   Qualification Attributes
   2.6   Relationship Attributes
   2.7   Attributes Describing System Entities
   2.8   Other Documentation Considerations (e.g., keyword capability, version control, etc.)

3. **Data Description Generation (Automated)** — evaluates the ability of the DD/DS to generate data definitions for various automated uses (e.g., DBMS, host language compiler, etc.)

   3.1   Generation of Host Language Description
   3.2   Generation of DBMS DDL
   3.3   Completeness of Interfaces

4. **Security Support** — the ability to describe user data base security, and facilities to protect the DD/DS data base.

   4.1   Attributes for Describing User Data Base Security
   4.2   Security Support for the DD/DS Data Base

5. **Integrity Support** — addresses the ability of the DD/DS to support, with specific facilities, the DBA responsibility for data integrity.

   5.1   Edit and Validation
   5.2   Audit/Derivation Functions
   5.3   Test Data Generation
   5.4   Distributed Data Base Support

6. **User Interfaces/Outputs**

   6.1   Standard Reports
   6.2   Ad Hoc Query/Update
   6.3   On-Line Facilities (retrieval/update)

7. **Ease of Use and Resource Utilization** — considered from both a personnel and operational standpoint.

   7.1   Ease of Learning
   7.2   Level of Expertise Required
   7.3   Compatibility with Existing Procedures
   7.4   Operational Impact

8. **Vendor Support** — includes all facets of vendor support

   8.1   Vendor Stability
   8.2   Commitment to Package
   8.3   Reliability and Quality of Support
   8.4   User's Group
   8.5   Documentation

Figure 9-3. Uniform DD/DS Selection Criteria—Major Categories

160

DD/DS SELECTION CRITERIA

In the evaluation and selection of a DD/DS package, the candidate packages are compared according to a uniform set of evaluation criteria. Developing this uniform set of criteria is an important step in the selection process. Figure 9-3 lists the eight major categories that comprise the uniform DD/DS selection criteria.

Mandatory Criteria

In identifying and describing the uniform selection criteria according to the foregoing guidelines, it is necessary to identify specific criteria that will be considered mandatory. DD/DS packages failing to meet minimum requirements for mandatory criteria would be eliminated from the evaluation process at this early stage.

For example, applying criterion 1.6, it may be deemed *necessary* to have a COBOL program scanner that would generate input for the DD/DS. This type of facility may be mandatory because of anticipated major conversion activity. Thus, DD/DS packages without this facility would be eliminated from contention (e.g., LEXICON).

The use of mandatory criteria necessitates classifying available DD/DS packages according to their dependency on a DBMS and/or the degree of control the packages afford the DBA once installed.

A given DD/DS package must utilize some mechanism to manage (i.e., organize, access and control) the DD/DS data base. This metadata base is often managed by a commercial DBMS; this requires the installation of the DBMS in order to run the DD/DS package. This can, of course, be an advantage if the metadata base and the DBMS directories are one and the same. Additionally, in organizations that are committed to the underlying DBMS, the fact that the DD/DS is dependent on the DBMS would be an advantage. Nevertheless, many DD/DS packages remain independent of any particular DBMS, allowing users to be somewhat more flexible with a DBMS.

Whether a DD/DS is dependent or independent of a DBMS, it can still provide a high degree of active control over the data base environment. This is accomplished by automated interfaces for the generation of data descriptions (see criteria 3). In doing so, the specification of all data descriptions can be controlled through the DD/DS. Packages not providing sufficient degrees of active control are referred to as passive DD/DSs. An alternative name for the active controlling DD/DS is the "integrated" DD/DS.

Figure 9-4 illustrates a typical classification of DD/DS packages in terms of:

- Dependence versus independence
- Relative active control versus passiveness

It should be noted that in Figure 9-4 it has been assumed that a DD/DS package is active (integrated) only if it includes a facility for generating DDL for at least one DBMS. Also, we have assumed that if a DD/DS package requires the access methods of a DBMS to operate, it is classified as dependent, even if the vendor does not require the prior *purchase* of the DBMS in question.

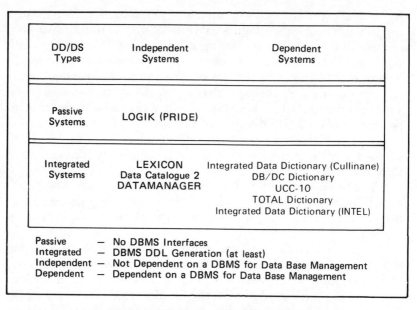

Figure 9-4. DD/DS Package Classification

Weighting of the Selection Criteria

Having arrived at a set of uniform DD/DS selection criteria, the next step is to assign weights to each of the criteria. This process represents the "tailoring" of the criteria to the particular needs of the data base environment in question.

The mechanical process of assigning weights is similar to the calculation of a weighted average and is hypothetically illustrated in Figure 9-5. Notice that weights are applied successively at each level of the criterion.

The task of deciding upon the values for the weights is difficult and critical. This task is the single most important activity of

CRITERIA	WEIGHTS – LEVELS					SCORES			NOTE
	1	2	3	4	5	(1)	(2)	(3)	
4. SECURITY SUPPORT	10								
4.1 Security Attributes of DB		32	42						
4.1.1 Included in DBMS Interface			58			0	0	10	
4.1.2 Independent Security Support						3	7	0	
4.2 Security Support (DD/DS)		68	62						
4.2.1 Password Control									
4.2.1.1 Global				58		5	0	10	
4.2.1.2 Data/System Entities				42		5	2	10	
4.2.2 Functional Access Control			38			5	0	10	

Figure 9-5. Example of Assigning Weights to Levels of Criteria

163

the selection team. Experience has shown that a workable approach is to have each team member assign a full set of weights individually and then convene as a group to negotiate differences.

The process of applying weights will reflect the need for particular features of a DD/DS. For example, an installation may already be using one or more DBMSs or a program library manager (e.g., Librarian), and special interfaces would be advantageous. The weights in category 3 should reflect these requirements. Another installation may be using TSO for on-line programming and therefore require a DD/DS with compatible on-line capability. The weights in category 6 should reflect this situation.

EVALUATION OF DD/DS PACKAGES

The next stage in the selection process is, for the most part, technical and completely independent of the particular needs of organization. At this point the evaluation concentrates on scoring each package against the uniform selection criteria. Ideally, this task should not be performed by the selection team. By assigning different individuals to do the scoring, an element of objectivity is introduced into the selection.

There are various sources of information available to develop these scores. Vendors, of course, are always willing to participate; however, one must be extremely careful of ambiguities and errors of omission. Independent sources of information are available in the literature (see References) or from consulting firms actively involved in the evaluation and implementation of DD/DS packages. An advantage to using external services is that time is not wasted considering packages that will not be used.

FINAL SELECTION OF A DD/DS

The final step in the evaluation and selection process involves the mechanics of calculating results and arriving at a conclusion. In this last phase it will become obvious why one DD/DS scored higher or lower than others. One of the advantages of using the weighted evaluation technique is that specific weaknesses and strengths can be isolated and analyzed for their effect on the total selection process. Thus, if a package lacks on-line update capabilities, its final score would clearly reflect the penalty incurred for the absence of this feature. Similarly, scores in particular categories can be compared to highlight further the relative strengths and weaknesses of the packages under consideration.

In the final stage of evaluation it is important to recognize that the attempt to minimize subjectivity does not completely eliminate individual bias. All the scores and weights were *assigned* not measured—these numbers are, therefore, qualitative not quantitative measurements. Thus, to be significant, a difference between the scores of any two packages should be at least five percent.

In situations where the selection methodology yields two high-scoring packages with less than a five percent differential, the more subjective evaluation criteria should be scrutinized. The evaluation criteria that may have caused some bias are in the last two categories:

- Ease of use and resource utilization
- Vendor support

The selection team should analyze and reevaluate the scores assigned in these categories.

Ease of Learning (7.1). Each DD/DS package is to be evaluated for the relative ease with which users can understand the instructions for using the system. It is difficult, however, to ascertain this qualitative aspect of the DD/DS without experience with the package. It is therefore recommended that the selection team consult with users of the package and rely on the experience of others.

Level of Expertise Required (7.2). This criterion focuses on the number of administrative and technical people required to support the DD/DS. The issue of experience with the package arises again. Here also this could be solved by consulting other users. However, the varying complexity of different data base environments must be taken into account.

Compatibility with Existing Procedures (7.3). This criterion relates to the ease with which a DD/DS can adapt to particular characteristics of the installation's DP environment. The installation, for example, may require that the DD/DS supplement or replace existing forms of documentation. Similarly, the DD/DS may have to be compatible with systems development methodologies.

The problem with this criterion is that it is vague in scope.

The selection team should enumerate the affected areas. They should then create sub-headings for each to refine the scoring further.

Vendor Stability(8.1). It is important to ascertain the ability of the vendor to maintain itself as a going concern. Because the DD/DS plays an important role in the data base environment, users want a vendor that is financially sound. Obviously, there is a qualitative judgment to be made. When arriving at a score, consideration should be given the following factors:

- Size of the company (people)
- Profitability
- Number of years in business

Commitment to Package (8.2). The DD/DS should be the central repository for data description and an important control mechanism for the DBA. Thus, the DD/DS must be closely coordinated with other software components (e.g., DBMS and TP) in the environment and should be enhanced periodically to stay current with technological advances. This requires vendor commitment to supporting a research and development activity. This assessment must be made on the basis of past history and future capability.

Reliability and Quality of Support (8.3). The vendor of the DD/DS software package must be capable of providing reliable support for the user. Personnel assigned should be knowledgeable and capable of solving user problems. The assessment of this capability will be largely subjective and must be based upon past history and the experience of other users.

User's Group (8.4). The majority (if not all) of the major DD/DS vendors organize conferences and meetings for their users.

Documentation (8.5). The importance of good documentation cannot be over-emphasized for the DD/DS package. Generally, the longer the package has been commercially available, the better the documentation.

SUMMARY

Many organizations recognize the need for automated support of the DBA function. Much of this support has materialized in the form of commercial software packages, generally referred to as Data Dictionary/Directory Systems. The process of evaluating and selecting a DD/DS from among these systems must be carried out carefully and with maximum objectivity. The methodology proposed in this chapter, based upon uniform DD/DS selection criteria, provides the basis for such an evaluation and selection procedure.

chapter 10

Criteria for the Selection of a Data Base Management System

INTRODUCTION

In considering implementation strategies with regard to the DBMS, the "make vs buy" decision is often debated. While it is true that in the late 1960s and early 1970s few commercial DBMSs were available, there are now about a dozen reliable DBMS packages available from various hardware/software vendors. Thus, availability is no longer a problem. Furthermore, the "make" effort has been accurately estimated at costs ranging from $500,000 to $3 million and requiring anywhere from 3 to 4 years for implementation. In addition, the required skills in data base technology and software engineering would have to be applied in such an endeavor. This argument, summarized in Figure 10-1, has caused most installations to opt for the "buy" strategy in the acquisition of a DBMS.

In order to select the best DBMS to satisfy a specific user environment, each of the candidate systems must be evaluated across a wide range of criteria from two different viewpoints:

- How well does the DBMS handle the criteria?
- How necessary is this capability to the user community as a whole?

169

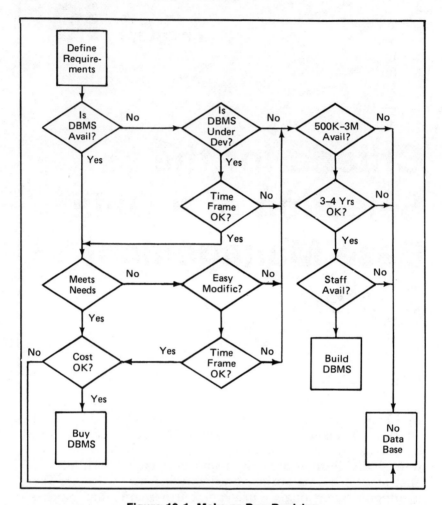

Figure 10-1. Make or Buy Decision

Before any evaluation can be made, a comprehensive list of criteria must be developed. This list should be derived from a combination of user requirements and available data base technology. Table 10-1 presents a representative list. Each category is described here along with the factors that influence the evaluation process.

FACILITIES AND CHARACTERISTICS

This section of the evaluation criteria addresses the capabilities and features of the DBMS, that is, what the DBMS can support and to what degree. Obviously, if a given DBMS does not support any single feature that has been identified as absolutely necessary during the initial analysis phase, then it should not be evaluated any further.

Table 10-1.   Evaluation Criteria

1. Facilities and Characteristics

> Data Definition/Representation
> Types of Conceptual Data Structures Supported
> Access Methods/Retrieval
> Security
> Physical Storage Management
> Operational Characteristics and Interfaces
> Backup and Recovery
> Other Services and Utilities

2. Ease of Installation, Use, and Implementing Change

> Ease of Installation
> Ease of Use
> Ease of Implementing Changes and Future Growth

3. Resource Requirements

> Memory
> Disc
> Performance Overhead
> Staff
> Direct Dollar Cost of Package

4. Vendor Support

> Training
> Documentation
> Vendor Position
> Vendor Assistance to Users

Data Definition/Representation

This criterion addresses the generality and flexibility of the DBMS with respect to the Data Definition Language (DDL). How the DBMS supports the various file, record, and item definitions and organizations that may be required is also considered. These key concepts may be defined as follows:

- *Data definition language:* overall characteristics of the DDL, such as level and detail, validation rules, security, physical storage strategies.
- *Data set (file) definition:* facilities for defining files to include: use of meaningful names, ability to describe files not

accessed by way of the DBMS (external files), and constraints on number of records or fields within a file.

- *Record definition:* facilities for defining records include use of meaningful names, support of variable-length records, and constraints on records' length or number of data items per record.
- *Repeating data:* facilities for defining multiple-occurring data. Evaluation criteria include restraints on the following: number of levels of nesting permitted, number of occurrences (variable or fixed) of a group, number of different group types, and size of a group in characters or components. The DDL must also be examined for the ability to define aggregates, that is, named collections of data items within a record.
- *Data item (field) definition:* facilities for defining data items. Specifically, length restrictions, naming conventions, formats, repeating group/aggregate membership, data compression, derived data elements (values derived from other elements instead of being stored in record).

Types of Conceptual Data Structures Supported

The structure of a data base refers to the relationships between record types. The two basic relationships are member and owner. For example, an order record would be a member of the set of orders for the owner record containing customer data. At the same time, an order record also may be the owner of all the item records generated by that order.

A *network* is a structure in which there are no restrictions as to the number of owner or member relationships for a record type. A subset of this structure is the *hierarchy,* in which a given record type is restricted to being a member in only one relationship but may be the owner of many member record types. Although the network structure is obviously a more general structure, the hierarchy has the advantage that there can never be more than one path from any given record type to another. This advantage makes this structure much easier to understand and to implement from the analyst/programmer's viewpoint. Figure 10-2 graphically represents network and hierarchy.

Each candidate DBMS must be evaluated on how it implements these two basic structures. The member-owner relationships may be implemented by way of direct or indirect pointers. Direct pointers involve the storing of disk record addresses in the records. This tends to optimize retrieval speed but makes the re-

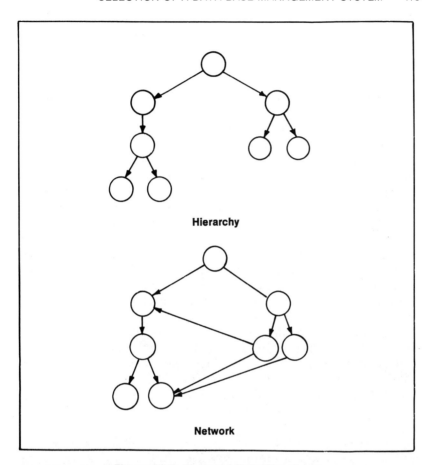

Figure 10-2. Types of Data Structures

lated files physically dependent. Indirect pointers are established using redundant keys in the owner and member records. These records can then be randomized or used to access index tables that point to related owner or member records containing the same value. This method slows down retrievals since an intermediate step is involved before the desired records can be located. However, reorganization costs are lowered since records can be physically moved, without causing records in related files to be modified in order to point to the new address.

Criteria for evaluation should include any limitations in the following areas:

- Number of member types for a given owner
- Number of owner types for a given member

- Complexity or depth of multiple (cascaded) owner-member relationships

Access Methods/Retrieval

This criterion is used to evaluate how well a system uses the four basic random access methods and how these methods apply to the specific application mix of the evaluator's environment.

Randomizing is the process of passing a record key through an algorithm that results in a DASD address within a predetermined range. Ideally, each key should randomize to a different address. This cannot be guaranteed, however, which gives rise to the major drawback of this access method that is, synonyms. A synonym occurs when the key for a record to be inserted randomizes to an address which is already occupied. Since the new record cannot be stored on top of the existing record, some mechanism for locating and maintaining available space to store synonyms must exist. Also, since the new record is not stored in its "home" location, the synonym procedure must also be able to locate this record on subsequent retrievals.

The randomizing algorithm must be evaluated on its effectiveness in avoiding synonyms and its flexibility in handling a variety of different key types. Most algorithms can be rated on their maximum recommended load factor (the maximum percentage of the file that can be filled before synonym resolution begins to degrade performance seriously). The method by which synonyms are resolved must be evaluated on resource effectiveness in the areas of physical I/O efficiency and on the overhead of pointer storage and maintenance. In addition, the ability of the DBMS to support multiple record types within a file and to support a mechanism for reading the files serially can be useful when optimizing specific application programs.

Direct addressing is the storage technique that solves synonym problems of randomizing by using the DASD address of a record as the key for the record. This method is very rarely used as the primary access method. In addition to the fact that this method requires a detailed knowledge of the physical storage of the records within a file, the key for a record has no significance to the record as data—both of these facts put an undue burden on the programmer. The basic criteria for evaluation concern the generation of the addresses and whether or not variable record sizes are allowed.

Imbedded link systems allow lists of related records to be chained or linked together using pointers stored in the record. The simplest form of this structure is accessed by following an owner-member pointer to the first record on the chain, called the head. This record then points to the next record, which points to the next, and so forth. There are three basic types of lists that can be supported:

- Associative: pointers between two records, such as husband-wife
- Chain: a list of linked records, beginning at the head and ending with a record with no next pointer, called the end-of-chain
- Ring: a chain in which the "next" pointer in the last record points back to the head of the chain

The pointers used to implement these relationships include the following:

- Forward: pointer to next record
- Backward: pointer to previous record
- Headed: pointer to head of list

A DBMS must be evaluated on the types of lists and pointers supported and on the user options available in their usage. Another consideration is the flexibility allowed in placement of records in a chain, such as maintaining a list of employees in a department in employee number sequence, or ordered by date of employment. Also, it may be necessary to maintain several sequences on the same group of records, such as chaining a group of orders by shipping date, due date, and customer number.

An extension of the imbedded link concept is the pointer array. In this type of list, all links are stored in the head record instead of being imbedded in the individual records. This technique can improve the processing time used to satisfy conditional retrievals but it involves the use of variable length records to hold the pointers.

Indexing involves the building of a table containing an entry for each unique value for a given key and a list of pointers to the records containing that value. Areas for evaluation include:

- Support of multiple keys per record
- Index processing efficiency (retrieval and update)
- Space management within the indexes (reuse and expansion)
- Support of sequential processing

Indexing provides the best support for ad hoc queries based on multiple keys because a query can be resolved entirely in the index tables without having to read any of the records in the data file.

Security

This subcategory deals with the available procedures to control access to both the logical and the physical data base. Security can be further subdivided into the following areas:

- *Types of user and terminal identification supported:* user password and/or hardware terminal ID.
- *Program/module identification:* security based on the name of the program making the request.
- *Control level supported:* security by file, record, or item type; security by record or item occurrence.
- *Functional control:* security by type of operation requested, such as modify structure or read, update, or qualify fields or records.
- *Encryption:* encoding and decoding capability when transferring data to and from the data base.
- *Output control:* selective control of output of sensitive information to unsecured terminals.
- *Data structure integrity:* preventing the user from updating internal control information, such as pointers and index tables.

Physical Storage Management

This is concerned with how the DBMS handles the physical aspects of the storage of data:

- *Allocation of data to physical devices:* user and/or DBMS controlled allocation of specific files to specific devices in order to minimize access conflicts among files and to maximize utilization of available storage.
- *DBMS space management:* options available to optimize the handling of available space within a file, such as padding of internal tables to allow for anticipated growth, overflow areas, buffer allocation.
- *Data base allocation of space:* DBMS contols over record placement within a file, such as within specified intervals, "place near," and reserved space for further growth.
- *DBMS garbage collection:* efficiency of techniques used by DBMS to recover and reuse space from deleted records. Factors include physical vs. logical deletion, packing of blocks

to force empty space to the bottom of the block, and reuse of space before reorganization of file.

Operational Characteristics and Interfaces

The DBMS must be evaluated, in the following ways, on how it interfaces with the various portions of the overall system and the constraints it may place on the operating environment:

- *Interface with operating systems:* ease of use with one or more operating systems
- *Interface with transaction controllers:* ease of use and the efficiency with one or more transaction controllers
- *Interface with query/report processors:* efficiency of interfacing vendor support, flexibility, and ease of use
- *Interface with Data Dictionary/Directory systems:* level of communication and control between DBMS and DD/DS, ease of use, and efficiency
- *DBMS hardware independence:* various hardware that supports the DBMS, communication with multiple CPUs possible, and compatibility with CODASYL Data Base Task Group (standards)
- *Operating environment:* ability to support batch/on-line operating mode, query language/report writer/host language processing, access to both data base and nondata base files

Backup and Recovery

A critical area of concern in many data base environments is the ability to restore a data base after it has been lost. This must be done within a very brief time and without errors. A DBMS must be evaluated with regard to the types of recovery mechanisms available and how these mechanisms function under various categories of failure, such as:

- *Journalizing:* transaction logging, checkpoints, before/after images
- *Backup facilities:* automatic dump facility, partial dump, full and/or partial restore of data base
- *Catastrophic failure:* mechanism for recovery when data base file is unreadable
- *Intermittent failure:* mechanism for recovery when the system fails but the data base is readable

- *Valid (but incorrect) data:* deletion and correction of incorrect data to include an audit trail of all affected updates and reports
- *Contention:* DBMS methodology that resolves conflicts when two or more programs try to access the same file/block record
- *Restart facility:* DBMS efficiency in backing out transactions or restoring selected records

Other Services and Utilities

This category is used to indicate the presence or absence of features or capabilities that usually are not mandatory but are very useful tools. These are tools that tend to simplify and/or optimize the tasks of the analysts and programmers who work with a DBMS:

- *Data base/file operations:* utilities to maintain entire data bases or specified files, such as dump, reorganize/restructure, and load
- *Sort:* facility to sort selected records as an internal DBMS function
- *Format, edit, validation:* automatic edit criterion incorporated into the DBMS, such as ranges, list of acceptable values, guaranteed unique, and presence/absence of specified fields
- *Data compaction:* internal compression of data records to remove fillers, strings of blanks, leading zeroes, etc.
- *Data structure display:* ability to display to the DBA, or a user, all or part of the data base structure in list or graphic form
- *Statistical monitoring routines:* DBMS facilities for gathering activity statistics, such as record access counts, response times, system performance, resource utilization, error counts, and associated users
- *Structure simulation:* facility to simulate proposed structure changes and to process pseudo-transactions against the simulated structures in order to assist in data base design and tuning
- *Other services:* any other services or tools, either provided by a DBMS or desired by the user

EASE OF INSTALLATION, USE, AND IMPLEMENTING CHANGE

The impact of a given DBMS on the data processing staff in the areas of system and application programming must be given serious consideration. Relative efficiencies in these areas have a very profound effect on cost justification and manpower utilization. This is especially true since one of the primary goals of a data base is to be more responsive to the needs of the user community. To accomplish this goal the DBMS must be easy to use and amenable to change.

Ease of Installation

The ease with which a DBMS can be installed and maintained is very important to the success of a data base environment from the standpoints of delay of the pilot application and manpower drain. The time period between first receiving a DBMS and the day the first pilot application becomes operational must be minimized if the full support of upper management is to be realized. Criteria for evaluation include:

- *Implementation procedure rules:* procedures for installing and maintaining the DBMS must be rated on the amount of training involved, level of technical expertise required, and degree of difficulty involved.
- *Utilities provided:* facilities provided to simplify building and initializing a data base, such as data conversion, preformatting of files, and initial load of the file.
- *Scheduling impact:* frequency of update to the DBMS package and the time and manpower required.

Ease of Use

The ease with which a DBMS can be used has a great impact on the effectiveness of a data base environment in meeting the needs of the user in a timely and cost effective manner. There are three functions within a data base environment that must be considered:

- *Designer/DBA:* ease of use of the Data Definition Language for data items, records, files and structures, physical storage options, performance monitoring and statistics, data base structure simulation, and security
- *Application Programmer:* depth of knowledge of data and structure required, ease of use of the Data Manipulation Language, ease of testing and debugging of programs
- *Operations:* ease of interpretation of DBMS messages and diagnostics to the operator and ease of implementation of recovery procedures

Ease of Implementing Changes and Future Growth

Another critical factor in evaluating a DBMS is the ease with which the data base can be modified in response to the changing needs of the user community. Each of the following types of changes must be evaluated for its impact on the data base administration function and on existing programs:

- *Change of indexes/pointers/access methods:* the effect that changing the file access method (to better fit a given application) has on other applications requiring that file.
- *Add/Delete a record type and/or its relationship:* modification of the data base structure.
- *Add/Delete/Change a data item:* modification of the format and/or length of a record, effect on applications that access the record but do not use any of the modified data elements (data independence).
- *Reorganization of data base/file:* impact of file reorganization on other files in the structure as well as on existing programs. Reorganization may typically be caused by garbage collection, file expansion, transferral of a file to a different physical device, or correction of fragmented chains.
- *Change physical placement of related record types:* impact of the modification of record placement strategy, such as, placing all orders owned by a given salesman physically close together as opposed to grouping them by customer name or due date.
- *Change primary key designation:* impact of the selection of a different element within a record as the prime key, such as, changing the key from order number to product number or salesman ID.

From the viewpoint of the DBA, the above changes must be evaluated in terms of the following: complexity and volume of work required, effect on related files, necessary reorganizations, and requirements for special conversion utilities. The critical question for the programmer is what effect a change will have on programs that do not reference the changed element/record/file; this is the degree of independence of the program from the data. Coding changes may involve complete redesign, modifications to I/O procedures and/or data descriptions, or possibly just a recompile.

RESOURCE REQUIREMENTS

The resources used by a data base environment must be evaluated in terms of hardware and personnel requirements. This is another area of evaluation where a given DBMS may be discarded because it does not meet any of the resource constraints of an organization.

Memory

The main memory requirements for a DBMS can be divided into two categories:

- *DBMS:* minimum memory required to hold the basic control and processing routines and tables, plus any additional features and utilities unique to the environment
- *Data buffers:* user or DBMS control over buffer size may either be dynamically based on processing demand or fully determined during initialization

Disk

This criterion is used to evaluate the DASD storage overhead requirements for the access methods available with a DBMS. Space may be required by any or all of the following elements:

- *Pointers/links:* pointers stored within data records
- *Indices:* tables containing key values and addresses of records containing those values. Indices are usually maintained separately from their associated data records
- *Redundant data:* duplicate data values used to indicate relationships instead of direct pointers
- *Expansion space:* extra space within a file to allow for the future addition of records to the file without causing reorganization (in randomized files, a certain amount of expansion space is required to avoid a prohibitive number of synonyms.)

Performance Overhead

The overall performance of a DBMS is measured in terms of CPU and DASD overhead to perform standard as well as utility functions, as follows:

- *DBMS internal overhead:* the CPU overhead imposed by the DBMS to interpret and execute commands
- *Access method/retrieval path:* the DASD overhead imposed by the access requirements within the DBMS, such as single key, multi-key, and sequential retrieval; table and pointer maintenance during updates; and suitability of high volume update processing
- *Service functions/tuning:* relative efficiency of the DBMS utilities, such as dumping and reorganization

Staff

This criterion is used to evaluate the technical staff requirements for administration and maintenance of the data base environment, such as:

- *Data base administration:* staff required to perform such functions of administration and control of the data base as data base definition, standards, design procedures, and interfacing among applications.
- *System maintenance programmers:* staff required to support and maintain the DBMS package and related support software such as interfaces with other packages (query processor, report writer, etc.), installation of software fixes, and maintenance of user-written utilities.
- *Application analysts/programmers:* relative size of application staff to support a DBMS. This can either be evaluated or can be incorporated into the criterion for ease of use.

Direct Dollar Cost of Packages

The initial cost of a DBMS alone varies from $60,000 to $190,000, and if such additional software as query processors, report writers, and/or transaction controllers are required, the cost will be much higher. The evaluator must be aware, however, that as the cost rises, the capabilities and features tend to increase also.

VENDOR SUPPORT

The amount of assistance available from the vendor of a DBMS has a very large impact on the smoothness of implementation and the support of a data base environment.

Training

Vendor supplied training must be evaluated for its quality and completeness. This is another area that is critical if the development time for the pilot application is to be minimized. (NOTE: In some instances, training may be available from sources other than the vendor.) Factors to consider are:

- *Amount of training required:* length of time required at various staff levels to become proficient in the use of a DBMS.
- *Courses offered:* evaluation of available courses in relation to requirements. Criteria to be considered include: availability of courses (in-house as well as public courses), cost, range and detail of training for management, DBA, system programmers, application programmers, and operators.
- *Instruction manuals:* availability, completeness and clarity of instructor manuals, self-teaching aids, student exercises, and course texts.

Documentation

This criterion includes reference manuals and other documentation that describe the techniques to be applied when using and/ or optimizing DBMS design, utilities, programs and computer operations. The following levels of documentation should be evaluated in terms of completeness, content and clarity:

- *General level:* introduction to data base concepts and overview of the DBMS.
- *Application design level:* specification of techniques for design of the data base structure and programs which utilize the structure. This level is directed primarily at the DBA and system analyst functions.
- *Technical level:* detailed documentation on how the DBMS package functions and the techniques for installing and maintaining the DBMS, coding and debugging programs, developing interfaces to other packages.

Vendor Position

This criterion is used to evaluate the amount and quality of support that a vendor supplies for its product. The primary source of much of this information is the community currently utilizing the DBMS. Things to consider are:

- *Reputation:* current vendor reputation toward the DBMS with regard to maintenance of the package, responsiveness to user requests for support, and the frequency and impact of DBMS enhancements.
- *Vendor commitment to DBMS:* view of vendor toward the product, specifically in the areas of maintaining upward compatibility with new versions of operating systems, hardware, and enhanced versions of the DBMS.
- *Accommodation to users:* mechanisms provided by the vendor for enhancements and/or extensions of the DBMS. These should be evaluated in terms of quality control and testing, and the degree of influence of the user on selection of priorities. The DBMS user group, if any, should also be evaluated concerning vendor interaction and support.

Vendor Assistance to Users

This criterion serves to evaluate the degree of technical support available from the vendor (both during installation and afterwards) in the following areas of consulting and programming:

- *Installation aid:* vendor support during initial installation and subsequent DBMS maintenance at the user site. This should be evaluated from the viewpoints of the willingness and ability of the vendor to supply sufficient experienced personnel as well as a commitment to assist with debugging and performance problems.
- *Vendor contract support personnel:* availability of highly skilled and experienced personnel to provide service to a user, on-site, for periods of time ranging from several days to several months.
- *Vendor continuing support:* access to quality personnel at the vendor's offices for customer support. This capability should be evaluated in terms of personnel availability, location of closest office, responsiveness of vendor, and backup support from the home office.

SUMMARY

There is obviously much work involved in evaluating and selecting the best DBMS for a given situation. The evaluation process involves drawing information requirements from management and end-users, utilizing highly technical information concerning data base management techniques, and extracting detailed information about the internal mechanisms of a group of DBMSs. Much of the necessary expertise, typically, cannot be found in house. As a consequence, consultants must be brought in or qualified personnel must be hired. However, if this evaluation is not done, and the DBMS chosen does not meet the needs of a company, the expenses that could be incurred far outweigh the cost of evaluation. It is important to be very sure, before undertaking this evaluation, that it has the complete backing of upper management. Otherwise, there is a possibility that the results of the evaluation may be ignored because of political commitments.

chapter 11

Alternative Approaches to Data Base Management System Performance Evaluation

INTRODUCTION

In this chapter, "performance estimation" is distinguished from what is usually understood as "performance evaluation." This distinction is important because many of the tools and techniques are the same. Performance estimation is essentially predictive and often hypothetical. The emphasis is often on obtaining estimates that are relative rather than absolute. Thus, it may be of primary importance to obtain estimates that enable performance differences to be established among competitive packages, and it may be of secondary importance to actually establish the absolute performance of the packages. The relative estimate allows discrimination for the purpose of a comparative evaluation, and the absolute estimate allows for bounding performance for the purpose of predicting actual execution behavior. The latter can be of great value in application data base design. The nearness to which estimated performance can be shown to correspond to real performance is of great importance in validating the estimation analysis.

When software is to be acquired, various approaches are used for comparing and evaluating the competitive packages. These approaches fall into two general categories: one addresses the functional capabilities of the packages, the other the performance capabilities. Essentially, the first category deals with effectiveness of the functions. Chapter 10, on criteria for selecting a DBMS dealt with this issue. The second category deals with DBMS efficiency. Efficiency generally involves measuring storage space, file maintenance time, and execution time. An objective here is to estimate the performance of a group of functionally related software packages, under the constraint that it is not possible—or at least not feasible—to actually measure their real performance over a sufficiently large sample of applications. This constraint is dictated by the nature and complexity of the packages under consideration, which are, namely, Data Base Management Systems.

The methods most often used for estimating the performance of the functional capabilities of software packages are *benchmarking, simulation,* and *modeling.* Benchmarking requires actual execution of the package on the hardware configuration and establishing performance by making appropriate measurements. The data extracted from the benchmark's execution is extrapolated to obtain estimates of more general performance. Simulation requires the iterative execution of a model (often what would have been the benchmark), and the collection of appropriate statistics. Modeling requires statistical assumptions, mathematical analyses, and empirical information to represent the real situation. Calculations are then developed from the representation. Performance estimates of specific package-supported functions are made by analytically (where possible) modeling situations that might otherwise have been developed as executable benchmarks. Each method is discussed here for the purpose of comparison.

Because of the potential impact on an organization of the adoption of a DBMS, a careful evaluation of competitive packages is usually made. It is particularly important to estimate comparative performance of the competing packages. Because of the complexity of a DBMS, as compared with most other types of system software, no one estimation method is clearly best, or most appropriate, in every case. The inherent complexity, or special nature, of some of the tasks performed by a DBMS severely limits the efficacy of any particular method for complete performance estimation. Therefore, it is necessary to determine and isolate those tasks of most importance in their effect on performance. As an aid in this process, there follows a brief outline of the relevant salient features of DBMSs that includes:

• Data description and manipulation

- DBMS usage
- Data access

DATA DESCRIPTION AND MANIPULATION

All DBMSs provide specific, logical data structures for expressing the relationships among classes of data and among elemental data types. Explicit description of a data base is made possible by use of the Data Definition Language provided by the DBMS.[1,2,3] The DDL allows the conceptual, or logical, view of the data base to be expressed as a collection of data, record, and file structures that may be combined according to definite, unambiguous rules. Any host language application program will have its own logical view of subsets of the DDL-defined data base. The Data Manipulation Language, also provided by the DBMS, allows these program modules to access data from the data base. The entire data base and all necessary relationships are mapped automatically by the DBMS from the logical representation expressed in the DDL into a physical representation on secondary storage. Thus, the addition of a DBMS to the complex of hardware, operating system, standard I/O routines, and host language compiler enables any program written in the host language, and using appropriate DBMS interface protocols, to share data in a common data base.[4,5,6]

Since the number of combinations of relationships and possible types of data access of a collection of programs using a data base is so large, it is prohibitively costly to test even a small part of them. Thus, in order to make performance projections for a specific DBMS, or to make comparisons among specific DBMS packages, only limited sets of logical data base structures and functions to be applied to them can be realistically tested.

DBMS USAGE

Determination of the aspects of performance to be measured will be made by considering the implementation of an application or class of applications using a DBMS. (For convenience; certain data base administration procedures that might be applied will be ignored here.) The implementation must go through the following steps:

1. The data required by the applications, the transformation of the data, and the required output must be defined.

2. A data base design using the data and data structures of the DBMS must be constructed. This design will express the logical relationships desired by the application programs using the rules for combination of records and files allowed by the DBMS. This representation of the schema is usually developed graphically or schematically. The data base will be designed to enable the multiple uses to be made of the data to be satisfied at the lowest possible cost. The appropriate definition of "cost" is extremely difficult and will be discussed in detail further on.

3. The data base is defined using the DDL.

4. The data base is loaded with data consistent with the DDL description and according to the storage strategies of the DBMS.

5. Application programs are implemented that satisfy user requirements by executing complex functions using data extracted from the data base.

6. During execution, application programs may read, write, add, or delete data from the data base. These functions must be expressed through the DML commands particular to each DBMS.

Although storage space and speed are used to measure performance, the particular aspects and context must be carefully defined. Storage space is comprised of primary (core) storage and secondary (disc, tape, drum, etc.) storage. Secondary storage is needed for application data, DBMS-required data, and the DBMS itself. Primary storage during execution requires data buffers, application program work areas, and DBMS execution space. "Speed" can refer to the time required to access, compress, update, add, and delete data during application execution. The times measured can be CPU time, attributable to DML commands, or each of the time intervals required to retrieve data from secondary storage. There is also the time cost of executing integrity and security functions (e.g., data format checking, execution of checkpoints, and log tape recording). Time intervals required for data base maintenance (e.g., loading and reorganization periods) are of great importance. Each of the preceding steps will now be examined with the aim of establishing criteria for performance measurement.

Steps 1 through 3 are of importance from the point of view of human (DBA) performance. They deal with the ease of expressing conceptual relationships using the DBMS data structures and with the linguistic power and flexibility of the DDL.

Step 4, data loading time, is important particularly if the data base might need frequent reloading. The amount of secondary storage required for data can also be ascertained at this step.

Step 5 is of importance from the point of view of the performance of the application program. Program implementation is much affected by the structure, power, and ease of use of the DML.

Step 6 is the step usually considered when estimating, or evaluating, performance. The active or functional interface of the application with the data base is through the execution of DML commands. Certain sequences of commands correspond to natural user functions (e.g., get, update, etc.). In some cases they are in one-to-one correspondence. Where these deal with access to a subset of the data base on, for example, the satisfaction of a query or the insertion of new data during execution, these fundamental user functions could be taken as basic "primitives" whose performance would be estimated.

The performance differences between packages, assuming the same hardware configuration, could then be taken to depend on the execution of the primitives. This, in turn, depends on the time of execution of the commands comprising the primitives and the time taken to read, modify, or move the data. In general all the time on a data access path must be considered.

DATA ACCESS

It is important for the subsequent analysis to consider the system's view of data access; that is, the operating system, the access methods, and the DBMS routines. At some point in the sequence of events that begins with a logical description of the data and ends with the use of the corresponding data values by the application program, the data description must be associated with the actual physical data value recorded on some storage device. This mapping and the return of the data item to the program is accomplished by the DBMS software.[7,4]

An application program, using a DML command, calls the DBMS to retrieve a record(s). During the execution of the command, there is a set of possible errors that might occur during the accessing of data; status codes corresponding to these are returned as arguments in the program's calling sequence. These codes alert the programmer to the nature of the conditions encountered. The program must supply the value of the key to identify the record and may supply other qualifying information as well as a privacy password. The DBMS, either by use of its own routines or by issuing calls to the operating system, performs the following sequence of actions:

1. The application program's subschema is scanned for the logical record description and necessary local logical relationships. (The *subschema* is the application program's logical view of that part of the data base to which it has access—the view of the application programmer.)

2. The schema is scanned for the desired record description and the necessary global logical relationships. (The *schema* is the logical description, or framework, of the entire data base, including the names of all data classes, their attributes, and their relationships—the view of the data base administrator.

3. The physical data base description is scanned and the physical record to be retrieved is identified (block number, address, etc.).

4. The physical record is retrieved and placed in a buffer.

5. The physical record is related to the data descriptions in the schema and subschema. Any translations into subschema-specified format are performed.

6. The record is moved from the buffer into the program work area and any status information is also placed into the work area.

Since it is reasonable to assume that the data definition files and the appropriate DBMS "intelligence" is core-resident during execution, then it is clear, on examination of each of the steps in the procedure, that only the fourth step, the retrieval of the physical record, might require data transfer from the secondary storage medium. Thus, the time cost of data retrieval will depend on the CPU time used by such step, plus the addition of I/O time for the fourth step. The number of I/O accesses and consequently the total I/O time depends on the manner in which the data is organized on the secondary storage devices. This, in turn, depends on the logical-to-physical mapping of data performed by the DBMS during loading of the data base, and on the accessing and buffering strategies used by the DBMS during execution.

In the following parts, benchmarking, simulation, and modeling are examined in the light of estimating overall predictive DBMS performance by estimating the performance of a carefully selected set of primitives and an appropriately defined data base. Each of the methods will use the same logical data base and the same mix of primitive functions. (Please note that retrieving a single data item is, of course, only one [the simplest one at that] of a set of primitives. However, more complex primitives can be defined and, in fact, appear in succeeding chapters.

BENCHMARKING

The only conceptual differences between the implementation of a benchmark and the implementation of an actual application are:

1. the care necessary in developing a representative job mix, and
2. the necessity for correct measurement.[8]

The first difficulty is, of course, also faced by simulation and modeling. It is attended to by applying the most careful analysis in the selection of the set of primitives and the data base structures on which they will be executed.

The second is unique to benchmarking. The points in the sequence of DBMS events at which measurements should be made are important; no less so is the manner in which the measurements are to be made.

Measuring may take the form of actually timing critical functions by hardware clocking or by software or hardware monitoring. Software monitoring is usually done by statistical sampling of the location counter, which determines where activity occurs and for approximately how long it continues. A software monitor is actually a software package that is loaded with, and runs with, a job. A hardware monitor is actually connected to specific hardware modules and samples the activities of those modules directly.

Distinctive aspects of benchmarking are:

- Representative functions (primitives) are actually implemented.
- Actual measurements of CPU and I/O times of the primitives are made.
- It is difficult, and usually expensive, to vary data base parameters (volume, block sizes, buffer sizes, record sizes, etc.) over a range sufficiently wide to make reliable predictions about performance in many situations.
- Many runs must be made and averages calculated; thus machine costs are usually high.
- Very little knowledge of DBMS internals is required.
- Experience in package use is gained if the work is done in house.

SIMULATION

Simulation requires that some, or all, of the DBMS events be initiated by specially designed computer programs.[9, 10, 11, 12] It is assumed that the DBMS itself is not used. Modeling of the execution-time behavior by expressing the functions in the DBMS's DMLs is not done. This would require knowledge of the internal architecture of the host compiler-DBMS interfaces and a knowledge of the code executed during run time. This information is usually not available. What is modeled is all the secondary storage data access activity required to resolve the function. For example, for a disk this would be disk-head motion (seek time), disk rotation, and channel activity.

As a simple example, consider the implementation of single-key random retrieval from a hash file. In benchmarking, a representative set of key values would be selected from the sample data base. A host-language program calling the DBMS would retrieve the records from the data base, and timings for various data base sizes and densities would be made. Averages would then be calculated. In performing the estimation by simulation, the sample data base would be loaded by a hash algorithm replacing that provided by the DBMS (hopefully equivalent). The algorithm would then be used to map records into the data base. As in benchmarking, actual timings would be made over various data base sizes and densities and averages calculated. Adjustments in the times of some events to more closely simulate DBMS behavior could be made. Each DBMS would have its appropriately adjusted hash algorithm equivalent. However, even in this simple example, unless the different DBMS vendors supply enough detailed information about their hash algorithms and their DML interfaces to allow for distinctions to be made, it may not be possible to discriminate among packages.

The distinctive aspects of simulation in this context are then:

- Programs must be implemented that imitate DBMS behavior.
- No DDL need be written and no data base loaded (nor does a theoretical logical-to-physical mapping have to be constructed).
- Many runs must be made and averages calculated over ensembles of values.
- Machine costs might be high.
- Extensive knowledge of DBMS internals is required. (If the work is performed in house, the development of expertise is of potential value.)

MODELING

Modeling replaces benchmarking measurements and simulation experiments with calculations based on statistical assumptions and mathematical idealizations of the DBMS activity.[13] Since simulation models often utilize mathematical modeling in their development, that which distinguishes each from the other should be noted.[13, 14]

Simulation usually denotes the process of conducting experiments on a model of a system. This is performed by executing a system of computer programs that emulate the expected activity of the system that the programs have been constructed to represent. Execution of the programmed system may be likened to the performance of an experiment on which measurements are made. Input to a simulation is nearly always generated from a statistical distribution; thus the results computed are not deterministic and must be validated on statistical grounds.

An analytic model, as opposed to a simulation model, usually denotes a mathematical description of a system with the purpose of predicting system performance under various conditions. The description may be expressible as a computable mathematical expression, and thus predictions of system behavior may be deterministic. That is, it may be possible to derive equations that, on numerical evaluation, will be used for predicting some behavior or specifying some properties of the system. Distinctive aspects of modeling for DBMS performance are:

- The data base constructed in the benchmark and simulation studies can be used. However, definite properties and statistical attributes of the data base must be established.
- The data base is hypothetically loaded; i.e., a complete physical storage layout is constructed though no DDL is necessary.
- Probabilistic, statistical, and combinatorial analyses of execution-time behavior are made whenever possible.
- Averages are computed directly from analysis rather than averaging over multiple experimental iterations.
- Programs are written that allow variation of relevant data base parameters. Families of curves are calculated to be used to estimate levels of performance.
- Moderate knowledge of internals is required, and that mostly of storage management.
- Machine costs are low.

- Conceptual and pragmatic understanding of DBMS activity should be developed, since the computational results are causally related to the analytic assumptions.
- The range of validity of the results is difficult to determine.

It may be possible to estimate only secondary storage access times. If CPU times are to be considered, specific computer experiments and measurements may have to be done. Analogous to the functional primitives used for estimating storage structure performance, identifiable and frequently executed blocks of instructions may be considered primitives of CPU activity. The values of the primitives can be realistically obtained only by actual measurement. The basic DBMS CPU primitives are:

Access method overhead (per block or page): the fixed CPU time overhead for each BDAM I/O is a basic primitive for systems using BDAM. This time can be measured and used in the model where appropriate. If other access methods are employed, the CPU time overhead must be measured. Note that this time is proportional to the I/O time, and thus should not affect the differences between systems. Thus, this refinement would be of value primarily for absolute estimates of DBMS performance.

Record location with a block: when a record is to be retrieved, there is a certain amount of time required to locate the record in its block and return all requested fields. These times can be measured. They may be sensitive to the number of fields, the placement of the record within the block, and any chaining of records within the block.

Randomizing algorithm: for systems using randomizing, there is a fixed cost of applying the randomizing algorithm. This time is either supplied by the vendor or can be measured; it may be sensitive to the length of the key.

The CPU time primitives can be established by measurement on a small data base. The values can then be applied to models involving data bases of various sizes.

SUMMARY

This chapter has presented distinctive aspects of three methods of performance estimation in the context of DBMS comparative evaluation and optimal performance data base design. None of the three methods is "best" in all circumstances. The advantages and disadvantages of each method may be summarized as follows:

Benchmarking has a place in estimation. Nothing can replace the certainty of actually measuring something—even if what should be measured is not quite known. The specification of a representative mix of jobs of potential data base applications on a "real" data base is, practically speaking, an insurmountable obstacle.

Simulation experiments can, if enough time and resources are devoted, imitate reality rather closely. The costs can, however, be appreciable. If in time, special purpose simulators for particular DBMSs become available (see reference [12] for an example of one) it would increase the desirability of the use of simulation.

Analytic modeling, where applicable, involves the lowest cost and possibly the shortest elapsed time of implementation. There is a small but useful body of theoretical literature available for use. Modeling provides insights into the performance require-ments without risking a large investment of computer and human resources. Even if the results are not as accurate as desired, they may be used as initial estimates to be further refined by application of the other methods. The difficulty with modeling is establishing the range of validity of the model. (This is discussed further in a subsequent chapter.)

The procedure recommended here combines modeling and benchmarking. A particular subset of modeled primitives would be benchmarked. The closer the benchmark results correspond to the model results, the greater the credibility of the model. The use of the non-benchmarked primitives can be enhanced by extrapo-lating the initial computations, as appropriate, by the empirical data obtained from the benchmark. The effort is clearly an iterative one that requires a substantial amount of intuition, analysis, and hard work.

Notes

1   R. A. Bassler and J. J. Logan, *The Technology of Data Base Manage-ment Systems* (Arlington, Va: College Readings Inc., P.O. Box 2323, 1974).

2   CODASYL, *Data Base Task Group (DBTG) Report,* (New York: ACM, April 1971).

3   CODASYL, *Data Description Language Journal of Development,* (Washington, DC: U.S. Department 1974).

4   James Martin, *Computer Data-Base Organization* (Englewood Cliffs, NJ: Prentice-Hall, 1975).

5   Ian Palmer, *Data Base Systems: A Practical Reference* (Wellesley, Mass.: Q.E.D. Information Sciences, Inc., 1975).

6   R. Rustin, "Data Base Management: An Overview" (unpublished paper, Chase Manhattan Bank N.A., New York).

7   C. J. Date, *An Introduction to Database Systems* (Reading, Mass.: Addison-Wesley, 1974).

8   E. O. Joslin, ed., *Analysis, Design & Selection of Computer Systems* (Arlington, Va.: College Readings Inc., 1974).

9   A. F. Cardenas, "Evaluation and Selection of File Organization — A Model and System," *Comm, ACM 16, 9* (Sept. 1973), pp. 540-548.

10   A. F. Cardenas, "Analysis and Performance of Inverted Data Base Structures," *Comm. ACM 18, 5* (May 1975), pp. 253-263.

11   F. S. Kenneth, "A Stochastic Evaluation Model for Database Organization in Data Retrieval Systems," *Comm. ACM 19, 2* (Feb. 1976), pp. 84-95.

12   V. Roach, "An Automated Technique for Designing Optimal Performance IMS Data Bases," *FDT — Bulletin of SIGMOD, 6, 2,* (1974).

13   J. W. Boyse and R. D. Warn, "A Straightforward Model for Computer Performance Predictions," *Computing Surveys, 7, 2* (June 1975), pp. 1-93.

14   A. Reiter, "Data Models for Secondary Storage Representations," *Proceedings of the International Conference on Very Large Data Bases,* ACM, 1975.

chapter 12

Alternative Architectures for Active Data Dictionary/Directory Systems

INTRODUCTION

Before discussing alternative design architectures of an "active" DD/DS, it is useful to review basic objectives of any DD/DS.

Objectives

As the primary tool for the administration and control of data resources, the DD/DS should support all phases of the System Design Life Cycle (SDLC).[1] In a data base environment, the fact that data are shared heightens the interdependence of the SDLC phases. If effective project control is to be maintained throughout the continuous modifications made during the SDLC, it is essential to have accurate and consistent documentation of the logical views and physical representation of data.

The basic stages of an SDLC are:

- System justification
- System design
- System implementation
- System auditing and monitoring

The following paragraphs describe the SDLC and how it can be supported by an "active" DD/DS.

System Justification. In Stage I of the SDLC, analysts and designers concerned with *what* data are needed in the system, must concentrate on the data dictionary functions of the DD/DS. Existing descriptions of data entities are referenced, new entries are proposed, and new usages of existing entries are justified. During the System Justification stage, the emphasis is on the *logical* definition and description of data elements as they exist or are proposed in the current environment.

System Design. Detailed data base design includes specifying data base access methods, physical placement of data, and other DBMS-dependent design specifications (i.e., the physical aspects of data description and definition). The data dictionary portion of the DD/DS is used to describe where and how data can be accessed by the new application system.

System Implementation. In Stage III, the implementor must create the physical data environment in such a manner that the system can produce the various users' logical views. Furthermore, in a data base environment, the principles of data independence mandate that:

- Changes to the physical representation do not affect existing logical views.
- Additional logical views can be added with minimal impact to the entire system.

The definition and description of these logical views and physical representations were created in System Design (Stage II). In Stage III, these definitions and descriptions are transformed into a working system. Both the dictionary and directory aspects of the DD/DS are required in this stage, the dictionary for meta information, and the directory for generating operational metadata in production software.

Using an active DD/DS as an integral part of the implementation stage can ensure that the DD/DS will operate as a control mechanism in the production-mode environment.

System Auditing and Monitoring. The activities associated with this phase are conducted while an application system is up and running. Having used the DD/DS as an integral part of system implementation, the analyst can be sure that the contents of the DD/DS precisely represent the application's environment; proposed data-related changes can be evaluated confidently and implemented directly into the DD/DS. Auditing and monitoring production systems are greatly facilitated by this accurate representation of data as they are processed and utilized.

SYSTEM ARCHITECTURE

Figure 12-1 illustrates the basic software components of a data base environment. The degree to which the DD/DS and other components are bound defines the potential control architecture of the environment. At opposite ends of the spectrum are "passive" and "active" DD/DSs.

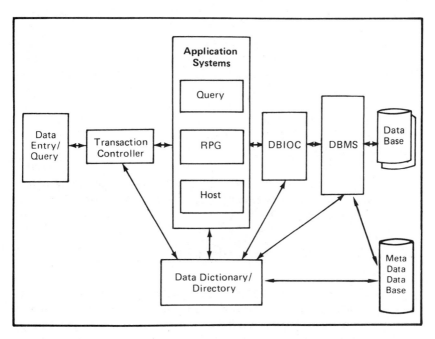

Figure 12-1. Basic Components of a DB Environment

Passive DD/DS

The passive DD/DS contains documentation of the data base environment *after* changes have been made to the processing environment. No direct, active link is maintained with any components of the data base system through the metadata maintained by the DD/DS.

Active DD/DS

Any active integration of the DD/DS with any (or all) components of the data base system is established and maintained by generating metadata for the components. The extent to which the DD/DS plays an active role in processing information requests in each component can ultimately determine the efficiency of the data resource management effort.

Using an active DD/DS can reduce costly maintenance and implementation of systems documentation. This reduction can be realized by a controlled implementation of all components. Automated interfaces between the DD/DS and other system components ensure that the physical and logical metadata are identical to the documentation; this increases the probability of a successful system.

Placing such interfaces between each component and the DD/DS also enhances data independence and permits management to evaluate each component without fear of an adverse impact on the data definition aspects of the remaining system. Thus, if a new technically superior component product is announced, it can replace the old component at a minimal cost—that of changing the interface. (The cost of the processing overhead, however, must be considered when installing the DD/DS as a component of the data base system. Nevertheless, with increasing CPU processing speeds, distributed processing, back-end computers, and other technical advances, the cost of the overhead should not be a major concern. Of far greater importance is the need to maximize the life expectancy of application programs and other user/system interfaces.)

ACTIVE DD/DS: METADATA GENERATION

An active DD/DS is more than a repository of metadata. It controls a metadata base that is shared by two categories of users, human and automated. A DD/DS is active with respect to its automated users *if and only if* these automated users depend on the DD/DS for their supply of metadata. For example, a COBOL application program uses metadata in the form of its File Definition (FD) Section. If the FDs can *only* be obtained from the metadata base, the DD/DS is said to be active with respect to the application program. Similarly, a DBMS is a user of metadata in the form of its schema. If the schema can only be obtained from the metadata base, the DD/DS is said to be active with respect to the DBMS.

The "scope of activeness" of a given DD/DS is measured in terms of the number of automated data base system components that depend upon the DD/DS for their metadata. Thus, a DD/DS upon which a large number of data base system components depend, is said to have a high scope of activeness. It should be noted that the data base system component *must* depend on the DD/DS for its metadata. If the same metadata can be acquired from other sources (e.g., manual input supplied by a programmer), the DD/DS is said to be passive relative to the component, with only a potential for this degree of activeness.

The following parts discuss selected data base system components that can be implemented to depend on a DD/DS for their metadata.

Host Language Application Programs

Application programs written in conventional programming languages require metadata in the form of data descriptions for the input/output/work areas of the program. In COBOL, this is the Data Division; in FORTRAN, the FORMAT statement. In order for the DD/DS to be active with respect to host language application programs, it must be the *only* source of data descriptions for the programs (see Figure 12-2).

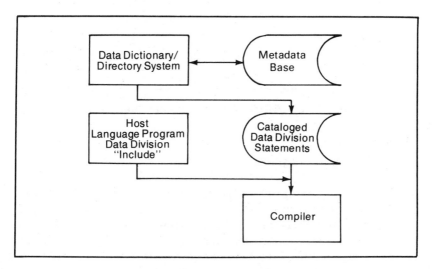

Figure 12-2. DD/DS Host Language Interface

Report Generation Programs

Report generation programs are a specialized type of host language application programs. In addition to the metadata required by ordinary host language application programs, report generation programs require complete definitions of reports to be produced. These report definitions are also a form of metadata. DD/DS that is active with respect to report generation programs would be the *only* source of data definition for the report generation program (see Figure 12-3).

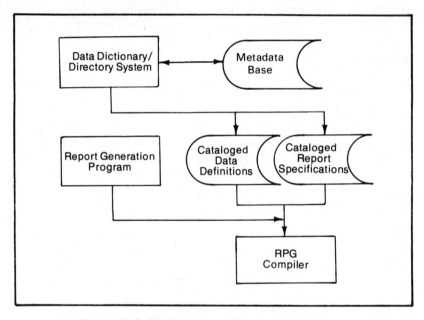

Figure 12-3. DD/DS Report Generation Interface

Query Language Programs

Query language programs (QLP) are different from host language programs in that QLPs are problem oriented and simply request a particular result. QLPs are, therefore, particularly well suited for ad hoc, quick-response requirements. The typical user of this "programming" tool is not a technician and has very little knowledge of either programming or data and storage structures. Nevertheless, a QLP requires metadata.

Data definitions can be supplied the context of a query by using a simple data definition language. An active DD/DS interface for the QLP would supply this data definition requirement from the metadata base. Queries would be formulated using DD/DS data names or acceptable (translatable) synonyms; appropriate references would be made to the metadata base, because they are required by the Query Language Processor/Interpreter.

The DD/DS can play an additional role (active or passive) in preparing an ad hoc query. As requests are formulated, users must know the data that are available from the data base; the DD/DS can be used as a "front-end" to a QLP and process queries related to data availability.

Figure 12-4 illustrates the active interface between the DD/DS and the QLP.

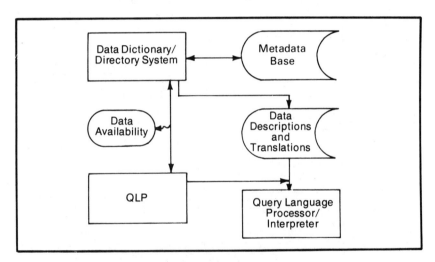

Figure 12-4. DD/DS-QLP Interface

Edit and Validation Programs (Routines)

An edit and validation program is a special kind of host language program requiring a specific type of metadata. These metadata are in the form of edit and validation rules to be performed on processed data within host language programs. Typical examples would include:

- Alpha/numeric check
- Range check

- Lateral check
- Check digit
- Zero balancing
- Batch/hash totals

Programmers often code these checking requirements (and others) into a host language program, thus embedding the metadata in the application program. A DD/DS should include these edit and validation rules in its metadata base. If the edit and validation program can be generalized and implemented as a "routine" driven by a series of metadata parameters specifying the rules, the DD/DS can be used to generate these metadata for the edit and validation routine. When the metadata base is the only source for edit and validation rules, the DD/DS is said to be active with respect to the edit and validation process (see Figure 12-5).

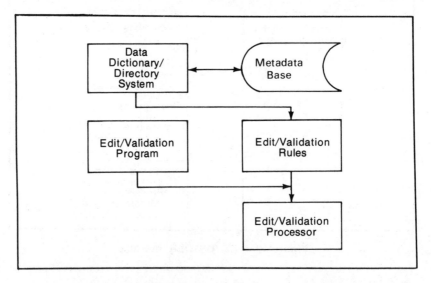

Figure 12-5. DD/DS Edit and Validation Program Interface

Data Access Control Programs

Data access control programs are generalized routines used to enforce security constraints by limiting access to data resources. Such programs are predicated on the concept of a security profile (see Figure 12-6) that specified the passwords required to gain access to data resources classified at various levels. This security profile is metadata, because it describes the privacy/security requirements of the data (i.e., it is data about data).

A metadata base containing security profiles can enable the DD/DS to generate the necessary parameters to drive a data access control program. If the data access control program depends on the DD/DS for this type of metadata, the DD/DS is said to be active with respect to the program. Figure 12-7 illustrates the DD/DS data access control program interface.

Levels of Security	Data Resource Entities																				
	Data Element				Record				File				DB				• • •	• • •	• • •			
	1,	2,	3,	• • •	1,	2,	3,	• • •	1,	2,	3,	• • •	1,	2,	3,	• • •						
Read-only																						
Read/Write																						
• • •																						
• • •																						

Note: The body of the security profile contains the passwords.

Figure 12-6. Data Access Control: Security Profile

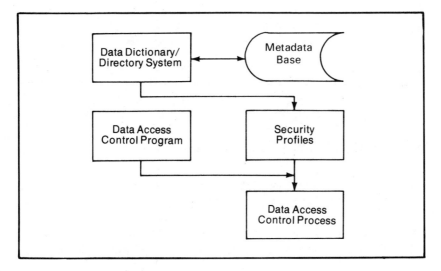

Figure 12-7. DD/DS Data Access Control Program Interface

DBMS

Data base management systems require metadata in the form of a schema and subschema in order to organize, access, and control data. All DBMSs are provided with a Data Definition Language to facilitate the specification of a schema and subschemas to the DBMS. These schemas and subschemas are metadata and should, therefore, be part of the metadata base.

A DBMS that depends on a DD/DS for its metadata would not require a DDL; the DBMS DDL would be superceded by the DD/DS DDL. Such a DD/DS is said to be active with respect to the DBMS.

Figure 12-8 depicts the interface between the DD/DS and DBMS.

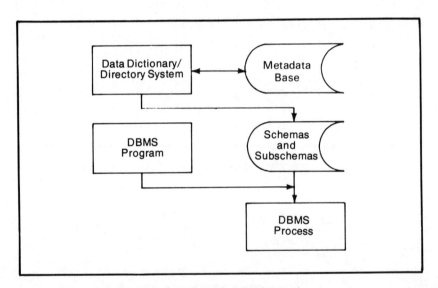

Figure 12-8. DD/DS-DBMS Interface

ACTIVE DD/DS: METADATA INTEGRATION

An alternative strategy in DD/DS architecture is to integrate the use of the metadata base among the components of the data base environment. Thus, a program that depends on metadata from the DD/DS would access the metadata base directly (see Figure 12-9). This approach implements a shared metadata base and requires careful planning on the part of the DD/DS developer/vendor. An example of such a DD/DS in the commercial marketplace is the Cullinane Corporation Integrated Data Dictionary (IDD).

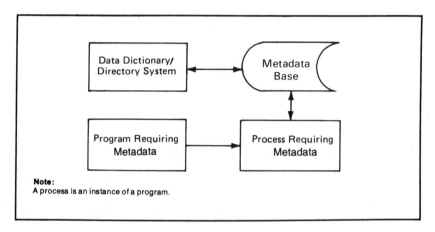

Figure 12-9. Active DD/DS: Metadata Integration

ACTIVE DD/DS: PROGRAM GENERATION

An extension to the concept of metadata generation in DD/DS architecture is the generation of the programs/processes requiring metadata. These programs/processes would eventually execute as would any application program. Based on the metadata description contained in the metadata base, the DD/DS would generate a code to process data. Thus, DD/DS-generated codes could:

- Access data bases (data manipulation language code)
- Create reports
- Edit/validate data
- Perform any data-related function

Generated programs might be in the source of executable form (see Figure 12-10). When actually executing as a process, the application would use metadata generated from the metadata base as would any program requiring metadata.

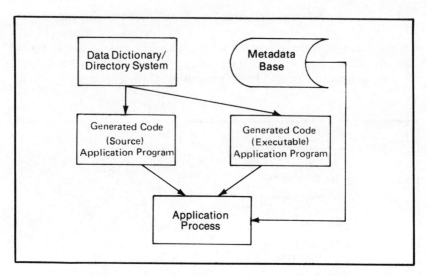

Figure 12-10. Active DD/DS: Program Generation

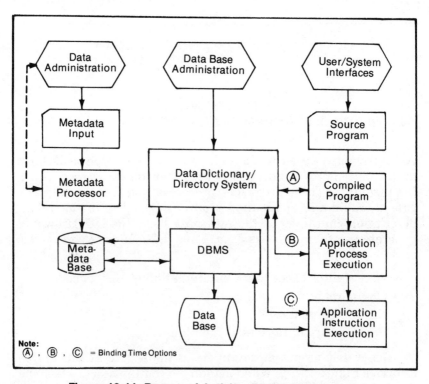

Note:
Ⓐ , Ⓑ , Ⓒ = Binding Time Options

Figure 12-11. Degree of Activity: DD/DS Architecture

210

DEGREE OF ACTIVITY OF THE DD/DS

The *degree of activity* of a given DD/DS is measured in terms of *when* the scope of the DD/DS's activeness is implemented. The concept of "degree of activity" is closely related to the sending time and data independence. Figure 12-11 illustrates three alternatives that relate to the degree of activeness:

- Compile time
- Program execution
- Instruction execution

If the DD/DS is bound to programs requiring metadata at compile time, the degree of activity is low; consequently, the level of control attainable with the DD/DS is limited. On the other end of the scale, if binding is accomplished at instruction execution time, the degree of activity and the level of attainable control is higher.

SUMMARY

It is generally recognized that automated dictionary interfaces are necessary for the adequate control of data resources. The current direction of DD/DS development is indicative of a general trend toward DD/DSs with the type of interfaces discussed in this chapter. Each organization can have a different approach to DD/DS architecture based on its particular needs and cost justifications. In assessing those needs, it would be advisable to keep this epigram in mind: "The only way to control automation is to automate the controls."

Notes

1   H. Uhrbach, "The Systems Development Life Cycle (SDLC) in a Data Base/Data Dictionary Environment" (North American Users Group; Nov. 1977).

PART IV

Administration of the Data Base Environment

No matter what the size of an organization, data base administration is beyond the scope of a single individual. The primary task is to carefully define the administrative function by creating job specifications that outline the duties required.

A most crucial, and recently acquired, responsibility of the Data Base Administrator is compliance with the Privacy Act of 1974. The privacy issue is a fact of life for the Data Base Administrator that is further complicated by increasing telecommunications processing, decreasing hardware costs, and the emergence of transborder data flow as a national concern.

The auditing function also figures heavily within a data base environment. Since their integration into corporate financial systems, auditors—both internal and external— have had a stake in computers and information systems. Including a data base system within a firm's information system creates yet another set of implications for the auditor, particularly when viewed in the context of the relationship between the administrative and auditing functions.

chapter **13**

Organization and Job Descriptions of the Data Base Administration Staff

INTRODUCTION

This chapter discusses job descriptions for the DBA staff. It explores organizational factors in creating a DBA staff and describes the differing staff functions/roles to be filled. It also suggests desirable levels of experience for senior- and junior-level personnel in the various positions. In contrast to Chapter 6, where the DA/DBA was introduced as a function, here we discuss it in the practical sense of a staff.

ORGANIZATIONAL ISSUES

In dealing with the issue of placement within the organization, it is especially important to recognize the necessity for evolutionary development. It is unreasonable to expect that the DBA function will grow in a short period of time into a fully staffed, highly capable, and well-defined organizational entity. For the long range, it is necessary to identify where the DBA function should be situated. Then, interim plans can be formulated and a gradual movement toward the longer range goal can be reasonably expected.

In the interest of establishing a hypothetical frame of reference, the organizational structure shown in Figure 13-1 will be used as a point of departure. While it is recognized there may be as many variations for possible organizations as there are boxes in Figure 13-1 it is still necessary to establish a point of reference. The following discussion should be appropriately modified to take into account the particular variations present in the DP organization under consideration.

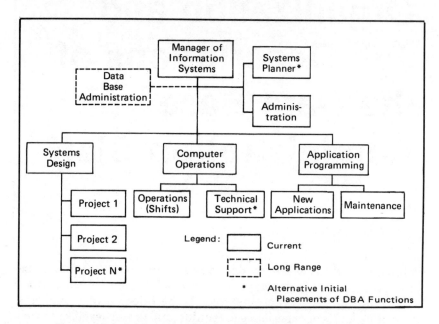

Figure 13-1. DBA: Hypothetical DP Organizational Structure

Long-Range Objective for DBA Placement

The long-range objective for the organizational placement of the DBA function for our hypothetical organizational structure is shown in Figure 13-1 by dotted lines. It is the considered opinion of many specialists in the DBA field that the administrator should be ultimately removed from the direct control of the users, application areas, computer operations, and technical support (i.e., systems programming). Ideally, the DBA should be situated at a high level within the DP function, reporting to the Manager of Information Systems. There are essentially two reasons for this conclusion.

Span of Control. The DBA function requires a wide span of control over the DP functions of an organization and a respectable organizational position with regard to user relationships. The functional responsibilities and, more importantly, the reasons for having a DBA function dictate that the function be organizationally placed both to achieve user-related objectives and to control the use of the components within the data base environment.

Biased Decisions. The DBA must be in a position to make decisions that consider the overall objectives of the data base environment. This objective cannot be accomplished if the DBA function is placed within a part of the organization that will exert pressure and cause a bias in the DBA decision process. The objective and benefits again support placement of the DBA function at a high organizational level so that he or she may concentrate on the task of managing the data base exclusively. Placement in a subunit of the organization will not allow this concentration and will thereby reduce the benefits of having the position.

DBA Placement in the Short Range

Placement of the DBA function in the short range should be viewed as an interim step toward the eventual realization of the long-range objective just described. It should be recognized, however, that in many organizations there is no conscious decision on where the DBA function should reside in its early stages of development. In these situations, it is a matter of coincidence and circumstance that determines the initial placement of the DBA function.

The alternative initial placements, as shown in Figure 13-1 are largely a result of limited experience with the data base environment and the uncertainties echoed by senior management on a new technology.

DBA in System Development. This strategy is usually the result of the functional orientation of the data base implementation. That is a project-by-project, application-by-application use of this new area of technology. As more projects and applications begin to utilize the data base tools, it becomes critical, and perhaps too late, to move the DBA to a more global position.

DBA in Computer Operations (technical support). The placement of the DBA functions in the technical support area of computer operations results from the strong advocation of a data base approach by technical personnel, such as systems programmers.

DBA in System Planning. The system planning function, as shown in Figure 13-1 is a staff function involved in the overall planning and coordination of system development and hardware/software acquisition. This strategy turns out to be the most advantageous for the short range for the very reasons of long-range placement (span of control and unbiased decision making). For an organization just entering into a data base environment, the DBA can conveniently be placed within this area. Furthermore, the eventual objective of placing the DBA in a position of reporting to the Manager of Information Systems will be more easily achieved with the DBA function in System Planning (a position already reporting to the chief DP officer in the organization).

The positions that must be considered in establishing a DBA staff are:

- Data base designer
- Data base technician
- Documentation specialist
- Data base standards developer
- Education and training specialist

Figure 13-2 lists the skills associated with DBA staff members. Each skill is ranked by its importance relative to each posi-

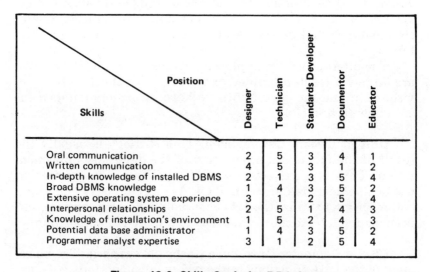

Skills \ Position	Designer	Technician	Standards Developer	Documentor	Educator
Oral communication	2	5	3	4	1
Written communication	4	5	3	1	2
In-depth knowledge of installed DBMS	2	1	3	5	4
Broad DBMS knowledge	1	4	3	5	2
Extensive operating system experience	3	1	2	5	4
Interpersonal relationships	2	5	1	4	3
Knowledge of installation's environment	1	5	2	4	3
Potential data base administrator	1	4	3	5	2
Programmer analyst expertise	3	1	2	5	4

Figure 13-2. Skills Scale for DBA Staff

tion (with 1 as the highest value). For example, no position requires more knowledge of DBMSs or knowledge of the installation's environment than that of Data Base Designer. Additionally, data base design is the most likely position leading to manager of data base administration.

It should be noted that some necessary functions of the DBA will not be considered here. These functions are left to the manager of DBA:

- Communicating with upper management
- Budgeting data base expenses and DBA staff
- Managing the DBA staff
- Establishing priorities for DBA staff efforts

Starting Up the DBA Staff

Experience has shown that the DBA staff should start with just one person (this introduces the DBA concept into an organization in a low-key fashion). This individual should be selected with the intention that he or she will become the DBA. Not only must this individual have the requisite skills in technical areas and user relationships, but he or she must also have strong administrative and leadership skills in order to manage the DBA staff.

Determining the size of the DBA staff is an imprecise process. However, as a useful rule of thumb, there should be one DBA staff member for every 25 DP application personnel involved in data base applications. This figure can vary with the complexity of the DBMS selected. Supporting a DBMS that uses an embedded link network usually necessitates a larger staff than that required to support a DBMS that employs the inverted index structure.

Organizations that balk at a staff of this size usually have an uncertain commitment to data base administration. These organizations also have a tendency to acknowledge only the technical aspects of the DBA position. These kinds of attitudes generally result in a staff that is not numerically adequate to the task. The organization cannot hope, therefore, to derive the full benefits of an integrated data base under centralized control.

JOB DESCRIPTIONS FOR DBA STAFF POSITIONS

The ordering of the detailed job descriptions that follow is arbitrary and implies no hierarchy of positions. In addition, the specific titles used in the following descriptions may vary from organization to organization. Specific titles, however, are unimportant. The important point is that all of the functions be provided for on the DBA staff.

Data Base Designer

The data base designer's main task is to construct data and storage structures that meet users' needs. This task is divided into two closely related activities: interpreting user requirements and establishing data base designs.

Interpreting user requests in terms of the data base approach is a prerequisite to the proper establishment of integrated data bases. The best tool for developing such interpretations is the access requirements analysis. This is a technique for identifying user requirements at the level of specific, definable services.

The access requirements analysis, performed by an installation's senior systems analysts, provides information about specific data that a user needs to perform his or her job. For example, for a typical user query, the analysis would identify:

- Necessary data elements
- Frequency of the request
- Time constraints placed on data availability

Results of an access requirements analysis are transmitted to the data base designer. On the basis of these results, the data base designer should create a design that reflects as accurately as possible the users' views and uses of data.

Figure 13-3 contrasts the access requirements analysis approach with the conventional application system approach.

In addition to an access requirements analysis, the data base designer uses supporting considerations to establish the physical characteristics of the data base design. Some of these factors are:

- Physical record size
- Blocking factors
- Data compression requirements
- Editing characteristics

The data base designer is also responsible for implementing changes to the data base structure. The impetus for change may come from within the DBA staff or from systems analysts. Data base changes initiated by the DBA staff may come from the data base technician and the standards developer. These changes can represent responses to performance inadequacies and access requirements variances. Requests for changes from systems

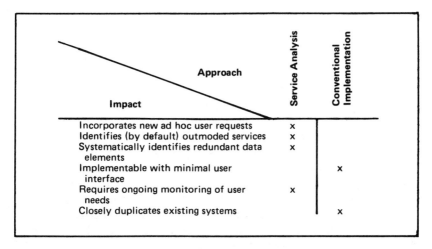

Figure 13-3. Access Requirements Analysis vs. Conventional Implementation Trade-offs

analysts will reflect changes in the user environment. In both cases the data base designer must negotiate and implement the desired changes to the data base.

The data base designer should also assume responsibility for "phasing" the data base into activity with a minimum of impact on existing systems. An attempt should be made to reduce "parallel processing" (i.e., using "spin-off" files to pass data between the data base and conventional files) until the data base is fully integrated and operational.

As the preceding description indicates, the data base designer must be an exceptionally able EDP professional. This person should be at least a senior systems analyst. He or she should also combine considerable knowledge of data base packages with a detailed understanding of the installed DBMS. If the data base designer is a junior-level individual, he or she should have a great deal of potential and prior experience on the DBA staff.

Data Base Technician

The data base technician is the technical "heavy" on the DBA staff. While the data base designer is concerned primarily with structural and organizational issues, the technician investigates overall DBMS considerations. This involves such areas as:

- Systems performance measurement
- Configuration evaluation

- Application appraisal
- Simulation

In systems performance measurement, the data base technician must implement measurement tools for the installed DBMS and keep abreast of performance figures being generated for data base packages at other installations. Additionally, this person must create and review on-line performance reports in such areas as terminal and line usage. He or she must also monitor the installation's audit trails, transaction logs, and the like.

As a result of the performance measurement analyses, the data base technician is in a position to determine if systems usage is actually or approximately equal to the projections made during analysis of user needs. Significant variances may require action by others on the DBA staff, including the data base designer and the data base standards developer.

Configuration evaluation involves the technician in analysis of the current hardware and software configuration. This analysis will determine if the configuration will permit optimal data base usage of each system component. The analysis will also determine if the configuration is capable of handling the data base load. A systematic cycle of review, evaluation, and recommendation has been found to be the best approach in this area.

The data base technician is also responsible for detailing, analyzing, and rectifying poor performance of applications. This brings the data base technician into contact with application designers and programmers. They will conduct a review of application programs that focuses on the data base interfaces. This analysis must be informed by the fact that, because of the nature of the integrated data base, a poor implementation of "data base calls" in one program can seriously degrade another program's performance.

A common source of erosion in data base performance is due to an expansion of the data base. Expanding a data base requires the creation of lengthier data chains or larger indexing tables (depending on the type of DBMS installed). The technician must then determine if a data base reorganization would aid performance, or if eroding performance can be resolved only through an iteration in the data base design.

In order to project the impact of change in the data base environment, the data base technician should also be skilled in modeling and simulation. Two common types of change are brought about by the effect of:

- Introducing new DBMSs and enhancing the existing data base

- Adding new user groups and systems to the existing data base

The DBA, in filling a senior-level technician's position, should lean toward a candidate with a background in OS internals and a good knowledge of the installed data base package. A junior or associate technician would have a similar background but would perform under close supervision of a senior technician.

The data base technician, by definition, is a highly skilled individual. The position, however, should not lead directly to that of a manager of DBA. The individual should first perform successfully in the data base designer's role.

Documentation Specialist

The documentation specialist performs varied functions on the DBA staff. The major function is to serve as the central source of the data base description. In so doing, this individual provides for the following documentation:

- Description of logical structures
- Description of physical structures
- Definition of data element attributes

This information, furnished primarily by the data base designer, provides the input for the installation's data dictionary/directory system.

The descriptions of logical and physical structures are essential for a coordinated and controlled data base environment. Further information on data base characteristics is contained in such attribute information as the element's length and its representation, editing characteristics, and user access capabilities.

The documentation specialist is also responsible for coordinating data-base-oriented documentation and distributing it to sections outside the DBA group. Major aspects of this task are encompassed in the following list:

- Maintenance of distribution control
- Release of access information
- Support of education and training specialist
- Documentation and release of standard procedures
- Preparation of data dictionary analysis reports

Maintaining distribution control involves providing current data base information to all relevant parties. Thus, the documentation specialist works closely with the education and training specialist in creating support tools and distributing educational materials. He or she must coordinate these activities with other

DBA staff members. The documentation specialist, for example, must work with the data base standards developer in creating and releasing systems support procedures. The documentation specialist must also work with the data base technician on the release of operations analysis documentation.

The documentation specialist position requires patience and meticulous attention to detail. The requisite talents are those of a senior technical writer and data specialist rather than those of a student versed in the theoretical foundations of data base. The position can lead to the DBA post only with extensive exposure to data base design. Junior-level personnel would perform the more mechanical tasks, such as data dictionary maintenance.

Data Base Standards Developer

The data base standards developer is responsible for the creation, implementation, and maintenance of appropriate data base standards.

The standards developer monitors three important areas in which standards must be established:

- Data definition
- Data manipulation
- Data base support procedures

In the data definition area, the standards developer works closely with the data base designer and the documentation specialist to ensure that data descriptions are consistent among the various users of data in an organization. For example, in the

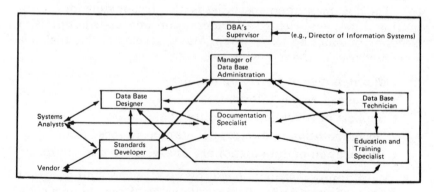

Figure 13-4. Key DBA Staff Interfaces

banking industry, the data base standards developer would guarantee that "account number" was defined and had a common format that was used consistently throughout the organization.

The standards developer should also strive for standard naming conventions within the organization. Common nomenclature will contribute toward the reduction of duplicate data and the identification of inconsistencies caused by the same data element being referred to by different names. This activity should be conducted with the close cooperation of the data base designer and documentation specialist (Figure 13-4).

Data manipulation standards involve the standards developer in the following three related activities:

- Data editing.
- Access control.
- Access patterns.

The common thread among these three activities is their relationship to the programming process. The basic objective and task of the standards developer is to establish guidelines, procedures, and constraints that will ensure a high degree of data integrity. Edit and validation requirements should be centrally and consistently specified and controlled through the data dictionary. Access controls using schema/subschema specification and password controls should be established. Finally, procedures should be established for monitoring data base access patterns against the original prediction made by the data base designer.

The standards developer is also responsible for developing procedures for the use of data base support procedures. These include such tools as:

- Recovery/restart.
- Data base initialization (load).
- Backup procedures.

In accomplishing this task the standards developer must work with the operations staff, the documentation specialist, and the data base technician.

The standards developer must be an individual with strong communication skills and patience. Additionally, the standards developer must recognize that standards need to reflect the users' input rather than being imposed on users.

A senior-level standards developer should have a strong background in systems analysis and a good working knowledge of the installed DBMS. A junior-level systems analyst will receive excellent exposure to data base technology through assignment as a junior-level data base standards developer.

Education and Training Specialist

The data base education and training specialist plays a key, albeit supporting, role throughout the data base installation effort. During implementation and development of the data base, the education specialist performs the following tasks:

- Introduces data base concepts to both data processing and non-data processing personnel (particularly upper management of these groups)
- Develops training schedules, training priorities, and in-house course plans
- Familiarizes himself with opportunities for data base education from both DBMS vendors and other sources
- Schedules in-house courses by both installation and non-installation personnel

Along with reading current literature, the education specialist should attend seminars, conferences, and the like in order to remain current in data base developments. He or she should report the information gained at these sessions to other members of the DBA staff. This should take the form of regular meetings of the group specifically for that purpose. These meetings should be supplemented by appropriate reading materials when available.

Skillful management of vendor relationships can have beneficial results for both the education specialist and the installation as a whole. By maintaining continuous contact with vendors, the education specialist can stay current with the latest DBMS refinements and possible drawbacks associated with these advances.

Strong oral and written communication skills are naturally the key to the selection of an education and training specialist. These skills should be supported with a solid background in systems analysis. Furthermore, a senior data base education specialist must be well-versed in the data base approach in order to establish credibility in dealings with both vendors and users. A junior-level individual must, of course, have the same communication skills but probably with less data base background. This lower position, however, is an excellent place to gain data base experience at an entry level.

SUMMARY

The preceding examination of the data base administration staff points up the following:

- Data base administration should not be treated as a homogeneous function; distinct and definable roles occur within it.
- These roles can be expanded or merged as the situation dictates without blurring the validity of the function as a whole.
- Due to the individual significance of these roles, none can be considered lesser or "fringe" functions.
- The interrelationships of these roles are important and require careful attention. (Figure 13-4).

Installations that adhere to these guidelines will be in a position to establish a coordinated and controlled data base administration function.

chapter 14

The Impact of Personal Privacy Requirements on Data Base Administration

INTRODUCTION

The data base administration function plays a key—and difficult—role in an organization's efforts to protect the privacy rights of employees, clients, and others. It is imperative that the data base administrator remain aware of state, federal, international, and provincial privacy laws so that he or she can effectively and legally manage the information maintained in the organization's data bases. Awareness of these laws and regulations is particularly important as users modify or migrate data base management systems, since

- Provisions for future privacy can be incorporated easily during the modification or migration process
- These laws can easily be overlooked by the technicians and managers charged with doing the modifications, given the pressing nature of their work.

Definitions

In order to understand the issues surrounding personal privacy, it is necessary to define it and distinguish it from data confidentiality. The definition most widely used by legislatures stipulates that *personal privacy* is the right of individuals, groups, or institutions to determine for themselves when, how, and to what extent information about them is communicated to others. According to this definition, each individual should be allowed to determine what personal information is private and to review personal information and challenge its correctness.

Data confidentiality and security are two concepts that are related to privacy. *Data confidentiality* is a status afforded data (e.g., top secret). Legislation, by defining the controls to be used in handling and protecting data, is creating a new status of personal information. *Data security* refers to the mechanisms required to protect data from unauthorized disclosure, modification, or destruction.

LEGISLATIVE BACKGROUND

The first legislation directly related to privacy, the Fair Credit Reporting Act, was passed in 1970 in the United States. The main impetus for the initial legislation came as a result of abuses in the credit and medical information industries. To enhance the usefulness of their data bases, many organizations sought to collect more data and more types of data; some of this data was collected from questionable sources, was simply incorrect, or was made erroneous in some way (e.g., by being taken out of context). (In one case in California, an individual was listed as having been the defendant in roughly a score of suits. In truth, he was listed as defendant solely because of his position as an official of the State of California and not because of personal actions.) Such errors can have a significant, even tragic, effect on the lives of individuals.

Privacy became a popular political bandwagon in the early 1970s; related efforts culminated in the Privacy Act of 1974, which initially affected only federal record systems. Privacy is now a universal issue, however, and most American states, most European countries, and Australia and New Zealand have passed or are considering legislation that will affect the private sector in some way. (There appears to be little public interest in privacy issues in Asia and the Third World countries.)

Generally speaking, most privacy legislation mandates the following:

- Information should be collected, as much as possible, from the source of the data.
- Personal information should be maintained in a manner that ensures completeness, accuracy, relevance, and timeliness.
- Individuals should be able to inspect the personal information maintained on them and correct it if it can be demonstrated to be in error.
- There should be appropriate data processing system safeguards to protect personal information.
- There should be appropriate civil and criminal penalties for abuses.

Despite this legislation, there are still abuses, with some organizations appearing to be unaware, unwilling, or unable to comply with legal requirements. For example, a study conducted in late 1979 by David F. Linowes, former chairman of the PPSC, found banks disclosing data without the consent of their customers. Banks and other organizations have also been known to disclose information to federal authorities without proper warrants. In addition, from time to time, individuals or organizations obtain unauthorized (usually fraudulent) access to data bases.

CHANGES IN DBA RESPONSIBILITIES TO MEET PRIVACY REQUIREMENTS

The DBA function has emerged as the logical one to be concerned with privacy requirements. Preparatory activities by the DBA, based on the anticipated passage of legislation, will save the organization time, trouble, and money. Areas that may be affected by privacy legislation are discussed below; suggestions to help prepare the DBA for the changes are provided.

Data Security

Privacy and related legislation will probably force organizations with computer operations (and therefore the DBA) to develop, describe, and install all possible security safeguards. Such safeguards include technical, physical, and administrative measures.

The first step toward implementing these safeguards entails quantifying the level of risk in the organization or installation. The steps required to determine this risk are:

- *Asset analysis*—Determine the value of the assets within the responsibility of the DBA function. Placing a value on information maintained by an organization is never easy, but the burden can be lessened by adopting a team approach and including users, auditors, and DP technicians on the team. The team should try to determine a realistic dollar value for all assets and should document the process by which the value is calculated.

- *Threat analysis*—Determine the most likely sources of threats, including natural disasters, and the probability that these threats will come to pass.

- *Expected annual loss*—Using an appropriate algorithm, determine the expected annual loss within the DBA function.

Although, realistically speaking, accurate predictions are quite difficult, this exercise can at least give the DBA a picture of the specific mechanisms in place for securing or replacing data. Moreover, now that privacy has become a business, there are many organizations that act as consultants and give seminars in this area.

Standards

Most conscientious systems organizations have formal standards for managing development and maintenance projects. These organizations should welcome the inclusion of appropriate privacy material in each category. Organizations that do not have such standards should. These standards should address privacy issues as follows:

- *Design and implementation*—In addition to discussing overall system design, the design plan should discuss how privacy considerations are addressed and how data privacy is to be implemented. In addition, auditability should be built in rather than having to be added on subsequently.

- *Maintenance*—Repetitive testing is often required during system maintenance. The plan should show how data privacy and integrity will be maintained during these periods.

- *Audit*—The plan should show how privacy and integrity will be maintained during audits.

- *Personnel*—In some ways, DBA personnel, as overseers or gatekeepers, are in even more sensitive positions than others associated with projects. Conduct standards, where they differ from those for other project members, should be clearly delineated.

- *Documentation and training*—Since the technicians and system implementers cannot reasonably be expected to be aware of privacy requirements, part of the charter of the DBA function should spell out the requirements for initial and continued employment in that function. Formalizing such standards is essential for a risk-free DBA function.
- *Education of others in the organization*—Realistically, people will occasionally seek to subvert, if only for their own momentary purposes, the privacy requirements. Written standards regarding the DBA's role in protecting privacy will serve as a safeguard and strengthen the DBA position.
- *Procedures*—In addition to describing system operation, documentation should detail such privacy operations as required paper shredding. The precise steps required should be specified.

A particularly ambitious standard might also outline which tests might be conducted to attempt nondestructive penetration. Military organizations routinely test security in this way with what are called Tiger teams. Nonmilitary organizations might wish to consider variations of this approach.

Required Control Procedures

In some cases, existing control procedures may be adequate to meet privacy requirements. Recommended procedures are as follows:

Data Collection. Personal data that becomes the responsibility of the DBA should be controlled to ensure that it has been collected and processed in compliance with existing standards. The controls should establish and record who collected the data, when, why, possibly how, and any special circumstances that could affect the status of the data.

There should also be some method of controlling data entry. Since the data entry process is often the weak link in the privacy chain, the DBA should be familiar with this operation even if it is not under DBA control.

Program Controls. The integrity of the data base cannot be verified or accredited unless the program development cycle is adequately specified and controlled. Control procedures must be in operation from the first request for program development until program completion. The user and designer must decide on the type and number of control points to be placed in the program in order to ensure that it has a high degree of integrity. Trade-offs between operational efficiency and adequate controls must be evaluated in light of the organization's environment.

Quality control must see to it that controls are tested for completeness, accuracy, and relevance. Users, designers, implementers, and the DBA should be involved in this process. The DBA and maintenance personnel should develop procedures that protect established controls from change during update or maintenance.

Operational Control Procedures. The DBA should establish operational controls that will provide for the handling of personal data through the operations cycle. Labels that clearly identify personal data should be provided for tapes and other storage media. Special handling controls such as sign-in/sign-out logs might be considered to maintain accountability.

CHANGING LEGAL REQUIREMENTS

For the most part, privacy legislation has focused on specific applications or industries; lawmakers have tended to avoid omnibus legislation. (The fact that the Privacy Act of 1974 was an omnibus bill is believed by many to have weakened it.) In the U.S., recommended legislation is directed at known problem areas that are uncovered through public testimony and/or individual awareness. For example, a large number of legislative changes for the insurance and credit industries were recommended in the Privacy Protection Study Commission's final report.

The purpose of the recommended changes is to ensure that individuals can identify, see, and (if necessary) change personal information maintained by an organization. These changes will affect the DBA function, primarily in the area of information retrieval. The DBA function should be responsible for establishing and enforcing rules that govern access to personal information.

The following country-by-country survey of the changes in personal privacy legislation highlights the likely impact of these changes.

United States—Framework for a National Policy

Federal. New legislation and other official activities were deferred until the PPSC issued its final report. That report was released in July 1977, after two years of study and public testimony. (For a copy of the report, write to the Superintendent of Documents, U.S. Government Printing Office, Washington DC 20402.)

The PPSC determined that it is very difficult for individuals to make certain that personal information is not misused. Consequently, the PPSC noted that public policy must focus on five aspects of personal data record-keeping in America. These are:

- Some organizations maintain personal records for reasons other than business. They also keep records for the purpose of documenting actions; this makes it possible for other organizations to monitor the actions of the individuals.
- There is an accelerating trend, most obvious in the credit and financial areas, toward the accumulation of personal details about individuals.
- An increasing number of records about individuals are collected, maintained, and disclosed by organizations with which an individual has no direct relationship, but whose records help to shape his or her life.
- Most record-keeping organizations consult the records of other organizations to verify the information they obtain.
- Neither law nor technology now gives individuals the tools to protect their legitimate interests.

This last item is most likely to have the greatest impact on the DBA function. It will probably result in legislation aimed at helping individuals protects themselves. Thus, it is likely that organizations in the private sector will be required to fulfill an individual's requests for personal information regardless of how the organization stores and retrieves that information. For example, a former employee of an organization might request all the information the organization maintains on him or her. If the organization has large data bases, it must still be able to retrieve all the information and present a hard copy of it to the former employee at a "reasonable cost." From a technical standpoint, it may not be too difficult to locate all the information; it may be very difficult, however, to put the information into an easily readable format.

The PPSC concluded that an effective privacy protection policy must have three concurrent objectives:

- *To minimize intrusiveness*—A proper balance must be created between what an individual is expected to divulge to a record-keeping organization and what he seeks in return.
- *To maximize fairness*—Record-keeping operations should

be modified to minimize the possibility that recorded information can be used unfairly.

- *To create and define legitimate, enforceable expectations of confidentiality.*

Each of these objectives is worth discussing because most of the PPSC's recommendations were within the three categories.

To *minimize intrusiveness,* the PPSC recommended that:

- Individuals be better informed of the information needs and practices of an organization before they provide information.
- A few specific types of information not be collected (e.g., arrest information, in certain instances).
- Limitations be placed on methods of collecting information.
- Governmental mechanisms be established to assist individuals in their attempts to secure their right to privacy.

This means that the DBA must be aware of the data collection practices of the organization when new personal information is added to the data base. The DBA, while not responsible for data collection, should influence the data collection practices of the organization to obviate future problems.

To *maximize fairness,* the PPSC stressed that the individual must have the right to access, correct, or amend information about himself. The recommendations generally call for reasonable procedures to ensure the completeness, accuracy, and timeliness of records. This set of recommendations will have the most direct effect on the DBA. In order to meet these requirements, some data base management systems may have to be modified, or new application systems may have to undergo design changes. In any event, the DBA will have to ensure that personal information under the control of the DBMS meets the organization's standards of accuracy, completeness, and timeliness. (In the event that such standards do not exist, the DBA must develop them.)

To *create legitimate expectations of confidentiality,* the PPSC proposed two types of legally enforceable statements. First, the record-keeping organization has a right to protect itself from improper actions by individuals. Second, individuals have a right to protect themselves against any improper or unreasonable demands for disclosure.

The issue of unreasonable disclosure, especially to the government, is a very important one. It has become apparent to those studying personal privacy issues that the government is one of the worst offenders in this area. Many organizations—most notably financial institutions—are all too willing to supply the government with personal information about customers or clients. The PPSC has taken steps that will require the government to use legal processes (e.g., subpoenas or search warrants) for most requests for information. Furthermore, when seeking access to records in which an individual has a legitimate expectation of confidentiality, the government should inform the individual so that he or she could contest within the legal framework. The DBA must see to it that the organization has well-defined procedures for dealing with third-party requests for information. These procedures should be known throughout the organization to prevent inadvertent disclosure of information to third parties.

Table 14-1 provides a summary of all PPSC recommendations. It should be noted that the PPSC did not recommend omnibus legislation but made specific recommendations by industry. Table 14-1 also shows that the largest number of recommendations were directed at the insurance and credit industries. These industries, along with the medical-care industry, maintain information that can seriously affect an individual's life. Testimony before the PPSC indicated that there are many potential problems in these industries; such problems can occur because of the way information is collected (in many cases from third parties) and used (to determine levels of credit or insurance costs, for example), and because of the manner in which the individual is forced to deal with the organizations maintaining it.

State. There is also privacy protection activity at the state level. California and Connecticut have enacted fair information practices legislation in the past two years, joining Arkansas, Massachusetts, Minnesota, Ohio, Indiana, Utah, and Virginia, who already had similar laws.

Also, Connecticut, Michigan, Oregon, and Pennsylvania have begun or enhanced legislation designed to allow employees to inspect portions of their employee records. Because many states are likely to pass additional privacy legislation in coming years, DBAs should be in touch with their state bar associations.

International. Politics, economics, and technology have combined in the international data privacy domain to present some particularly difficult, and interesting, problems involving data crossing national borders. Moreover, this area of pressing interest has already acquired a name, *transborder data flow,* as well as a legal following and several dedicated newsletters. Decreasing telecommunications costs are sure to add fuel to this fire.

For multinational firms, the position can be quite confusing. For example, data accessed by a terminal in Country A from a

Table 14-1. Summary of PPSC Recommendations

	General*	Minimize Intrusiveness	Maximize Fairness	Expectation of Confidentiality	Total
Consumer Credit (Comm Credit)		2(1)	9(5)	2	19
Depository (EFT)	3	1	6	1	11
Mailing List		1	1	1	3
Insurance		3	13	1	17
Employment	2	3	26	3	34
Medical Care	4	—	5	5	14
Investigative Reporting	—		—	—	—
Government Access to Personal Records	7	—			7
Record-Keeping in Education	15				15
Citizen and Governmental Assistance	2	—	7	7	16
State Role					—
Citizen and Government					
Privacy Act 74	3	—	—	—	3
Taxpayer Perspective	5	—	—	—	5
Research & Statistics	13	—	—	—	13
Social Security Number	4	—	—	—	4
Totals	58	11	72	20	161

Note:
*This category includes recommendations that do not fall into any of the other categories
— None

computer in Country B and dealing with citizens of Country A can, in some cases, come under the purview of the privacy laws of Country A. Because of inexperience with these laws and the lack of legal precedent, however, the question of inspection of the data base by officials of Country A appears muddled. This clearly means that DBAs in multinational companies must be aware of the data privacy laws relevant to their foreign operations. It is not inconceivable that computer-based order entry systems, for example, could ultimately be touched by these overseas privacy laws.

Fair information practice laws have been proposed in Belgium, Austria, France, Denmark, Luxembourg, Norway, Finland, and the Netherlands. The United Kingdom has issued a white paper, and Canada has passed a Human Rights Act.

France. The French privacy law of 1978 provided that data indicating racial origin, union membership, philosophical or political opinions, and similar categories could not be stored without the express consent of the subject, except by religious and similar organizations. Data gathered by fraudulent, unfair, or illicit means was prohibited, and provisions were made for contesting the accuracy of the stored data. The subjects of data must be informed of their right of access to the data; some other civil rights were granted in addition.

Germany. The German Federal Republic Data Protection Law of 1977 regulated the handling of personal data in DP systems. The law has different provisions, depending on whether the subject organization is a government agency, government-controlled business, a private organization processing data for itself, or a private organization processing the data of others. This law seems to have the same general provisions and goals as the U.S. laws; for example, limiting access by unauthorized individuals and auditing the source and handling of data.

Switzerland. Three cantons have established fair information practice laws, and a federal law is being considered. More interesting, perhaps, is the fact that the Swiss are writing security and confidentiality legislation that is stronger than personal privacy legislation. Geneva's Law on Protection of Computer-Processed Data requires that:

- The files, data, and results covered by the law be established, transmitted, and stored in a protected manner.
- A Council of State decides, on a case-by-case basis, to what extent the canton and community administration services

can consult or extract files, data, and results.

- A State Computer Information Control Committee be established to enforce and monitor actions under the law.

Denmark. A 1978 law prohibited maintaining data on race, skin color, political affiliation, or gender, except with the express consent of the subject. The law, however, does *not* apply to information maintained by or for a public authority. Moreover, negative information more than five years old cannot be stored or transmitted unless it is "clearly important" for evaluation purposes by the organization. Subjects on whom data is maintained must be notified within four weeks of the data being stored. There are provisions for right of access by individuals and penalties for violating the laws.

Luxembourg. A 1978 bill established a national catalog of data banks; the typical rights of individual access and correction apply. The provisions of the bill also cover data bases located outside Luxembourg and containing data on Luxembourg citizens, if accessed from within the country.

Spain. In mid-1979, a data base privacy bill was under consideration in Spain. Its current status is unknown.

Norway. A 1978 Norwegian law established a seven-member Data Surveillance Service. Under the provisions of the bill, personal data registers cannot be transferred abroad without government permission. An organization maintaining data is responsible for the acts of persons acting in its behalf.

Sweden. The Swedish Data Act of 1973 was the first legislation anywhere that addressed the protection of personal privacy. It took effect on July 1, 1974, covering automated files only, in both the public and private sectors. The Swedish Data Act is very similar to the U.S. Privacy Act of 1974 with two major exceptions:

- It established a Data Inspection Board (DIB) that grants licenses for all personal information systems except those dictated by the government. DIB does, however, review the requirements of all government-dictated files.
- It created a new type of offense—data trespass. Anyone who modifies, destroys, or discloses *any type* of DP record without authorization can be fined or imprisoned for a term not to exceed two years.

Most experts believe that future privacy legislation in many countries will provide for a DIB-like enforcement agency and will address general data security in a manner similar to the data trespass article.

SUMMARY

Given the increased activity in privacy legislation in the U.S. and abroad, all organizations will probably have to comply with some established guidelines for protecting the privacy rights of individuals on whom they maintain information. Although federal and international legislation affecting the private sector may be a few years away, state legislatures and consumer groups are forging ahead now.

It is difficult to predict the precise impact future legislation will have on the DBA function. Two areas, however, will be greatly affected—data security and accountability. The DBA will have to quantify the security mechanisms in use (physical, administrative, and technical) and justify their adequacy for the environment. Accountability will require establishing an extensive set of controls to ensure that information can be traced from its source to its users; such requirements will affect system design and implementation.

In order to diminish the impact of personal privacy legislation, it is recommended that the DBA develop a privacy impact plan. The plan should address the effect of legislation on the specific environment in which the DBA operates; it should include:

- A review of the organization's awareness of personal privacy requirements—Determine whether anyone in the organization has established a privacy library and is following current legislation. Determine whether any general organizational plans have been developed.
- A review of federal and state legislative proposals—Determine whether any existing or proposed legislation affects the organization. It is likely that state legislation will affect an organization in the private sector before any federal legislation will. In addition, the DBA should obtain a copy of the PPSC final report and use it to develop a training course for the organization's users and managers.
- A review of current and proposed international regulations— Organizations that store data in a foreign country or that process data collected or generated in a foreign country can

be adversely affected by privacy legislation in these countries. The DBA in such an organization is well advised to keep abreast of such legislative activity.

- A review of present data collection and data security controls—Determine what organizational standards have been established to define protection mechanisms and procedures for all DP operations.
- A list of the estimated costs for complying with current or proposed legislation—Goldstein describes a cost model that may be useful in estimating the cost of compliance with privacy legislation.[1]
- An action plan that describes a step-by-step program for upgrading the DBA function to meet privacy requirements— The plan should establish a priority for each step, according to the value returned for the dollars spent.

The data base administrator who waits until specific legislation is passed is doing a major disservice to his or her organization. Planning now for personal privacy may be the most important step a DBA can take to ensure smooth and economical compliance with privacy regulations.

Notes

1   Robert C. Goldstein, *The Cost of Privacy*. Honeywell Information Systems, 1975.

Organizations, Publications, and Other Sources of Information

- Attorney General's Department, Administrative Building, Government of Australia, Canberra, Australia.
- Computer and Business Equipment Manufacturers Association, 1828 L Street N.W., Washington, DC 20036. CBEMA provides a privacy update newsletter and updates of state legislation.
- *Computerworld,* a weekly newspaper, is a good source of timely news on privacy legislation in the U.S.

- Department of Communications, Government of Canada, 100 Metcalfe Street, Ottawa, Ontario KIA OC8. This agency monitors privacy issues.
- Information Gatekeepers Inc., 167 Corey Road, Brookline, Mass. 02146. This company publishes a newsletter dealing with transborder data networks and generally tracks developments in this area.
- *Information Privacy.* Sussex, England. This publication emerged in 1979.
- Organization of Economic Cooperation and Development. 2 Rue André Pascal, 75775 Paris, France.
- National Bureau of Standards, Institute for Computer Science and Technology, Washington, DC 20234. This organization has formed Task Group 15 to establish computer security standards and address privacy guidelines. It produces many good computer security/privacy documents.
- Privacy Protection Study Committee, Suite 424, 2120 L Street N.W., Washington, DC 20037. This committee was established by the Privacy Act of 1974 and has been the source of federal privacy legislation.
- United Nations Commission on Human Rights. This organization has published a report called "Uses of electronics which may affect the rights of the person."
- The University of Western Ontario, London, Ontario. The Social Sciences Computer Laboratory is running an academic research project related to personal privacy.

chapter **15**

Data Base Supported Systems and the Auditing Function

INTRODUCTION

The concept of a data base and the related topic of DBMSs represent key design features of advanced information systems. Some indication of the impact of DBMSs on the information processing environment can be gained from a sales figure for some of the major systems. Canning estimates that approximately 1,000 to 2,000 copies of "true" DBMSs are in use throughout the world[1]. In reality, there are more users, since many of these systems exist in service bureaus and have multiple users. The impact of DBMSs, however, is far wider than even these statistics would indicate. The information processing literature of recent years shows a pervasive concern with the philosophy of data base management. This level of interest signals a substantial increase in the use of DBMSs.

This chapter examines data base management from the perspectives of the DBA and the auditor. It includes an extended survey of the objectives and current technological status of data base management. This survey will help to focus the DBA's attention on those aspects of data base management that have a direct effect on the auditing function.

245

THE OBJECTIVES OF DATA BASE MANAGEMENT AND AUDITING

Data base management can be described as a special approach toward the management of data for information processing. The data base management approach is best expressed in terms of its objectives. Four major objectives of data base management have been suggested (see Figure 15-1)[2].

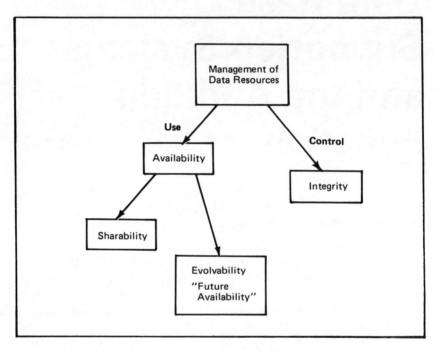

Figure 15-1. Objectives of Data Base Management

Sharability

Traditionally, separate application systems have maintained their own files for their own use. This can be attributed, in part, to the lack of available technology to support the objective of data as a shared resource. However, individual application files cause several problems. The primary problem is that discrepancies arise between files containing the same data items. For example, employee information is normally maintained in both a personnel file and a payroll file. Inevitably, an employee resigns and one of the files is not updated. When such events occur, the user begins to doubt the validity of the information processing system.

Secondary problems involve the storage space required and processing inefficiencies that result when data are duplicated. Redundant data means that increased storage space must be consumed. Additionally, more than one program is often needed to update the same data item stored in different files, even with the same transaction data.

Data base management attempts to remedy these problems. Special file structures are used by DBMSs to minimize data redundancy[3]. A single, logical-level definition is permitted even though the physical processing may necessitate more than one storage location for the data item. The objective of shared data is consistent with the view that data belong to the organization, not to an individual user.

The auditor and the DBA are concerned with sharability of data because of the impact it has on the integrity of the information that is produced.

Availability

"The objective of availability encompasses the responsiveness and performance of the system in a timely and economic manner to an environment of diverse users, operating in diverse modes, using diverse languages, to satisfy diverse needs"[4]. A primary concern of data base management is to make data available to a variety of users. These users range from system programmers to organization managers. This requires a system of interfaces suited to the different users. A variety of interfaces is especially necessary if the objective of shared data is to be achieved.

A DBMS also provides for diverse modes of use. These modes encompass traditional batch processing as well as the more advanced on-line and communications-oriented approaches. The on-line and communications aspects, in turn, dictate the need for different interactive languages to enable various levels of dialogue with the data base.

The DBA must be concerned with making the data base available to the auditor. This must be done in a manner consistent with the auditor's objective (maintaining independence) and the DBA's responsibility for data integrity.

Evolvability

One of the problems facing the DP manager is the rate at which systems become obsolete. Several surveys have suggested that 50 percent of the DP budget for programming is spent on maintenance of existing application systems[5]. Information processing systems should be able to evolve so they can adapt readily to changes in the environment. If evolvability can be achieved, the budget for maintenance of existing systems should be reduced. In addition, users should be more satisfied with an application, since it will be more readily adaptable to their changing needs.

Two primary methods for achieving evolvability are data independence and the use of programming facilities. Data independence refers to the separation of data from the programs that access them. If a single data item is to be accessed by multiple users, the physical storage of data must not prevent users with different views of the data and different logical processing requirements from each accessing the same logical data. This objective is achieved by separating the logical definition of data (as described by a user program) from the logical and physical definitions of data (as stored on the physical storage devices). The DBMS uses a data dictionary/directory or schema to extract data from the physical storage device and make them available according to the logical description provided by the user program (see Figure 15-2).

The data *dependence* aspects of traditional systems can be thought of in terms of data being passed through programs. The data *independence* aspects of a DBMS can be thought of in terms of programs being passed against data.

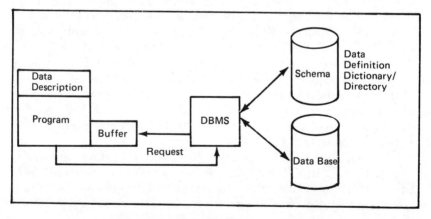

Figure 15-2. Data Dictionary or Schema

The provision of programming facilities also enhances evolvability. A DBMS is assumed to provide generalized facilities for update, query, and report writing. Programming facilities involve higher-level languages and standardized modules for the programmer writing in a conventional programming language such as COBOL or FORTRAN. Such facilities reduce the system development effort and make it possible to extend and modify the overall capability of the DBMS.

Integrity

Integrity of data refers to their essential soundness, validity, correctness, and completeness. There are a number of dimensions to integrity:

- *Validation.* Data (including both input transactions and stored data) should be submitted to various validation tests at different times during the processing cycle. These tests ensure appropriate levels of data quality.
- *Backup.* Techniques for restoring a damaged or destroyed data base should be available.
- *Privacy.* Techniques for complying with privacy laws should be employed.

The integrity requirement is linked to the objective of shared data. A DBMS attempts to achieve integrity in two ways. The first method involves the use of the data base control system software; this provides internal control over access to data. The second method, which is external to the actual hardware/software system, is to use the data base administration function to maintain data integrity.

The DBA's responsibility for data integrity is very closely related to the auditor's objectives. In a sense, the auditor can be considered as an independent reviewer of the DBA's performance in this area.

GENERAL IMPLICATIONS FOR THE AUDITOR

In general, the advantages and disadvantages of a DBMS will be the same for the auditor as for the DP community. Both the advantages and disadvantages for the auditor will be discussed in turn.

General Benefits from Using a DBMS

A significant advantage in using a DBMS is data consistency. The auditor, assessing the design or operation of information processing systems, will find that DBMSs generally enhance the accuracy and reliability of retrieved data. Data are more current, and various facilities are provided for exploring complex data interrelationships. The opportunities for ad hoc retrieval are also greatly increased.

From the auditor's viewpoint, the potential for increased data accuracy is an obvious advantage. The provision of facilities to explore interrelationships between data items with relative ease should also enhance the quality of the audit and provide support for analytical auditing techniques.

With increased experience with DBMSs, the systems design and implementation process for applications shoud be faster and more accurate. The use of the programming facilities of DBMSs enables applications to be written and modified faster. Also, standardized modules will have undergone rigorous testing by many users; systems developed using these facilities should be less prone to error.

General advantages should be derived from structured efforts to control and manage data. The implementation of DBMSs forces data management to become a formalized discipline. This is likely to result in the development of better information processing systems.

General Disadvantages and the Challenge to Auditors

The impact of failure with a DBMS is more catastrophic than with traditional systems. This should be a matter of concern for the auditor. Because the auditor is interested in maintaining accurate information processing systems, he or she should actively seek solutions to potentially disastrous problems.

The auditor, for example, could become actively involved in determining effective methods of implementing DBMSs. Practical experience in this area suggests that the success or failure of DBMS is strongly related to the method of implementation. It is in their own interests for auditors to participate in developing effective implementation methodologies.

The acquisition and use of a DBMS also involves substantial costs. The initial installation cost may be substantial because of the large-scale systems analysis and design effort to prepare applications for a DBMS. The maintenance costs may also be substantial. Some current DBMSs entail large administrative overhead to maintain correct functioning of the system. Input from auditors could help to reduce those costs.

Another area in which auditors could actively participate is in devising effective measures for maintaining data integrity.

Establishing effective data integrity involves a trade-off between processing time and storage space efficiencies—a trade-off that many are unwilling to make. Data integrity is the primary concern of the auditing function. Since the auditor is already skilled in methods of internal control, he or she should be active in finding solutions to the problems of data integrity.

SPECIAL IMPLICATIONS FOR THE AUDITOR

There are three facets of data base management that will have special ramifications for the auditor.

- The role of the data base administrator in the data base management environment
- The ability of the auditor to use generalized audit software when accessing the data base
- The changed scope and timing of the audit that will be required

Data Base Administrator

Relatively early in the development of data base management technology, it was recognized that a function was needed to perform centralized data resource management. This need was a natural consequence of the shared data concept. If data were to be shared by a number of different users, it would be necessary for someone to act as a coordinator and mediator.

There are several functions that the DBA must supervise that have an impact on the auditor[6]:

- Definition, creation, and retirement of data
- Maintenance of user availability
- Maintenance of data integrity
- Maintenance of communication with users
- Monitoring of operations

Definition, Creation, and Retirement of Data. When an organization recognizes a need for more data, the DBA (or someone in the data base administration unit) must design a logical data structure that meets the needs of multiple users and allows for evolvability. The DBA must then reconcile these logical needs with any restrictions imposed by the hardware and software environment.

Unfortunately, little work has been done in developing design methodologies to assist the DBA. In many ways the design process is still intuitive—the success of various design strategies is largely dependent on the skills and capabilities of the DBA and his or her staff. The role of the DBA also involves resolving conflicts among various users or between a user and the organization.

Even when the design process is complete, the DBA is still responsible for creating the data and establishing suitable retention policies. All of the problems with file creation and retention in traditional systems are still present in the data base environment. In fact, to the extent that data are now a shared asset, it is most important to ensure that data are created correctly and suitable retention policies are established. When an existing data structure is modified, the DBA must ensure that reorganization of the data base is undertaken correctly and that users are notified.

Maintenance of User Availability. The DBA must provide the various system and programming facilities needed to achieve the objective of availability. The DBA will either have to purchase or develop the necessary tools for implementing and accessing the data in the data base. A primary function of the DBA is to evaluate such tools and establish their validity before they are used in production processing.

Maintenance of Data Integrity. This function not only involves establishing preventive measures for ensuring privacy but also making suitable provisions for backup and recovery when the inevitable failures occur. Recovery from the destruction of data is even more important with multiple users in a shared data environment. The DBA must also design and implement suitable measures for controlling access to and updating the data base. Various levels of authorization might be instituted to enable the selective accessing and updating of data.

Maintenance of Communication with Users. The shared data environment requires that all users of data be aware of any changes to the data base. The DBA is responsible for documenting such changes and for providing user education services. These services include training sessions on facilities and providing suitable documentation on these facilities.

Monitoring of Operations. The DBA is responsible for the efficiency of operations. The monitoring system must be effective in detecting any threat to the integrity of data, whether it be deliberate or a consequence of inefficiency elsewhere within the system.

Again, the shared data concept makes it absolutely necessary to detect any inefficiencies or dangers before they can affect data.

What implications does the role of the DBA have for the auditor? Two major implications are:

- The DBA is a key employee in the data processing control environment.
- The auditor will have to interact frequently with the DBA in auditing DBMSs and the data bases.

The DBA is probably *the* key variable in determining the success or failure of a DBMS. It seems almost impossible that any single person could ever fill the job specifications for the DBA. In fact, data base administration groups are evolving to meet the imposing job specifications. Effective communication is required within the group as well as with the organization and its environment. If the auditor is to rely on the validity of data, the DBA or group is the key variable for rigorous examination and analysis.

The data base administration function, therefore, needs to be well-defined. Currently, the technology is just advancing to the stage where data base administration functions are being defined at a detailed level. However, the auditor will inevitably be forced into developing a methodology for assessing performance within the data base administration function. It seems illogical to wait for others to define precisely the DBA's role. Since auditors have a major interest in the correct functioning of data base administration, they should actively cooperate with CODASYL, GUIDE, SHARE, and other interested groups in attempting to define this role.

The Demise of Generalized Audit Software Packages?

A recent paper under this title examined at some length the implications of DBMSs for generalized audit software[7]. Currently, those auditors charged with the responsibility of maintaining and updating generalized audit software are faced with a problem. They must determine what approach to choose in modifying this software to handle the files created by a DBMS.

Currently, available generalized audit software is designed to handle file structures typically created under the sequential, indexed sequential, or the random method. However, DBMSs often utilize data and storage structures that are far more complex than these traditional methods. The purpose of these complex structures is to integrate and eliminate data redundancies, improve access to data, and implement better control procedures over data.

A number of solutions exist to the problem posed for generalized audit software by complex file structures. One approach is to modify existing generalized audit software to access the data base directly (see Figure 15-3). This approach, however, is problematic. The complex data and storage structures used by DBMSs are not implemented in any consistent manner. It seems unlikely that a single generalized audit software package could be devised to handle all the possible variations of the present complex data and storage structures. However, if an industry standard for DBMSs is eventually established, the appropriate modification of generalized audit software might be possible.

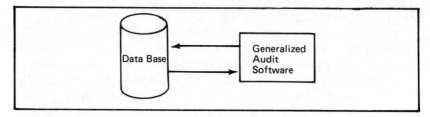

Figure 15-3. Direct Accessing of a Data Base by Generalized Audit Software

A second approach is to devise a standard interface between generalized audit software and DBMSs (see Figure 15-4). The auditing profession would be responsible for the specification of this standard interface. Measures would then have to be taken to ensure that the various vendors included the standard interface in their DBMSs.

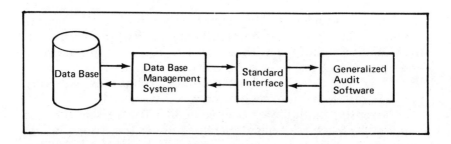

Figure 15-4. Providing a Standard Interface between the Data Base Management System and Generalized Audit Software

A third approach is to modify existing DBMSs to include required audit functions (see Figure 15-5). This would eliminate the need for modification of generalized audit software. Some existing DBMSs[8] already provide a substantial number of these required functions. (Figure 15-6 lists some major audit functions and indicates their inclusion in the DBMS SYSTEM 2000.) This approach would necessitate liaison between the auditing profession and the various vendors of DBMSs.

Of the three possible solutions, the most promising appears to be the modification of DBMSs to include the required audit functions, since many of these functions are already contained in DBMS packages. They are needed not only by the auditor but also by other users of the data base. In fact, some vendors are marketing existing DBMS packages to auditors under different names (CULPRIT as EDP Auditor, and DATA ANALYZER as AUDIT ANALYZER).

The other alternatives appear less attractive. The prospects

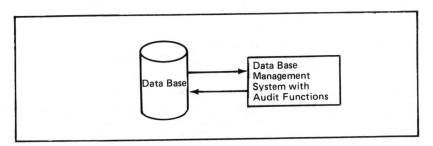

Figure 15-5. Accessing a Data Base by a Data Base Management System Containing Audit Functions

Audit Function	Available?
Record selection using simple logical expressions	Yes
Record selection using compound logical expressions	Yes
Mathematical computations	Yes
Producing subtotal	Yes
Testing footing and extensions	Yes
Sorting	Yes
Comparing 2 files for duplicate data	No
Categorization or stratification	Yes
Table look-up functions	No
Aging of accounts	Yes
Statistical sampling	No

Figure 15-6. Audit Functions Contained in SYSTEM 2000

of modifying existing generalized audit software seem dim. The auditing profession has already spent substantial funds on developing generalized audit software. The cost of modifying this software would probably be prohibitive because the technology of DBMSs is extremely complex, varied, and not yet standardized.

Changed Scope and Timing of the Audit

The data base approach will change the scope and timing of the audit. The phenomenon of shared data resources and the use of common systems software will be the primary contributing factors to this development.

The current scope of an audit is defined in terms of the information produced by a system and the underlying data from which it is derived. With the present application approach, an auditor can clearly define the information, system, and data relevant to the review because the data are dedicated to the particular application. With the advent of the shared use of data, the task of scoping an audit will be much more difficult. A given application system will be difficult to isolate from the effects of other application systems sharing common data bases.

Consider the audit of an Accounts Receivable System (ARS) sharing a customer data base with a Customer Services System (assume that the two systems share the data base shown in Figure 15-7). The auditor will be primarily concerned with the debits and credits made to a customer's account generated as a result of transactions processed in the AR system. However, these very same records are also affected by a transaction generated in Customer Services as a result of returned merchandise, for example. Thus the Customer Service System must also be scrutinized. This situation would not arise, of course, if two applications were not sharing the same data base.

It has been suggested that, in the future, auditors may be required to concentrate on the audit of the data base in addition to the audit of application systems. Should the scope of the audit change in this manner, auditors will need to know much more about data base design and analysis.

Requirements for additional knowledge and training may be counterbalanced by the effect that DBMS software will have on the audit process. In this case, the auditor will no longer need to investigate application programs at the technical level of procedure-oriented languages such as COBOL[9]. If a full DBMS is implemented, application systems will be developed using generalized software—the systems and programming facilities of the DBMS. The auditor may rely on the validity of this software. In general,

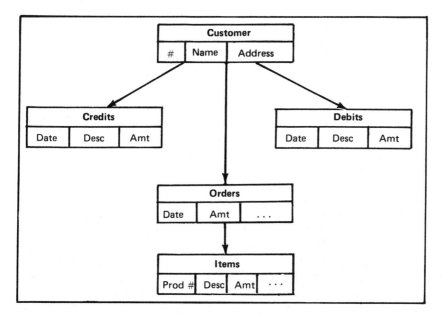

Figure 15-7. Customer Data Base—Partial Data Structure Diagram

the level of detailed, technical knowledge required by the auditor is the same as that used by the client personnel in designing, implementing, altering, and operating their system[9]. Figure 15-8 shows how the level of technical support for application systems has been changing in the information processing environment.

When client DP functions are performed by a DBMS that is not alterable by client personnel and is supplied by a reputable independent vendor, the auditor may rely on the processing validity of the system. (Independent certification of software by institutions such as the AICPA may be needed in the future.) This will alter the scope of the audit. The auditor will be less concerned with the accuracy of program processing in application systems. The emphasis, instead, will be on the nature of input and output, their relationship to the data base and its users, and the adequacy of the installed controls.

The timing of the audit will also be affected. In a complex data base environment it is important to ensure that controls are present in the system *before* it is implemented. Shared data increase the risk of violation of data integrity. The auditor must become involved in the initial design and implementation of a DBMS to ensure that adequate controls are present. Once the system is running, the complexity of a DBMS makes it increasingly difficult to detect violations of data integrity.

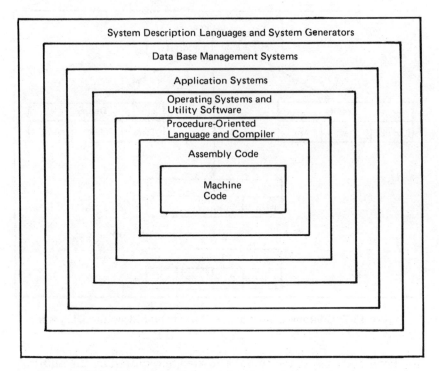

Figure 15-8. The Increasing Automation of Computer Processing Activities

SUMMARY

The auditing profession should actively supply suitable input to those in information processing, particularly in such areas as data integrity, the role of the DBA, and the use of DBMSs as generalized audit software. Continuing task force groups on DBMSs should be maintained within professional organizations such as AICPA. Those task force groups should be responsible for:

- Investigation and research into the implications of DBMSs for the auditing profession
- Monitoring and documentation of developments within the data base field
- Research on data integrity

- Research on effective methods of implementing DBMSs
- Research on the role of the DBA, including relationships with auditors
- Research on appropriate methods of auditing DBMSs, including the use of generalized audit software
- Liaison on the topic of DBMSs between the auditing profession and such institutions as CODASYL, GUIDE, SHARE, and ANSI

For their part, developers and vendors of DBMSs should attempt to understand the requirements of auditors and incorporate the needed functions into their commercial offerings.

Notes

1 Richard G. Canning, "Problem Areas in Data Management," *EDP Analyzer,* XII (March 1973), p. 1.

2 Gordon C. Everest, "The Objectives of Data Base Management," *Information Systems,* ed. Julius T. Tou (New York: Plenum Press, 1974), pp. 1-35.

3 James Martin, *Computer Data-Base Organization* (Englewood Cliffs, NJ: Prentice Hall, 1975).

4 Everest, "Objectives of Database Management," p. 20.

5 Richard G. Canning, "That Maintenance Iceberg," *EDP Analyzer,* X (October 1972), p. 1.

6 Gordon C. Everest, *Database Management: Objectives, System Functions, and Administration* (McGraw-Hill, in press).

7 Charles R. Litecky and Ron Weber, "The Demise of Generalized Audit Software?" *Journal of Accountancy* 138 (1974), pp. 45-46.

8 Donald L. Adams and John F. Mullarky, "A Survey of Audit Software," *Journal of Accountancy* (September 1972), pp. 39-52.

9 Gordon B. Davis and Ron Weber, "The Impact on Changing Information Technology on Auditing" (unpublished paper presented at the New York University/Peat, Marwick, Mitchell and Co. Audit Research Conference held in New York, May 1974).

PART V

Design and Development

Data base design spans activities ranging from identifying end user needs to assigning and ordering data values. The design phases encompass the theoretical description of the entities and their relationships as well as their physical representation for efficient data storage and processing. Errors in the design phases or distortions of the various types of interaction often result in suboptimal design.

The evolution from a file environment to a data base environment is significant. Merely forcing files into a data base framework is not the answer. Such an approach will produce unnecessary complexity resulting in inefficient operation. Defining the keys by which data will be structured is a complex task crucial to the effective functioning of the ultimate data base system.

chapter 16

Data Base Design Methodology—Part I

INTRODUCTION

This chapter concerns data base design and development. Stressed throughout are the conceptual, procedural, and technical differences that must be understood and integrated into all plans in order to develop a responsive and flexible data base environment. This first section discusses the meaning of data base design and the steps involved in developing the design. It presents a methodology to define and structure the keys and attributes of the Logical Data Base design and discusses the cost/performance decisions that must be made during this translation process.

DATA BASE DESIGN VS. FILE DESIGN

It is appropriate to begin this chapter by discussing the differences that exist between the objectives of the data base environment and the file environment and how these differences have an impact on the design process itself.

The objectives of the data base environment are to:

- Provide a base of all data elements relevant to the organization.
- Make these data elements easily available to all appropriate users, both current and future.
- Ensure the integrity of all data elements.
- Stabilize the organization's information environment.

In contrast to the data base environment, the objectives of the file environment are to:

- Create records of data required by each application.
- Tailor the design of each record and file to the needs of an application or program.
- Optimize the efficiency of each file according to the processing needs of the application.

Although the differences between the file and data base environments are readily apparent, it is important that they be thoroughly understood in terms of their effect on the process of designing each.

Scope

In the file environment, designs are developed to serve the current data needs of only one application or program. In contrast to the limited scope of the file environment, the data base environment attempts to serve all aspects of the organization's data requirements. To accomplish this, the data base designer must develop a design that takes into consideration how each functional area of the organization could potentially interact with the data base. Since the size of such an undertaking could be overwhelming, even in a medium-sized business, the data base designer is faced with the problem of developing a design both detailed enough to serve current users and flexible enough to serve the needs of future users.

Integrity

Understanding and ensuring data integrity is perhaps the largest and most complex issue facing data base designers. Since the data base will contain "all data" and make it available to "all appropriate users," it is essential that relationships between all data accurately reflect multiple viewpoints of individual users (i.e., even though an airline may cancel a flight and it no longer appears in the aircraft schedule portion of the data base, it is essential that the flight still exist in other areas of the data base for persons concerned with canceling services such as catering, fuel, etc.). The issue of integrity is not of concern to the designer in the file environment since, by its definition, most data will exist in multiple files, each tailored to the specific needs of one application.

Flexibility

The issue of flexibility is concerned with the ability to easily expand or manipulate data stored in a current file structure without affecting existing users and their associated production costs. Accomplishing flexibility within the file environment is extremely difficult, as the design of each record and file is intimately tied to the type of information being provided to the existing users. Linking the design of file content and structure to existing information implies that, as information needs change, so must the data content and structure of the record. In order for the data base designer to create a flexible data base, the content and structure of each file must be independent from the users' current information needs. To accomplish this independence, the data base design must be based upon data relationships as defined by the way data is created and utilized within, as well as across, the various functional areas of the organization.

Performance

Performance is the ability to retrieve the data required in an acceptable timeframe for a reasonable cost. Achieving performance is perhaps the easiest job of the file designer, as he is free to select the file structure and access methods required to optimize a single application's use of a file. In the data base environment, however, achieving performance is far from an easy task. Each data base contains data elements utilized by multiple applications in multiple ways. To achieve some level of performance for all users, the data base designer must be concerned with the cost/performance trade-offs associated with each potential use of the data base and choose those that optimize overall.

Although other differences exist between file design and data base design, the preceding outline describes the major issues affecting the definition, scope, and complexity of the tasks to be performed during the design process itself.

DATA BASE DESIGN PROCESS

Data bases are designed in two major phases: logical data base design and physical data base design.

Logical Data Base Design

Logical data base design is the planning and analytical phase of the design. It includes:

- Definition of scope
- Identification of data elements
- Identification of the relationship of data elements
- Identification of the organization's operating rules and their implications on data relationships

The product of logical design can best be described as a model that depicts all pieces of data and how each relates according to its many uses across the organization. As a by-product of the model, a list is produced that outlines the capabilities and limitations of the data base in terms of data dependencies. These rules describe how an organization conducts its business and should be carefully verified.

The logical design is totally independent of any particular DBMS. The design may be thought of as a set of specifications, much like a blueprint, for which a DBMS will provide the file structures and access methods required for implementation.

Physical Data Base Design

Physical data base design involves the translation of the logical design into the file structures and access methods of a specific DBMS. This design phase includes:

- An analysis of how data elements cluster physically
- A specification of major transactions and how they will utilize the data base
- A calculation of the costs associated with different file structures and response times
- A generation of all necessary file descriptors and control blocks

Although the scope of the logical design may include the entire organization, the physical design will most likely include only the parts required to implement a current application. Because the physical design uses as its base line the logical design, there are few if any problems associated with expanding the physical files to accommodate future applications.

DEVELOPING THE LOGICAL DESIGN

The logical design should be created separate from any application development efforts and should include in its scope all functional areas of the organization. Developing a design in this manner will allow data bases to be implemented for current applications while retaining the capability of easy expansion for future applications.

In most organizations, management has shied away from developing logical designs that include the entire scope of the organization. Instead, organizations have developed and implemented data bases on an application-by-application basis. The environment resulting from this fragmented approach closely resembles that of the file environment, with the exception of the added cost and complexity of the DBMS software. If it is impossible to develop an all-inclusive logical design, it is imperative to spend a great deal of time defining the scope of the current effort so as to minimize the possibility of creating another file environment and need for future redesign.

Defining Scope

If a logical design is to be developed for a current application only, it is necessary to determine which functional areas should be included in its scope. The best source of information for this determination is the organization's information plan. Information plans can vary widely in content; they should contain, however, a definition of the organization's current and future information requirements, as well as diagrams of the dependencies between major systems (both manual and automated) and groups of data (Figure 16-1). Utilizing the system and data diagrams as a guideline, it is possible to determine which functional areas of the organization should be included in the design's scope. The example shown in Figure 16-1 represents a small portion of the systems and data groups required to support a distribution organization. Assuming that the logical design is being developed for the Accounts Receivable application, the diagram would be used to first identify the major groups of data required by Accounts Receivable—Order Data and Customer Data—and then used to identify other applications requiring that same data—Order Processing and Credit Management. The scope of the Accounts Receivable logical design effort would then be defined as including the functional areas of Accounts Receivable, Order Processing, and Credit Management.

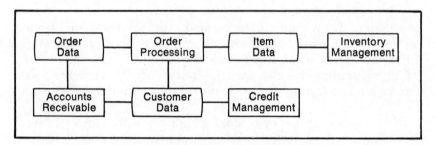

Figure 16-1. Information Plan—Data and System Dependencies

Miniature Information Plan Study. If an organization does not have an information plan or if the plan does not contain diagrams of system and data dependencies, it is the responsibility of the designer to determine the scope of the design effort. To accomplish a definition of scope in this situation, it is necessary to conduct a miniature information plan study. The study is based upon a series of interviews within the functional area for which the application is being designed. The main objective of these interviews is to determine how this area interfaces with the rest of the company. Additional interviews are then conducted within the interfaced areas to determine the extent to which data is shared with the application currently under design. At the conclusion of the study, the scope is defined to include all functional areas that share data with the current application.

Future Considerations. Another factor that will affect the definition of a design's scope is that of current versus future considerations. Future considerations, in the context of logical design, include both major changes in the business (e.g., new products, markets, etc.) and major changes in operating policy (such as centralized versus decentralized purchasing and warehousing). Changes such as these could potentially affect the relationships between major groups of data. Consequently, their impact should be fully considered, if for no other reason than to assess their potential effect on the stability of the design.

Information About Data

Once the scope of the logical design has been defined, the task of collecting information about data may begin. Before discussing the type of information that must be collected, however, it will be helpful to gain an understanding of the theory behind the logical design process. It will then become extremely clear why certain types of information must be collected in very specific ways and why other information is not collected at all.

The theory behind the logical design process is based on the thought that, even though a business may undergo many changes over a period of time (e.g., organizational restructurings, product mixes, and the market segments served), both the basic functions that a business performs and the data utilized by those functions remain fairly stable. Taking this thought a step further and applying it to the task of generating information (which is the ultimate purpose of any data base), it will be found that information needs change as a business changes, but the basic data required to create the new information remains the same.

For example, assume a company was established in the early 1920s to manufacture and sell sewing machines. Further assume that the company is still in business today but has grown to employ 4,000 persons and to manufacture 15 different types of sewing machines, with markets across the United States, Canada, and Europe.

To say that change has taken place in this business is obvious: new products are manufactured; assembly lines are now automated; and salesmen enter orders on-line. But to concentrate on these changes alone is to be misled since many things have remained constant (Figure 16-2):

- The basic functions that must be performed to conduct business (e.g., selling, manufacturing, maintaining records, etc.) have remained the same as those performed in the early 1920s.

- The relationship between functions has also remained the same (e.g., an order must be placed before an item is shipped; before an invoice is created; before a balance is posted to accounts receivable, etc.).

- Each of the basic functions still utilizes a constant set of data (e.g., customer name, account number, invoice number, invoice date, and amount of payment are still required to post a payment to the accounts receivable journal).

Utilizing these relatively stable functions and their related sets of data as its foundation, the logical design process can create a stable information environment.

Collecting Information

The following outline presents the three types of information required to develop the logical design:

1. The first type of information describes the business' basic functions and their related sets of data.
2. The second type of information identifies the explicit and implicit operational policies that determine when and how basic functions are performed.
3. The third type of information identifies additional data elements required to forecast, measure, or maintain a history of the data utilized by basic functions.

If the types of information required to build the design are reviewed, it can be seen how each type contributes to the creation of a stable and responsive data base environment.

CHANGED	REMAINED FAIRLY CONSTANT
How functions are done (i.e. technology)	Functions performed to do business (e.g., take orders, maintain accounts)
Number of products and markets	Type of business being conducted
Number of persons performing each function	Relationship between various functions
Information required to manage	Data required to perform basic functions

Figure 16-2. Basic Changes and Constant Factors in a Company

Identifying Basic Functions and Their Associated Data

This identification is accomplished by conducting interviews within the operational areas of the business. In the context of logical design, operational areas may be considered as those functions essential to conducting business. For example, shipping, selling, or manufacturing all represent functions that must be performed to actually conduct business. On the other hand, inventory planning, market analysis, or auditing all represent functions that are necessary and essential to planning and controlling profitability but are not necessary to conducting business. (Note: The latter are functions that will change over a period of time according to the internal and external business environments.)

In order to determine who should be interviewed within the

functional areas included in the scope of the logical design, request that each manager or supervisor provide a list that denotes: the job titles within his or her area of responsibility; the basic functions performed within each job; and a brief idea of what would occur if the job no longer existed. From these lists it should be fairly easy to identify jobs that have to do solely with planning or controlling and to eliminate them from the interview list (Figure 16-3). After deciding which job titles should be included, each manager should select *two* persons who perform each function to be interviewed.

JOB TITLE	FUNCTIONS	RELATIONSHIP TO DOING BUSINESS
*1. Order Picker	Gathers items on order from warehouse	Fills customers' orders
*2. Inventory Planner	Buys items to stock inventory	Stocks inventory
3. Inventory Manager	Determines optimum time and amount of items to buy	Minimizes investment in inventory
*4. Order Clerk	Records orders and adjustments	Takes customers' orders
*Represents an operational function		

Figure 16-3. Job Titles and Functions

Conducting Operational Interviews

The purpose of conducting operational interviews is to gain a complete understanding of the

- Tasks performed within each operational area
- Data associated with performing each task
- Explicit and implicit rules associated with when and how the task is performed

Interview Procedures. Since the information collected during these interviews will be input to an analysis to create parts of the logical design, it is extremely important that the interview be documented in a predefined format. The following set of interview procedures will ensure that the required information is gathered and correctly documented.

Begin each interview by asking the interviewee to describe the functions that he or she performs on a daily basis. As the interviewee describes the major actions, decisions, and interfaces performed, document them in a flowchart (Figure 16-4). The flow-

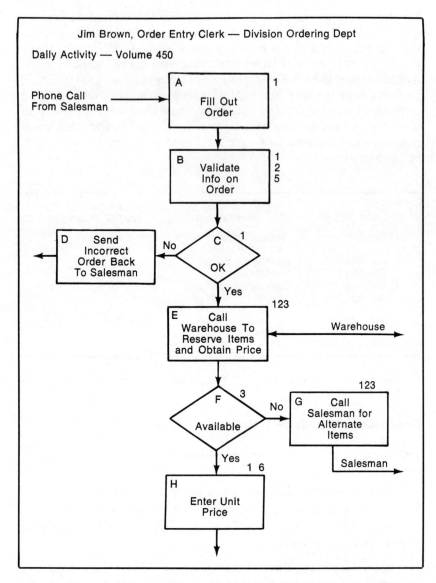

Figure 16-4. Documentation Flowchart of Operations Interviews

chart may also be used as a communication tool to verify that all the basic steps and their sequence are correct. (Repeat the same procedure for weekly, monthly, yearly tasks, etc.)

As the flowchart is being developed, keep a running list of the documents, files, or references mentioned, such as:

1. Order
2. Item book
3. Warehouse call (item number, quantity ordered, quantity available, expected date of next shipment, etc.)
4. Salesperson's call
5. Customer log
6. Pricing form

Once the interviewee understands and agrees to the content of the flowchart, discuss each action, decision, and interface point to determine what documents or references are used. Place the appropriate document number(s) (e.g., 2 for item book) next to the symbol on the flowchart (Figure 16-4). After each symbol on the flowchart has been related to a source document, request a copy of each. If none exists, as in the case of a phone call, record the data content next to the reference itself (see Warehouse call).

The final step in the interview process is to associate the actual data utilized on a document to the action, decision, or interface being performed. This can be easily accomplished by assigning each symbol on the flowchart a unique identifier (Figure 16-4) and placing the identifier next to the data actually used on the document.

There is no specific format for documenting the explicit and implicit rules associated with when and how the flowcharted steps are performed (e.g., a salesman can only submit orders to the warehouses in his division). It is essential, however, that they be recorded for later use.

Conducting Management Interviews

Other information required to develop the design includes a more indepth understanding of the organization's operational policies and rules, a definition of the type of additional data that will be required to control and plan the business, and an idea of the business' future plans. There is no rigid format in which the information must be documented, but it is essential that it be collected and thoroughly understood.

Top Management Interviews. Interviews involving management personnel are broken down into two distinct levels. Top management interviews should be conducted with persons whose responsibilities include defining the goals and objectives of the business, formulating strategies to achieve these goals, and managing plans to implement these strategies. The objective of these interviews is to gain an overall understanding of the

- Basic components of the business and how they interact with one another
- Internal environment (e.g., organization, locations, etc.)
- External environment (e.g., regulatory agencies, number and type of markets)
- Information currently used or required to plan the business (obtain examples if available)
- Forecasted changes that would affect either the type of business or the scope of the business being conducted

Middle Management Interviews. These should be conducted with persons who are directly responsible for the performance of one or more operational areas. The objective of these interviews is to gain a more detailed understanding of the

- Interfaces between operational areas
- Rules and policies governing daily operations
- Effect of forecasted changes on operational areas
- Additional types of information required to measure and control performance

IDENTIFYING COMPONENTS OF THE LOGICAL DESIGN

The logical design consists of three major components: keys, attributes, and relationships.

Keys

Keys are data elements used throughout the organization to identify objects, create other data, or reference other data. There are two types of keys:

- Unique keys are data elements that identify a particular and distinct thing or object (e.g., social security number, order number, customer number, etc.).
- Nonunique keys are collections of data elements, unique in their use, that receive their identity through two or more

unique keys (e.g., an inventory that is identified through the unique keys, item number, and warehouse location).

Attributes

Attributes are data elements that must be qualified by a unique key in order to have any meaning (e.g., address and quantity received have no useful meanings unless they are respectively qualified by the keys, customer number, and item number).

Relationships

Relationships represent dependencies between two or more data elements and are divided into three categories.

Key Relationships. These describe the qualified or unqualified ownerships between keys. For instance, the key "Vendor Number" in an unqualified sense owns the key "Vendor Items." This implies that a vendor's items will never exist in the data base unless the vendor number exists. An example of a qualified relationship is the relationship between the line item of an order, the order itself, and an invoice number. The ownership of the line item belongs to the order number as long as the item is not shipped. As soon as shipping occurs, the ownership of the line item transfers to the invoice number. Hence, ownership of line items is qualified according to the occurrence of shipping.

Key-Attribute Relationships. Such relationships are always unqualified and describe the data elements directly owned by a key (e.g., the key "Customer Number" owns its attribute's customer address credit status). Implied by a key-attribute ownership is that none of the attributes may exist if the key does not exist.

Attribute-Attribute Relationships. Unqualified dependencies between the attributes of a specific key are represented by an attribute-attribute relationship. For example, the key "Accounts Receivable Number" may own the attribute "Total Balance Owed." Conversely, the attribute "Total Balance Owed" may own another attribute, "30-Day Past Due Balance." Implied is that the attribute "30-Day Past Due Balance" will never exist unless the attribute "Total Balance Owed" exists.

In order to develop the components described in the preceding, it is necessary first to consolidate the information collected during the interviews and then to perform a series of analyses. The process of consolidating the information consists of two steps—defining unique data elements and identifying task/data relationships.

Defining Unique Data Elements

In order to thoroughly analyze the flowcharts developed during the interviews, it is necessary to develop a list of unique data elements and definitions. The problem most often experienced in creating such a list is trying to determine which data elements are, or are not, redundant. One way to reduce the magnitude of this problem is to extract individual data elements from documents obtained during the interviews and categorize them in generic lists (such as a list of dates, amounts, names, etc.). Two major efforts are accomplished by following this procedure. First, the categorization of data elements into generic lists reduces the possibility of duplication. Second, when questions arise as to whether two similar data elements may really be one, the source document from which each is extracted can be used to determine the context in which each data element is utilized.

Once generic lists are created and questions of redundancy resolved, the data elements should be input to a data dictionary and assigned both a unique identifier and a description.

Identifying Task/Data Relationships

After a dictionary of unique data elements has been created, it is possible to analyze the flowcharts and define task/data relationships. On the lowest meaningful level, task/data relationships represent the basic static functions performed by the organization and their usage of data.

A task is defined as *a unique unit of work that consists of a set of performed steps, all of which are directed toward a common goal and all of which utilize one common set of data.*

The following outlines a set of rules that will aid in dividing the flowcharts into tasks consistent with the foregoing definition.

- A task must be performed within one functional area of the company (i.e., tasks are always defined within each flowchart and never span two or more).
- The task must consist of serially performed steps (or serially positioned symbols on the flowchart). If a decision point occurs and one path of the decision includes a new action, the first task should be ended and a new task begun.
- Each step within the task must use the same set of data. If new data is created in one step of the task and used by the

next step, it may be considered the same set of data.

- Each step within a task must always be performed. There is one exception to this rule. If a task includes a decision, such as that described in Figure 16-5, all paths from the decision are to be one task; since the different paths of the decision do not change goals, use new data, or include different functions.

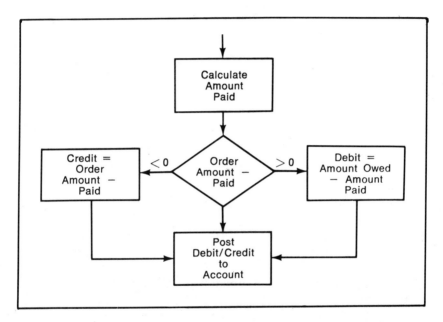

Figure 16-5. Example of Steps Included in a Task

Using the rules stated in the preceding as guidelines, the flowchart illustrated in Figure 16-4 has been divided up into the following tasks.

- Task 1 consists of only symbol A since the data required and the goal of the next symbol are different from that of the first.
- Task 2 includes symbols B and C since they both utilize the same data and both have the same goal.
- Task 3 includes symbol D only since it represents one path of a decision that is not always executed.
- Task 4 includes symbols E, F, and G since they are all directed toward the goal of reserving items and prices and utilize the same set of data.
- Task 5 includes symbol G only since it is not performed all the time and has a different goal.

After all tasks have been defined, they should be further described (Figure 16-6) to include a description of frequency, volume, usage of data (e.g., creates, deletes), functional area (i.e., where it is performed), and data element usage (obtained from the cross-reference between flowcharts and documents).

TASK DEFINITION	FREQ	VOL	FUNCTION	DATA ELEMENTS*
(1) Create Order	DA	2,000	Order Entry	1-45, 50, 67
(2) Validate Order	DA	2,000	"	4-17, 22, 27, 50, 202, 117, 120-124
(3) Fill Out Error	DA	25	"	4-10, 200-204
(4) Reserve Item, Price	DA	6,000	"	7-9, 62, 65
(5) Request Alternate Items	DA	75	"	7-9, 2, 15

*The numbers shown under Data Elements represent a unique identifier assigned to each element.

Figure 16-6. Definition of Task/Data Relationships

Analyzing Task/Data Relationships

The task data relationships are input to a series of analyses that will identify the basic components of the logical design—keys and attributes.

The analyses to be performed are based upon the following hypotheses:

A data element will most likely be a key if it is used

- In a large number of tasks
- With a large number of other data elements
- With each individual data element a low percentage of the total time it is used

A data element will most likely be an attribute referenced and owned by one key if it is used

- In a relatively small number of tasks
- With a few data elements
- With each data element a high percentage of the total time it is used

A data element will most likely be an attribute referenced by many keys but owned by one key if it is used

- In an average number of tasks
- With an average number of other data elements
- With each data element an average number of times

Summarizing Relationships. The first step of the analysis consists of summarizing relationships in a matrix that reflects the relationship between each piece of data (Figure 16-7). Also developed during this step are a series of vectors (Figure 16-8) that reflect the three ways in which data elements will be measured: usage across tasks; usage with other data elements; and relative usage with all data.

Data IDs	Col 1	2	3	4	5	6	
Row							•••
1	0	10	107	2	0	18	
2	10	0	94	3	1	5	Each cell represents the number
3	107	94	0	120	26	99	of times the data ID in
4	2	30	120	0	6	8	the row is used with
5	0	1	26	6	0	12	the data ID in the col.

Figure 16-7. Data Relationship Matrix

Data Element	Total Tasks	Total Data Relationships	Relative Usage With Data
1	75	120	20%
2	40	97	45%
3	150	241	1%
4	10	50	97%
5	65	101	30%
6	140	211	2%

Figure 16-8. Summary of Data Element Usage

After the task/data relationships have been summarized in the proper matrix and vectors, frequency distributions are created. The frequency distributions will be used to define the three categories required to identify keys and attributes. This will be accomplished by inspecting the distributions and dividing them into ranges of low, average, and high. A sample of a frequency distribution of data element usage across tasks is shown in Figure 16-9. The low range is shown as $>0<11$.

The average is $>10<50$. The high range is >50. Translating these ranges into the criteria stated in the previous hypotheses of keys and attributes, the following is obtained:

- A data element will be a key if its task usage >49.
- A data element will be an attribute owned by one key and referenced by many keys if its task usage is $>10<50$.
- A data element will be an attribute referenced and owned by one key if its task usage is <11.

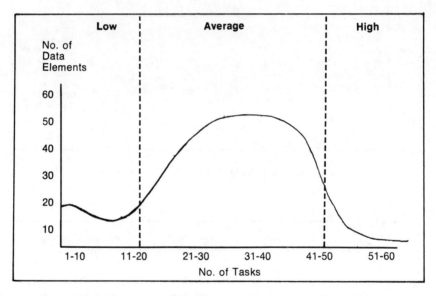

Figure 16-9. Frequency Distribution of Data Element Across Tasks

Categorization. After the low, average, and high ranges of each distribution are identified and expressed in terms of the criteria for keys and attributes (as shown in the preceding), each data element is categorized. Since the categories are derived through the statistics of the analysis, they should not be considered as hard-and-fast rules. Borderline cases should be identified and given special scrutiny.

Assigning Keys. After data elements have been categorized as keys, attributes referenced by one key, and attributes referenced by more than one key, each attribute is assigned to its owning key. Because of their limited use, it is easiest to begin with data elements in the category "referenced and owned by one key." Assignment of attributes to keys is accomplished by identifying the individual data elements that are related to the attribute being assigned and assigning the attribute to the data element that has been identified as a key. (The matrix shown in Figure 16-7 may be utilized to identify the data elements related to a specific attribute.) If it so happens, as it will in many cases, that the attribute is related to more than one key, the following criteria may be used to determine which one it should be assigned to.

- If there is a wide range in the number of times the attribute is used with each key, assign it to the one with which it is most frequently used.
- Refer back to the list of task/data relationships and identify the task that created and deleted the attribute. Assign the attribute to the key present in those tasks.

If different keys were used in the creation and deletion tasks, assign the attribute to the key present in the task in which it was deleted.

Identifying Relationships Between Attributes. At the end of the preceding exercise, all attributes will have been assigned to keys. The next step in the design process involves a further analysis of both the task/data relationships and the flowcharts from which they were defined. The objective of this step is to identify the relationships, or interdependencies, between the attributes of a key itself. To determine the relationships between a key's attributes, it is necessary to identify the tasks that created the attributes and order them according to their occurrence.

Having completed the ordering of the tasks, it will be possible to identify how groups of data are created. For example, assume that 22 tasks are associated with creating the attributes of the key "Accounts Receivable Number." After tasks have been ordered in sequence of occurrence, it will be found that the first creates basic description data such as name, address, age, etc. The next series of tasks adds data that describe activity such as purchase amount, tax, discount, and amount owed. Still later in this stream of tasks other summary type data will be created such as 30-, 60-, and 90-Day Past Due Balance. As shown in this example, there is a very distinct pattern in which most attributes are created. Once identified, these interdependencies should be expressed in a hierarchical diagram (Figure 16-10).

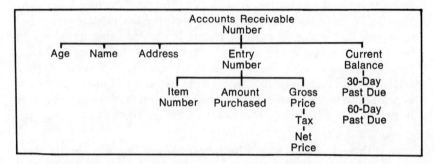

Figure 16-10. Hierarchical Diagram of a Key's Attributes

SUMMARY

We have discussed the basic issues involved in designing data base environments. The presentation of the basic components of a logical design has stressed the planning and analysis of the organization's data usage that must occur before physical files are designed. It is only through this process that an effective and responsive data base environment can be developed. Part II will show how the logical design is completed, validated, and translated into the file structures of a DBMS.

chapter **17**

Data Base Design Methodology—Part II

INTRODUCTION

This chapter presents a methodology for completing logical and physical data base designs. The steps that must be performed to transform the logical design into a physical design are emphasized. These include structuring the design to reflect the major operational policies of the business and verifying the design's implied capabilities and limitations with users. The physical design is further developed by translating the logical design into the physical file structures and access methods of a specific data base management system. Stressed throughout this discussion are the numerous cost/performance trade-offs that must be identified and resolved in order to create a responsive, flexible, and cost-effective data base environment.

COMPLETING THE LOGICAL DESIGN

The components of the logical design include keys, attributes, and relationships. The processes involved in identifying keys and attributes and in structuring the relationships between attributes were discussed in a previous chapter. In order to complete the logical design, it is necessary to identify and structure relationships between keys and to verify the design's implied capabilities and limitations with users.

Symbols of the Logical Design

Prior to discussing the processes involved in completing the logical design, it is appropriate to define the symbols used in its construction. The two symbols used to construct the logical design are rectangles and arrows. Rectangles represent keys. The attributes associated with each key are not explicitly shown within the rectangle. Unique keys are denoted by rectangles with a double bottom line.

Nonunique keys are denoted by rectangles without a double bottom line.

Arrows are utilized to show relationships between keys. The arrow used in the following example shows that the key, "Vendor Item," is related to the key, "Vendor." This implies that vendor items may not exist in the data base without being related to a vendor. It also implies that each vendor may be related to many items, but each item can be related to only one vendor.

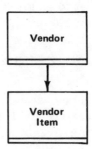

Relationships between keys are rarely as simple as the one shown in the previous example. In order to express other, more complex relationships, special combinations of arrows and delimiters are used.

When the relationship between keys is conditional, the arrow is qualified. As shown in the following example, Sales Agreement is related to items only when the item is participating (or included) in the terms of the Sales Agreement.

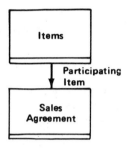

Oftentimes a key may be related to one of two or more keys, depending upon their status. In the following example Inventory will be related to either Item or Discontinued Item but never to both.

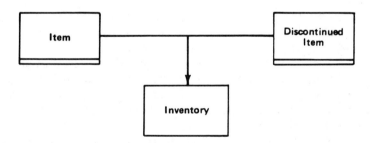

Nonunique keys are dependent upon one or more unique keys in order to derive their identity. Multiple arrows are used to show this multi-relationship. The example on page 286 implies that a specific piece of inventory will never exist in the data base unless it is related to both a Warehouse key and an Item key.

Identifying Relationships Between Keys

Relationships between keys reflect the following conditions.

Owner: In many situations a key may be totally meaningless

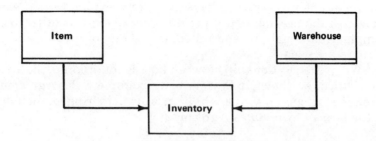

unless it is related to another key. This type of key relationship is termed *owner*, because the dependent key must always be related to the owning key in order to exist in the data base.

Status: Groups of data may take on different characteristics because their use and meaning change over a period of time. Under these conditions, a group of data may be owned by one of several different keys, depending upon its current status.

Regulations: Outside regulatory agencies often determine the way in which part of a business is conducted. The rules enforced by such agencies normally create relationships between keys. These relationships are termed regulatory relationships.

Policies: The policies of an organization (i.e., major rules that regulate how different areas of the business must function, either separately or together) represent yet another type of relationship between keys. Policy statements usually fall into two categories: organizational and functional. Functional policies tend to be fairly static over a period of time while organizational policies change frequently. For this reason, organizational policies are not usually included in developing key relationships.

Structuring keys and their associated attributes into the symbols of the logical design is an iterative process. Key relationship identification is the single most important phase in structuring the logical design because these relationships define the rules that control what data may or may not exist in the data base. For this reason, each of the four types of relationships should be identified separately.

The information required to identify relationships between keys will have been gathered, for the most part, during the interview cycle. The following example will be used throughout the rest of this chapter so that the process involved in structuring keys may be easily understood:

- The design example is a chartered airline.
- The functional areas within the scope of the design include Aircraft Scheduling, Sales, Contract Administration, Catering, Ground Handling, Maintenance, and Passenger Representatives.
- All keys and attributes have been identified. The keys include Flight Number, Affiliated Organization, Contract Number, Airports, Aircraft Number, Countries, and Engine Hours.

Each of the four types of key relationships will be identified separately using the previous example.

Owner Relationships. Owner key relationships represent explicit dependencies between one or more keys. The easiest way to identify owner relationships is to scan the list of task/data definitions and find those tasks that either create or delete keys. In the airline example, four tasks were found that either create or delete the key, "Contract Number." The task that creates the contract uses the pair of keys, "Contract Number" and "Affiliated Organization." Of the three tasks that delete the contract, two use Contract Number only, and one uses both Contract Number and Affiliated Organization. In no circumstance was Contract Number either created or deleted through any key other than Affiliated Organization. With this information in hand, it should be assumed that Affiliated Organization is the owner of Contract Number. The manner in which this owner relationship is displayed is shown in Figure 17-1. This diagram implies that:

- A Contract Number must be related to one Affiliated Organization.
- An Affiliated Organization may have many outstanding contracts.
- When an Affiliated Organization is removed from the data base all of its related contracts must be removed.

Status Key Relationships. Identifying status key relationships is a difficult task as most keys change status

- Over a long period of time
- As a result of a document moving from one functional area of the company to another
- As a result of one key being used in several different ways

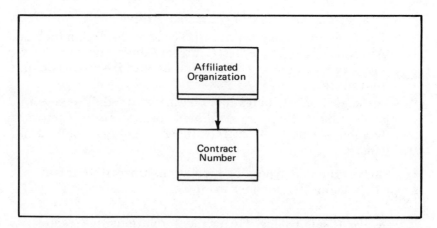

Figure 17-1. Ownership Relationship

The preceding type of change is documented in the interviews but is difficult to extract. To identify different statuses of keys, the list of task/data definitions should be reviewed along with the written interviews and notes taken on the different circumstances in which each key is utilized. For instance, it was found in the chartered airline example that the key, "Flight Number," was used to identify a customer flight, to schedule a customer flight, to schedule a training flight, to schedule a ferry flight (i.e., a flight without passengers), and to schedule crew members. Several statuses of Flight Number can be extracted from this list. The most obvious status of Flight Number is that some flights are generated by the airline itself (i.e., training and ferry flights) and are not contracted. This implies that more than one type of flight must be shown in the logical design, as only customer flights need to be contracted. Another status that is derived from this list is that flights are assigned to an aircraft number as they become scheduled. With further research into the interview notes, it is also discovered that each flight number may contain many legs (i.e., multiple take-offs and landings on the same or different days). In circumstances in which two legs of the flight are on different days (i.e., either a return flight or a layover), each leg may be scheduled on a different aircraft number. This implies that the individual legs of a Flight Number must be related to an Aircraft Number. The key relationships that display both the statuses of Flight Number and the statuses of a Flight Number's legs to an Aircraft Number are shown in Figure 17-2.

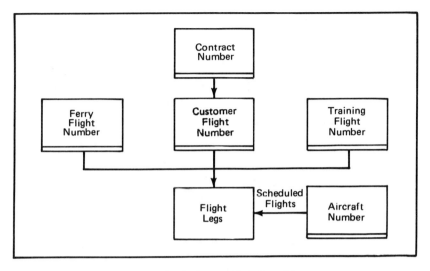

Figure 17-2. Status Relationships

Regulation Relationships. The information required to identify key relationships imposed by regulatory agencies is available from middle- and top-management interviews. For example,the Civil Aeronautics Bureau has stated that chartered airlines cannot sell seats on a chartered flight to individuals but must sell the entire flight to an affiliated organization such as the Boy Scouts of America or the American Medical Association. Implied by this rule is that each flight must be related to a Contract Number key that is in turn related to a valid Affiliated Organization key. As the relationships between Affiliated Organization, Contract Number, and Customer Flight have already been established in Figures 17-1 and 17-2, all that needs to be done is to combine the two diagrams.

Policy Relationships. Statements of policy are available from middle- and top-management interviews. Such statements define how business is conducted either within or across functional areas. For example, assume that the airline has experienced problems in the past obtaining fuel and other supplies at various airports. To alleviate this situation, management has decided to enter into long-range contracts with the most commonly used airports. In order to comply with the terms of the contracts, all flights must follow a route in which the first departure and the last arrival are at an airport covered by a service contract. To reflect this key relationship in the logical design, it is necessary to add the key, "Airport," and relate it to the first departure and the last arrival of all flight legs (Figure 17-3).

The logical data base may be considered complete after all key relationships have been identified and reflected in the design. The final step in the logical design phase is to verify, with all users, the capabilities and limitations implied by the design.

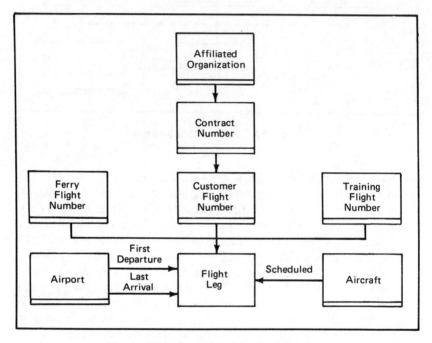

Figure 17-3. Completed Logical Design

Identifying Capabilities and Limitations

The process of identifying the capabilities and limitations of the logical design involves a step-by-step interpretation of the three types of relationships (i.e., key-key, key-attribute, and attribute-attribute).

The capabilities and limitations implied by relationships between keys can be determined by identifying the circumstances under which the design forces individual keys to relate to one or more other keys. For example, the design in Figure 17-3 implies that the following capabilities and limitations will be enforced in regard to the key, "Contract Number."

- Contracts can be made only with affiliated organizations, and contracts to any other type of customer will not appear in the data base.
- Each contract must be for one affiliated organization.
- Contracts cannot be made for training flights or ferry flights.
- Each contract may include an unlimited number of flights.
- Each affiliated organization may have an unlimited number of contracts.

To identify the implications of key-attribute and attribute-attribute relationships, it is necessary to refer to the attribute structure diagram associated with each key (Figure 17-4). Key-attribute relationships are represented by the attributes directly related to the key (i.e., attributes that appear along the first line in the structure diagram). Each attribute of the key that stands alone (i.e., is not further related to other data, such as longitude) implies that only one value of that attribute may exist for each key. Attributes that relate to other attributes may have multiple values. The following key-attribute implications have been derived from Figure 17-4.

- Each airport will be described by one longitude, one latitude, and one altitude.
- Each airport may have an unlimited number of different runways.
- Each airport may have one or more different fuel types available.

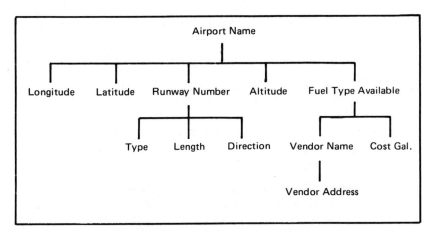

Figure 17-4. Attribute Structure Diagram

Attribute-attribute relationships are represented by attributes that relate to other attributes. The following implications have been derived from the diagram shown in Figure 17-4.

- Each airport may have an unlimited number of runways, and each runway will have a unique type, length, and direction.
- For each type of fuel available at each airport there is
  —One cost per gallon regardless of the vendor
  —Multiple vendors for each type of fuel

The list of capabilities and limitations verbally describes the data relationships and dependencies that will be ensured by the data base. Once this list is completed, it should be thoroughly reviewed by users. Following the review process, the design will be adjusted to accommodate the capabilities and/or limitations that were found to be inconsistent with the business environment.

PHYSICAL DATA BASE DESIGN

The physical data base design will provide the structures and access methods necessary to implement all or part of the logical data base design. While the logical design phase concentrates heavily on the business environment, the physical design phase is directed toward the technical environment. The physical design will duplicate the logical design if the software of the DBMS is capable of supporting all data structures while providing the required performance. As this is rarely the case, it is necessary to translate the logical design while taking into consideration the following:

- Data structures and access methods supported by the DBMS
- Type of hardware utilized
- Performance requirements of each application utilizing the data base
- Time allowed to recover from system and security failures
- Risks associated with maintaining redundant data, giving up data integrity, and losing flexibility

Before any efforts are expended on translating the logical design, two types of information should be gathered and thoroughly understood. The first type involves the capabilities and limitations of the DBMS itself. This information will be used to assist the designers in developing a cost-effective and high-performance data base environment. The second type is the performance requirements of the various applications. These requirements will be used to determine the effectiveness of alternate physical designs.

Analyzing the DBMS

The purpose of analyzing the DBMS is to gain a thorough understanding of its capabilities, limitations, performance, and cost of performance. The analysis should cover the following points:

- Capabilities and limitations
    - —Types of data structures (e.g., hierarchical, network, inverted)
    - —Types of access methods (e.g., direct, sequential, indexed)
    - —Level of security (e.g., data element, groups of data, files, application, terminals)
    - —Degree of recoverability
    - —Degree to which multi-views of data are allowed (i.e.,ability to retrieve data through secondary or tertiary keys)
- Performance and cost
    - —Cost associated with each file structure and access method expressed in terms of response time, recovery limitations, reorganization requirements, and flexibility
    - —Cost associated with multiple uses of the data base expressed in terms of security problems, operating system limitations, and file structure considerations
    - —Cost associated with different levels of data relatability

User Performance Requirements

User performance requirements should be defined and carefully verified before any portion of the physical data base is designed. Performance requirements should be categorized as follows:

- *Individual transactions* defined to include:
    - —Response time boundaries (i.e., desired, minimum)
    - —Data base requirements (i.e., sequences in which various groups of data are either required or created)
    - —Volumes (i.e., low, peak, and average)
- *Environment* should be defined to include:
    - —Number of different applications that will simultaneously

access the data base

—Mode of operation (e.g., on-line, remote job entry, batch)

- *Availability* should be defined to include the cost incurred by the user if the system is not available for specific and varying lengths of time.
- *Security* should be defined in terms of:

—Sensitivity of data

—Risks associated with data

- *Individual capabilities* of the applications should be separated into those that are required and those that are desired but not essential. These two categories will be utilized in the design process to assess alternate implementations of various high-cost sections of the data base.

Translating the Logical Design

The logical design is translated into the DBMS in the following three steps:

1. Select the main storage structures to store keys and their relationships to one another.
2. Assign attributes to key storage structures.
3. Select access methods for each storage structure.

Storage Structure Selection. Selecting the storage structures to represent keys and their relationships can be simple or difficult, depending upon the DBMS. The objective of selecting storage structures is to duplicate, as closely as possible, the keys and relationships displayed in the logical design. For example, if the DBMS provides network storage structures, the logical design shown in Figure 17-3 would be translated into one data set or record type for each unique key and either direct addresses or cross-reference data sets for each nonunique key or relationship between keys. It is important to note that the actual method of implementation (e.g., data sets, record types, pointers, addresses) will always be unique to the DBMS being utilized.

Depending upon the range of capabilities provided by the DBMS, it may be possible to implement keys and their relationships in a number of ways. If this is true, each alternative should be evaluated to determine its cost and performance and then compared with the requirements set forth by the users.

Assigning Attributes. Once the storage structures are selected to represent keys and their relationships, attributes should be assigned. The process of assigning attributes requires a further analysis of the task/data definitions because the logical design does not take into consideration how data are used together to process transactions. Groups, or clusters, of data are identified by performing the same analysis that was used to develop the logical design, with the exception that each task will be weighted by its volume and frequency. Such an analysis will identify clusters of data that are almost always utilized together (Figure 17-5). This

---

DATA CLUSTER ANALYSIS

15 — Date of Departure

Data Element ID	Percent Usage*
12 — Contract Number	92
17 — Flight Number	62
19 — Day of Departure	100
20 — Time of Departure	100
27 — Number of Passengers	92
28 — Meals Served	95
42 — Beverages Served	80
51 — Airport	51
73 — Tons of Luggage	87

*Represents the percent of the time Date of Departure is used with another data element.

Figure 17-5. Data Cluster Analysis

information is used to adjust the attribute structure diagrams. For example, assume that an attribute structure diagram exists for each of three keys shown in Figure 17-3 (Contract Number, Flight Number, and Airport). Reviewing these diagrams it is found that:

- Date of departure is related to Contract Number along with the attributes, day of departure, and time of departure.
- The remaining attributes—number of passengers, meals served, beverages served, and tons of luggage—are all related to Contract Number.

The data cluster analysis shows, however, that the attributes related to Contract Number (as listed in the foregoing) are used more often with Flight Number and, specifically, with the group of data—date, time, and day of departure. In order to maximize performance, all of the preceding attributes should be physically stored together under the key, "Flight Number."

Every time an attribute of a key is stored with another key, the question should be raised as to how its integrity will be guaranteed. In the preceding example, integrity will be guaranteed, even though the attributes are stored with Flight Number, if the storage structures previously selected reflect the relationship between Contract Number and Flight Number. If the storage structures do not reflect this relationship, the attributes of Contract Number should not be stored with Flight Number.

The process described in the foregoing is repeated for each data element. It should be emphasized that two major questions must be asked during the process. The first question is whether integrity, as defined in the logical design, is ensured. If integrity is not ensured it is necessary to discuss the risks and associated performance trade-offs with project teams and users. The second question concerns the cost/performance trade-offs associated with alternate means of implementation. As each data element is assigned a place in the storage structure, a cursory analysis should be performed to determine its associated cost.

Access Method Selection. The last step in developing the physical design involves selecting access methods for each portion of the storage structure. The following criteria should be used in this selection:

- User requirements
  - —Types, frequency, and volume of accesses
  - —Response times
  - —Allowable recovery time
- Environment
  - —Size and volatility of file
  - —Backup and recovery implications
  - —Mode of operation

Measuring Cost/Performance

The final phase in the physical design process is cost/performance measurement. The purpose of this exercise is to identify those parts of the design that cost the most and do not contribute to maximizing overall performance. Cost/performance measurements can be accomplished either by hand calculations or by software simulation. Regardless of the mode chosen, the following variables should be included:

- Cost to process each major transaction
  - —CPU time
  - —Number of calls to the DBMS
  - —Number of actual I/Os
  - —Message queue processing
  - —Transmission time
- Cost to process each application
  - —Storage space
  - —Log device
  - —Operating system and DBMS overhead

The results of the calculations will be used to fine tune the high-cost portions of the data base and forecast both the time and cost associated with processing all applications.

SUMMARY

The processes involved in data base design are directed toward two major objectives. The first is to provide a stable design capable of serving the data requirements of both current and future users within the organization. The second objective is to provide management with the information required to make cost/performance trade-off decisions prior to implementation.

The vast differences between file design and data base design have been exemplified by each step of the design process itself. It is essential that these differences be thoroughly understood and acted upon if an organization intends to derive its data from data base information systems.

chapter **18**

Trade-offs in Data Base Design

INTRODUCTION

In its broadest sense, data base design encompasses activities that range from the identification of end-user requirements to the final arrangement of data values on a physical device. The first phase of the design process, logical design[1], aims to develop a formal description of the entities and relationships that must be captured by the data base to meet user requirements. The second phase, physical design[2], determines how the logical data base (the data base schema or data submodel[3]) should be represented physically for most efficient data storage and processing. Many design decisions must be made during both phases of the data base design process. Further, decisions made in one phase may affect the choices that can be made in the other. Errors in either phase or ignorance of their interaction can result in a suboptimal design.

The critical nature of the data base design process is now being recognized. Business organizations are moving from the traditional approach of developing data files in support of specific applications to developing large, integrated data bases that may be shared by many users. In such an environment, design errors can be costly, not only to one application system but to any systems that share the same data. Design errors can cause excess or inefficient processing, excess device capacity, lengthy application development times, frequent data base reorganization, or reprogramming of application programs.

Unfortunately, many organizations approach the data base design process with little or no understanding of the trade-offs involved. Design decisions are made by relying on the designer's intuition or experience with non-data-base systems. If the designer would view the data base design process as a series of trade-offs, then the risk of design errors could be minimized.

The identification and evaluation of trade-offs provide a structured way of dealing with complex problems. A trade-off is the result of a knowledgeable assessment of the costs versus the benefits of a decision or action. It usually involves the trading of one benefit for another, when the latter is deemed more desirable or of higher priority. Trade-offs thus require a knowledge of the interrelationships among factors involved in the decision.

Two classes of trade-offs can be identified for the process of data base design: general and operational. General trade-offs are those that relate to the designer's approach to the overall problem. They should be acknowledged by the designer and used as guidelines for the selection of feasible alternatives for data base logical and physical structure. Operational trade-offs[4] are specific choices regarding design tools or among actual or proposed alternative data base structures.

The designer should compute trade-offs for the alternatives considered and use the results to compare, and ultimately select, an implementation that meets the objectives. This chapter covers the general trade-offs related to data base design and discusses the interrelationships among factors involved in the process as a basis for the evaluation of operational trade-offs.

GENERAL TRADE-OFFS

There are five general trade-offs that should be acknowledged and applied where relevant during the data base design process.

Specialization vs. Generalization

The traditional approach to file design was focused wholly on the needs of a specific application, that is, a group of related processing requirements. Data required by more than one application was often duplicated rather than shared. Following this approach, the storage and access decisions made could customize the files for their primary user. In a data base environment the emphasis is on managing the data as a resource. The data base thus becomes a repository of shared information, and customized representations or implementations are inappropriate. The question of cost and performance in a data base environment becomes more complex since the overall objective is a kind of global optimum, which may indeed be suboptimal for any given application.

Extent of Analysis

For most data bases some degree of analysis is worthwhile, considering the severe and continuing penalties of inefficient implementation. However, the effort required for additional analyses must be weighed against its benefit. For example, in selecting a data compression method for a textual data base, it must be determined whether the cost of content analysis is justified or whether similar information could be gained through published works on character frequency in English text.

Capabilities vs. Requirements

In matching the structural and usage requirements of the data base with the capabilities of the DBMS, access methods, and data storage devices available, the data base designer should attempt to make an economic trade-off between the power of the configuration and the requirements of the applications to be supported. The configuration should meet the requirements but should not provide unused capacity.

Present vs. Future

The data base designer should try to select design alternatives so that implementations based on them will remain tenable for the future. Considerations that bear on this trade-off include the expected useful life of the data base and trends in DBMS software and data storage devices. Design decisions today must consider the storage and access potential of new devices, for example, mass storage devices or bubble memories, and of new data structuring ideas such as relational or set-theoretic DBMSs.

Planned vs. Ad Hoc Processing

It is valuable for the designer to know the proportion of planned versus *ad hoc* processing that will be required of the data base.

Design decisions favoring planned processing will put less emphasis on nonprocedural interaction with the data base than those made with a view toward supporting spontaneous, unplanned processing. Similarly, the storage overhead (indices, pointers, and so forth) necessary to facilitate *ad hoc* processing would be unnecessarily burdensome in an environment where applications were well known and repetitive.

The data base designer should keep these general trade-offs in mind throughout the data base design process. Primarily, they form a design philosophy that can be used as a guide in the formulation of implementation alternatives. The designer can also use these trade-offs to evaluate the general feasibility of different approaches to the implementation of the data base. The final decisions, however, must be based on the evaluation of operational trade-offs.

OPERATIONAL TRADE-OFFS

Operational trade-offs are encountered during both phases of the data base design process. During logical design they relate primarily to the strategies and tools selected for developing the data base schema. During physical design the trade-offs are related primarily to alternatives for data base implementation. Certain trade-offs cross the boundary between design phases and relate to the interaction between logical and physical design.

Trade-offs in Logical Design

Logical data base design begins with an investigation of user requirements and ends with a logical description of the data base that will support those requirements. The schema, or logical description produced, is "logical" because it does not contain details about how the data are to be represented. The schema becomes input to the physical design phase which follows.

Logical design[1] is broken down for trade-off analysis into four activities: requirements analysis, data modeling, view integration, and schema development (see Figure 18-1). Requirements analysis involves the determination and documentation of user needs. These requirements are then expressed as an abstract, formal data model that represents the user's environment as realistically as possible. Since the data base must support a number of users, each with different views of the data, the user views must be integrated into one global data model. Finally, the global data model is transformed into a DBMS-dependent schema representation.

Logical design decisions have an immediate impact on how data are collected and how they are assembled to meet users' needs. In making these decisions the logical designer faces several types of trade-offs.

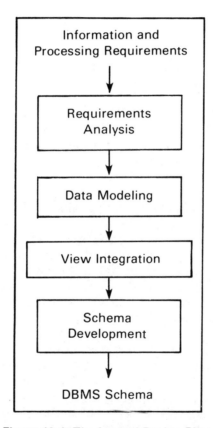

Figure 18-1. The Logical Design Phase

Application vs. Global Modeling. Two activities in logical design, data modeling and view integration, assume that the designer attempts to model each user's view, or application, separately and then merges these views into a global model capable of supporting them all. This approach has the advantage of being easier, with respect to the collection of user requirements and model development, but gives no guarantee that the view models will be successfully integrated. Since the development of the full data base may occur over time, with applications being added in succession, incompatibility of application models could cause data base redesign with its attendant costs.

To avoid this problem, the designer could choose to develop a global model initially and define application models as subsets of the global model. The disadvantage of this approach is that, to develop a global model, the requirements analysis must also be global in scope, thus increasing the complexity of the design task and the time and resources required to accomplish it. It also delays the expected benefit of the data base implementation, since no applications can come "up" until the full data base has been specified.

Most designers today feel the solution is a middle ground in which a high-level global model is sketched for the enterprise[5] and used as a guide during the development of application models. This can reduce the risk of incompatibility while not inordinately adding to the complexity and cost of the design process.

Choice of a Data Modeling Technique. Many different data modeling techniques[6] are available for use by the data base designer. All contain constructs and notations for representing data entities and relationships among them. In choosing a modeling technique, the designer must weigh the capabilities of the technique for use in requirements specification and communication with users against the ease with which models developed with the technique can be mapped into appropriate DBMS schemas. Normally the more user-oriented the technique, that is, the easier it is to represent and interpret its models, the less rigorous and complete it is. Thus, models of this type must be augmented and revised before they can be mapped to DBMS schemas.

Process vs. Information-oriented Design. The traditional approach to data file design emphasized the processing requirements over the data. Only data elements required by the processing were included, and these elements were grouped in a way that maximized efficient execution of the processes required. While this approach is not appropriate in a data base environment, the question of how much influence processing requirements should exert during data base design still exists. This trade-off can be explained as a balance between completeness and adequacy.

A complete data base must contain all information relevant to the enterprise, that is, be a faithful and complete model. A data base designed with a process orientation contains only that data necessary to make it adequate for support of processing requirements. A complete data base is perfectly flexible—able to support all existing and future processing needs—at the cost of excess data collection and maintenance. An adequate data base is less costly and is customized to existing requirements, but it would require redefinition should it become inadequate for new processing requirements.

DBMS-dependent vs. DBMS-independent Design. The debate here is how early in the data base design process the DBMS should be introduced. To achieve short-range efficiency, one could argue that the logical constructs of the DBMS should be used as early as requirements specification and data modeling. In that way, all information necessary to the data base schema for the DBMS would be collected and extraneous information would not. However, a data model expressed in DBMS constructs cannot be mapped easily into the constructs of another DBMS. Should the software environment change, additional analysis and design work would be necessary. Each DBMS also imposes its own logical view of how data should be grouped and structured. By following this view early in the logical design phase, the designer risks missing opportunities for representing the data requirements that may eventually be better than those offered by the DBMS.

Trade-offs in Physical Design

The physical design phase begins with the logical schema representing user requirements and information on the existing processing requirements. It results in a plan for the physical implementation of the data base that will achieve the best performance at the least cost. Physical design is divided, for trade-off analysis, into four activities:

1. Determining and documenting data representation
2. Selecting and documenting access modes
3. Allocating data to devices
4. Loading and reorganizing the data base (see Figure 18-2).

Each data element and group in the schema must be assigned a data type and size and documented using the data definition language of the DBMS. Next, the access methods by which the elements and records will be stored and retrieved must be chosen. Then each element, record, or file must be assigned to a data storage device and these assignments recorded in the DBMS internal schema[5] or Device Media Control Language (DMCL). Finally, the physical designer loads the actual data into the data base and is prepared to revise decisions regarding the physical aspects of the data base as changes in data or processing requirements dictate.

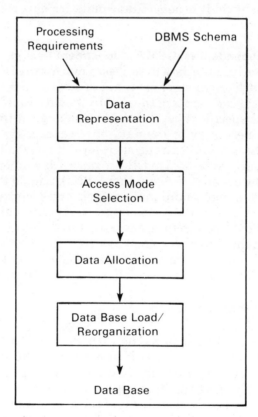

Figure 18-2. The Physical Design Phase

During physical design, trade-offs arise that balance data base costs against data base performance for both data storage and processing. Unfortunately, improvements in either cost or performance usually result in detriment to the other.

Impact of Data Allocation. Access to data on secondary storage devices is efficient when the data that are used together are stored in close physical proximity. Clustering data in this way improves the chances that a physical block of data transferred to main memory will have more than one required data record. Further, when multiple blocks must be retrieved, I/O time will be minimized if access can be restricted to tracks within one disk cylinder or, at worst, on adjacent cylinders. The trade-off here is that, in a data base environment, many processing programs share the same data, yet the optimal data allocation for each may, and probably will, be different. The physical designer must plan data allocation in response to application priorities, given a minimum standard of acceptable performance for each application.

Choice of Access Methods. Many DBMSs give the designer a choice of access methods for each physical file in the data base. When making this choice, the designer is trading off storage efficiency and access-method simplicity against flexibility and immediacy of data access. Methods with minimal storage and processing overhead, for example, a sequential access method, have constraints on data placement, such as requiring a physical or logical sequence of records, and such processing restrictions as no direct record retrieval or in-place updating. Methods that allow flexible and direct retrieval, such as indexed or inverted list methods, require additional storage (for pointers or indices or directories) and more complex processing operations for overflow handling, record addition and deletion, and the like.

Redundancy vs. Efficiency. Though minimum redundancy is an objective of the data base approach, with current hardware and software controlled redundancy may be necessary for efficient processing. For example, ideally a data element such as Product Name should be stored once within a data base, say with the other attributes of the product it describes. An order referring to this product might contain the product identifier, but the Product Name would not be stored redundantly. Duplicating the Product Name data element as an attribute of Order may save enough I/O accesses to more than offset the cost of the additional bytes of storage. The physical designer must make such trade-offs explicitly and ensure that proper controls are in place to guarantee consistency among duplicate instances of the same data element. In the preceding example an update to the product data involving Product Name would have to trigger a similar update of related orders.

Data Compression. Compressing, or compacting, data before it is stored can save valuable storage space. This is especially important in conjunction with access methods, for instance, inverted lists, that add substantial overhead information to the data base. The price of this saving in storage is increased processing time for encoding or decoding the data on addition to or deletion from the data base. The balance can be tipped in favor of data compression by selective compression. That is, only certain portions of the data (such as non-key fields) are compressed so that many searches can be performed without decoding until the final set of records is selected.

Interaction Between Logical and Physical Design

Although logical and physical design are two distinct phases of the data base design process, there is interaction between them. The designer must be aware of this interaction and of the effect it may have on the structure and implementation of the data base.

DBMS Constraints on Physical Design. Ideally, the constructs used to represent the logical schema for a data base are independent of implementation details. However, in most commercial DBMSs this ideal is not achieved. The constructs that represent groups of related data items (records, segments) in fact represent physically stored records; the relationships described define actual access paths; and, in some cases, even data allocation is specified in the data base schema (the DBTG Area or Realm concept, for instance). When this overlap occurs, the physical designer has less flexibility in selecting implementation methods. Further, a change in implementation has far-reaching ramifications, since the logical schema and programs written based on that schema may be affected.

Impact of Processing Optimization on Logical Design. Concern for the performance of data base applications can result in constraints on the logical design. The designer may choose to use only those DBMS constructs or relationships known to provide fast access. For example, an IMS designer may express most data base views as independent (physical) data bases and not make use of the IMS facility that allows a logical view to span two or more physical data bases. A DBTG designer may choose to avoid the use of the DBTG set type and instead represent the relationship between two types of records using imbedded (and redundant) data values. Unfortunately, allowing physical considerations to constrain the logical design in this way obviates the benefits of data independence and prevents the logical designer and the application programmers from taking full advantage of the power of the DBMS.

These interactions between logical and physical design appear to be the result of shortcomings in existing DBMSs and currently available storage devices. Advances in either of these areas should promote true data independence and eliminate the trade-offs.

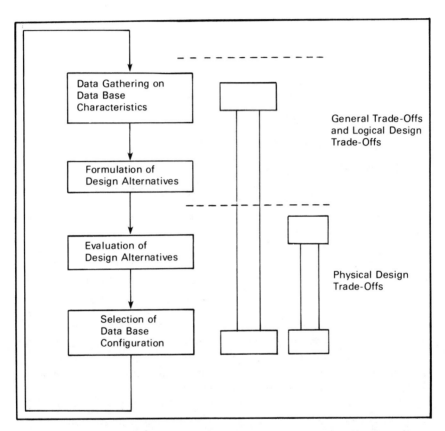

Figure 18-3. The Relationship of General and Operational Trade-Offs to the Data Base Design Process

TRADE-OFF APPLICATION AND EVALUATION

The two classes of trade-offs discussed previously can be specifically related to the phases of the data base design process (see Figure 18-3). As the figure shows, the general trade-offs are applicable throughout the design process, while the operational trade-offs are encountered in the more analytical steps that follow.

In the formulation of alternative designs, the general trade-offs can be of use to the data base designer in three ways:

- They may be used to set practical limits on the resources (personnel, time, and funds) expended on the design process. This function is served primarily by the "extent of analysis" trade-off.

- Whenever choices must be made, the designer may fall back on the general trade-offs for guidance. For example, the generality of a particular data modeling technique may recommend it, or a device may be removed from consideration for lack of desired capabilities.

- Perhaps most important, the general trade-offs may be used in the development of an acceptance standard (possibly a set of criteria) to be used in the evaluation of operational trade-offs. For example, to be acceptable, a design may be required to meet retrieval needs over a time span of five years.

The result of the operational trade-offs in logical design provides the data base designer with a logical design approach and tool(s) for specifying data requirements. The approach selected determines the scope of the logical design process and the types and extent of data collected during this phase. The data model selected and its relationships to the DBMS in use further define the type of requirements data to be collected and will govern whether or not a schema mapping step is required as part of logical design.

Ideally, the data base designer should be able to evaluate the operational trade-offs among alternative physical configurations in an iterative fashion. He or she should be able to change design parameters and reevaluate each alternative easily. Further, the designer should be able to stratify the evaluation of a given data base, that is, apply different constraints and design alternatives to different portions of the data base. To illustrate, it should be possible to evaluate the impact of using a mix of devices, such as a storage hierarchy. The best way to accomplish a systematic evaluation of this type is to simulate or model the data base in question.[7]

In any case, the evaluation of the operational trade-offs for each design alternative should result in the identification of one or more designs that meet the acceptance standard. If only one configuration is acceptable, selection is complete. If more than one meets the standard, a final decision is required. Here again the designer may rely on the priorities established by the general trade-offs to aid in the final selection. For example, if two equally acceptable designs differ in the support they provide for *ad hoc* inquiry, the "planned versus *ad hoc* processing" trade-off could determine the design selected.

Once selected and implemented, a data base design should be monitored during its lifetime to assure that it continues to meet the criteria that resulted in its selection. Both classes of trade-offs should continue to guide the data base designer and serve as indicators of the need for redesign.

SUMMARY

The factors involved in data base design are both numerous and interrelated. In considering all factors and relationships, the data base designer may become enmeshed in a never-ending analysis and overlook the best data base configuration for the requirements specified. However, by recognizing and confronting the trade-offs inherent in the data base design process, the designer can impose a structure on this complex task and can proceed step by step, using his or her skills more effectively to reach the final implementation.

Notes

1   S. B. Yao, S. B. Navathe and J. L. Weldon, "An Integrated Approach to Logical Data Base Design," *Proceedings of the NYU Symposium on Data Base Design,* p. 1-14, New York University, May 1978.

2   J. Martin, *Computer Data Base Organization* (Englewood Cliffs, NJ: Prentice-Hall, Inc., 1975).

3   C. J. Date, *An Introduction to Database Systems* (Reading, Mass.: Addison-Wesley, 1977).

4   J. L. Weldon, *Data Base Administration* (New York: Plenum Publishing Co., 1981).

5   ANSI/X3/SPARC Study Group on Data Base Management Systems, *Interim Report 75-02-08,* ACM FDT 7(2), 1975.

6   G. Wiederhold, *Database Design* (New York: McGraw-Hill, 1977).

7   J. L. Weldon, "Data Storage Decisions for Large Data Bases," *NTIS Publication* No. AS/A-023874 (Springfield, Va.: U.S. Dept. of Commerce, 1976).

PART VI

Current
Directions

Low-cost direct-access mass storage, rapid technological advances, and favorable cost/performance ratios have led to increased interest in and acceptance of data base systems. Current trends in data base system research at the logical, physical, and architectural levels are modifying the thinking of data base developers. These evolving technologies and methodologies include bubble and charge-coupled storage and centralized and distributed data base systems.

There is danger in implementing a data base management system on an already heavily loaded computer. Such a move may result in operational degradation of the data base management system as well as of the present application programs. Employing a backend computer with the requisite hardware and software may provide the solution.

Distributing the data base may be a trap for the unwary who find themselves lured into rocky waters by this siren's song. The problems inherent in distributing a data base are complex, involving many technological and operational issues.

chapter 19

Current Trends in Data Base Systems

INTRODUCTION

The current status of data base systems can be characterized by two closely related, significant trends:

- Rapidly increasing user acceptance
- Rapidly improving technology at the logical, physical, and architectural levels

Increased user acceptance has come about, in part, because of the availability of low-cost, direct-access mass storage. This has encouraged users to move away from tape-oriented sequential files to structures that support direct access efficiently. A recent survey has indicated that about half of the medium- and large-scale systems now being procured will have data base applications.

In addition, the large market for data base systems has itself spurred research and development to provide continually better technology. The basic value of data base systems to the end user and the absence of substantive barriers to further technological improvement are fundamental to the efforts and advances being made.

Although the overall cost/performance ratio of systems is improving, the needs of computer users are growing even faster. Consequently, computer architectures that are more efficient in information storage and retrieval applications are needed. Essentially all current architectural design activity in this area is directed at data base systems. This activity has resulted in the following:

- Storage design is independent of specific applications.
- Explicit data definition is independent of application programs.
- Users need not know data formats or physical storage structures.
- Integrity assurance is independent of application programs.
- Recovery is independent of application programs.
- Keeping a single copy of the data eliminates the redundancy and inconsistency of multiple files.

Although a number of approaches to data base systems exist, three data models appear to be gaining dominance: the network model (as specified in the CODASYL data design language and *Journal of Development*), the relational model, and the hierarchical model.

This chapter considers technological advances in four categories related to data base systems:

- Mass storage hardware
- User interfaces
- Distributed data base systems
- Data base computers

MASS STORAGE HARDWARE

Current storage systems include a hierarchy of random-access (or main) storage, direct-access storage, and sequential-access storage.

Main Storage

Although main storage is generally ignored in discussions of mass storage, main-storage technology has a major influence on how other elements of the storage hierarchy are used.

Main storage provides the buffer area necessary to operate direct-access or sequential-access storage; it is provided today in capacities that would have qualified for mass storage only a decade ago. (In the early 1970s main storage units of more than four megabytes were rare in large systems; main storage units of less than four megabytes are now rare on the same systems.) As main storage has become less costly, optimum system balance has shifted toward larger main stores; as a result, processor use has increased dramatically from the 50 to 60 percent common in the early 1970s to the 85 to 95 percent common today. The increased main store size has also decreased the amount of I/O performed because more data is kept in main storage as opposed to being moved to a lower level in the storage hierarchy. This data can be retained as hardware or software pages or as complete files or data bases.

Figure 19-1 shows how the cost of main storage has fallen as the technology has moved to progressively higher levels of chip integration for dynamic MOS. Overall, the price dropped from 1.0 cent/bit in 1970 (using 1K-bit chips) to 0.1 cent/bit in 1978 (using the current industry standard 16K-bit chip). In general, the number of bits on a chip has quadrupled every three years; this has cut the price approximately in half every three years (this is nonlinear cost reduction since cabinets, cables, power supplies, and interface logic have much more constant costs). Samples of 65K-bit chips are now available, and products containing these chips

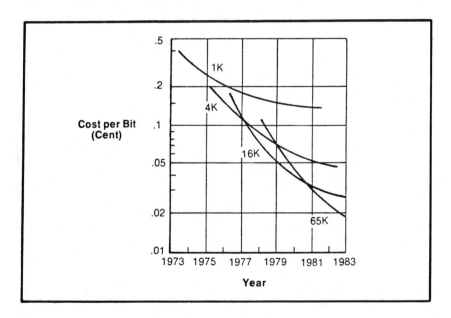

Figure 19-1. Trends in Costs of Main Storage

should be in mass production in the 1980s, continuing the trend.

Current improvements in photolithography suggest that the 262K-bit chip will be feasible, with samples likely in 1982, and that a one megabit chip may even be possible. At these levels of integration, the cost of main storage lies mostly in the interface and in support equipment; it is almost independent of the size of the store. The low cost of these devices is leading to ever-larger main stores in all classes of computer systems.

Direct-Access Storage

The requirement for direct-access storage has traditionally been satisfied by magnetic disk, with either fixed or moving heads. More recently, two solid-state direct-access technologies have appeared: charge-coupled devices (CCDs) and bubbles. Optical storage devices using lasers have been proposed, and some prototypes have been developed, but it does not appear likely that a viable optical-based product will be available in the near future.

Disks. The capacity of magnetic disks has increased rapidly because of increases in recording density. Storage capacity for a state-of-the-art moving-head disk, as shown in Figure 19-2, in-

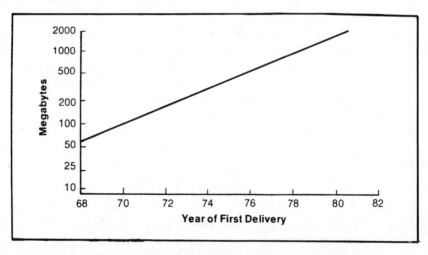

Figure 19-2. Increasing Capacity of Moving-Head Disks

creased from about 30 megabytes in 1965 to 600 megabytes in 1978. Recording density has increased from 300 bits/square centimeter (2,000 bits/square inch) in the early 1960s to the current million bits/square centimeter (6 million bits/square inch). Recording density is determined by the thickness of the oxide coating on the disk, the flying height of the head, and the gap in the head. These three dimensions must be roughly similar in size and are currently in the 0.6-micron (25-microinch) region. They will be reduced by new techniques to provide increased recording density. The magnetic coating on the disk will be upgraded to support the increased resolution, either by better control of granule characteristics and orientation or by the use of pure-metal-plated surfaces[1].

The technology for read/write heads continues to receive considerable attention, with particular emphasis on thin-film heads. Thin-film heads offer both lower cost and higher performance: lower cost because they are made by batch fabrication techniques, and higher performance because they offer more precise control over dimensionality.

The result of these advances is that the cost reduction per byte (by a factor of two every 30 months) will continue for at least several years. Disk capacity should double again to 700 megabytes and then reach more than one gigabyte by 1982, with a proportionate decrease in cost per on-line byte stored.

Sequential-Access Storage

Bubble and charge-coupled devices, both serial access at the chip level, have also increased rapidly in density. Bubble devices with 250K bits per chip have been announced, and there is strong evidence that a 1-megabit chip will be available soon. As bubble chips have gotten larger and cheaper per bit, however, they have gotten slower (current devices have a 7-millisecond access time). They probably will not be used as mass storage on large mainframes, but it is likely that they will be used on small systems. Recent improvements by Bell Labs avoid the coils required to obtain the rotating magnetic field that is needed to shift the bubbles along the latttice structure. This new development should improve the shift rate by a factor of five and provide an access time approaching that of CCDs.

Charge-coupled storage is now available in 65K chips, with 262K-bit chips likely soon. Access times for this technology are in the half-millisecond range. The 18- to 24-month lead of CCDs over RAMs may make the former attractive in high-speed swapping stores and as disk caches for large mainframes. The rapid advance of RAMs, however, makes this a close race.

USER INTERFACES

A user interface is the logical interface into a data base system. The following areas of research appear especially significant:

- Data models
- Data base access approaches
- Common data base architecture supporting multiple views of data, schema-to-schema translation, and schema, sub-schema, and storage schema separation

Data Models

Among the several dozen user interfaces proposed for data base systems, the two principal approaches are the relational data model and the network data model. The network model is more mature (it was developed around 1970). This model, as characterized by the CODASYL data base task group specification, provides relatively high performance but requires the user to specify storage structures, access paths, and data structures in considerable detail. In addition, the network approach is inflexible: access paths not predefined at data base load time cannot be used, limiting queries to those that can be satisfied by the predefined access paths. The storage structures, generally constructed of pointers to linked lists, tend to be quite complex.

In contrast, the relational approach generally spares the user the complexity of storage structures, data structures, and access paths. Access paths need not be predefined, although options may allow users to do so. Without predefined access paths, however, performance can suffer badly. The storage and data structures are very simple: they are treated as a series of one-level records. A more detailed description of this approach is provided by Astrahan et al[2].

Although the network model dominated data base technology for almost a decade, interest is now growing in the relational model, whose attractive features include a simple yet powerful interface and the ability to process *ad hoc* queries (i.e., those without predefined access paths). Although the relational approach may be less efficient, the declining cost of hardware, coupled with the rising cost of manpower and the very real value of fast response to *ad hoc* queries, makes relational data models increasingly attractive. In addition, associative storage devices described below offer the potential of greatly improving the efficiency and, therefore, the performance of relational systems.

Although the network and relational data models exist as

supported products, the network approach has a large existing user base and is gaining momentum. The network approach can be characterized as a host-language (usually COBOL) embedded network system; it supports indexed sequential, hashed, direct, and set-location access modes. For example, a record about a city could be accessed through the state in which it is located (via set), alphabetically (indexed sequential), or through the country in which it is located (via set). The advantage of the network approach is high performance because all the access paths can be defined and built, by using pointers, at data base creation time. The disadvantage of this approach is that it uses a relatively low-level language and involves the user in storage management and detailed record access. As mentioned previously, it is also limited to queries that can be satisfied by the predefined access paths.

On the other hand, the relational data model approach uses a high-level data retrieval and manipulation language that shields the user from data formats, access methods, and storage management. Access paths do not have to be predefined. A typical query might look something like:

list employees where department
= design and skill = engineer

Because physical access paths need not be predefined, relational data bases must be searched exhaustively to satisfy a query. Since this searching is very slow on conventional computers, users are often allowed to specify a prior access path to obtain acceptable performance.

A third model is the hierarchical approach, which is a subset of the network approach in that groups of records (structures) can be addressed by only one logical path.

Hierarchical Approach. In the hierarchical approach, records with some characteristic in common are grouped into sets. For example, a university curriculum data base might contain records of information on the courses given by a Department; these records might be grouped into sets by Department. The same data base might contain records of information on students; these might be grouped into sets by Adviser. The complete structure might be as shown in Figure 19-3. In this example, each Department record is the owner of a Teacher set and a Courses set. The Department set is, in turn, owned by the Curriculum record. If one wanted to access data about a given course (for example, Statistics) within a given department (for example, Mathematics), the set belonging to the Curriculum record would be searched until the Department record was found. The Course set belonging to the

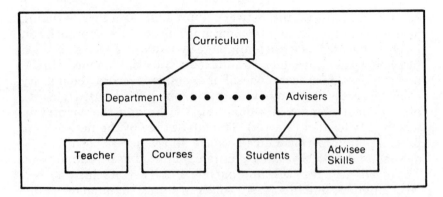

Figure 19-3. A Hierarchical Data Base

Department record would be searched until the Mathematics record was found. The set belonging to the Mathematics record would be searched until the Statistics record was found. The process of following logical paths from owner sets to member sets and to records within member sets is called *navigation*.

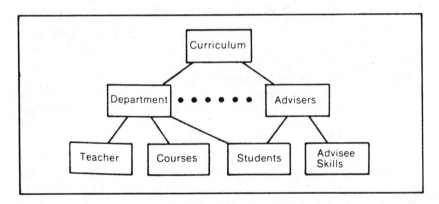

Figure 19-4. A Network Data Base

Network Approach. A network data base is a generalization of a hierarchical data base. A hierarchical data base is restricted to a single owner for each member set; a network data base, however, can have multiple owners for a member, as shown in Figure 19-4. In this structure, the Students set can be reached through either Department or Advisers.

Relational Approach. In a relational data base, the information is stored in the form of relations, with each entry in the rela-

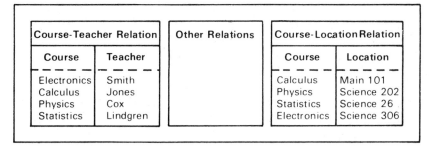

Figure 19-5. Organization of a Relational Data Base

tion called a *tuple*, or record. Our sample data base could include the relations shown in Figure 19-5. To find the name and location of the teacher of statistics, the course-teacher relation is searched to find the Statistics record from which the teacher name "Lindgren" is obtained. Then the course-location relation is searched to find the Statistics record from which the location "Science 26" is obtained. The answer from the data base then is "Lindgren, Science 26," obtained from the record value Statistics held in common.

Common Data Base Architecture

A movement toward unification and simplification of the various approaches to data base systems is now in progress. This is similar to the movement that has taken place in computer languages in the last few years. An example of work in this direction is the common data base architecture[3] that provides a unified basis for the various approaches to data base systems. In addition to providing a unified basis for understanding and description, the common data base architecture makes the following possible:

- A demonstration that the features in network and relational systems are equivalent to each other
- Translation of data definition and data manipulation statements from one data model to another
- Translation from one data model schema to another
- Superposition of the data description and data manipulation constructs from one data model onto the schema constructs of another
- Support of a single data structure in a system
- Translation of data manipulation commands in a heterogeneous distributed system

A common data base architecture shows the commonality that exists among different data models and at different levels within the same data model.

As an example of the functional equivalence among different data models, consider how interrecord relationships are handled in the network and relational data models. In the network model, interrecord relationships are explicitly defined by the declaration of set relations in the schema. The set relation logically chains together records having some common relationship; for example, all employees in a department could be logically associated by defining them as members of a set occurrence. In the relational model, interrecord relationships are defined implicitly by having the same value in a field. Each employee record, for example, could contain a department field, and all employees in the same department would have the same department number in that field.

Thus, the two models provide the same functional capability by different mechanisms. If we wished to translate from a network to a relational model, the linked-list pointer in the employee record would be changed to be a department field, and the values in the field would be copied from the owner of the set. If the relational model were translated to the network model, the department value would be inserted in the set-owner record, and the department field would be changed to be the linked-list pointer. On a higher level, the statement-type set in network models corresponds to common field names for records in a relational model.

More explicit examples of the correspondence between constructs in the network and relational data models are:

Network	Relational
Record Type	Table (relation)
Item	Column (component)
Record Occurrence	Row (tuple)
Unique Record Key	Candidate Key
Principal Key	Primary Key

It is noteworthy that pointers and common key values provide the same information and can be used interchangeably. If a relational model were built with pointers, the pointers would be used to associate records with a common field value and would, in fact, replace the field value, which would now appear only once, at the start of the set. (This capability is being provided on an optional basis in some experimental data base systems to improve performance.) Similarly, a network model could be implemented by using common field values rather than pointers and "copying" the field values into all members of the set. Thus, either storage structure (pointers or common field values) can support either data model (network or relational). Research is currently being done in both these areas.

Support of Multiple Views of Data. In the current implementation of data base systems on von Neumann computers, network data models are supported by pointers, and relational data models are supported by table searching. There appears to be little or no current research in designing architectures that are better at following pointers; however, there is considerable research in the area of faster searching of tables. This is described in more detail in the section dealing with trends in data base architecture.

Single Data Base Structure. Another result of the common data base architecture is that a single structure is used for data within a system, rather than separate file and data base systems. An example of this is the current use of files for such languages as COBOL. The common data base architecture shows that language "files" can be supported just as well by a data base. If the network data model is used as an example, the file declaration would generate the data base subschema, schema, and storage schema. The reads and writes would generate data manipulation commands that wuld be compiled by the data manipulation language compiler. The COBOL program would operate normally and would see no changes in the interface to the data. The data, however, could now be accessed for other purposes through the data base interface. Just as language files can be incorporated into a data base, any file system could be incorporated into a data base by the same general techniques.

A close connection exists between the common data base architecture and data base computer technology. In order to be economically viable, a data base computer must support several data models, including relational and network. The common data base architecture provides the underlying mechanism to accomplish this.

DISTRIBUTED DATA BASE SYSTEMS

It has been suggested that a distributed system is not very useful unless the data is distributed. In the past, systems have been implemented with centralized data bases even when other functions have been distributed. The few organizations that have implemented distributed data bases have developed their own systems, because the necessary software has not been available from manufacturers.

Objectives and Requirements

The objectives of distributing data over the nodes of a distributed computer system are generally the same as those of distributed systems as a whole. The following objectives, however, are especially relevant to the distribution of data bases:

- *Performance*—to obtain faster response to user queries
- *Lowered cost*—through reduced communications use
- *Shareability*—to permit data sharing among geographically separated nodes
- *Access transparency*—to provide uniform logical access to all locations
- *Reliability*—to ensure that the system will continue to function adequately despite the loss of one or more nodes
- *Tunability*—to permit data to be distributed to, and stored at, the location of heaviest use
- *Expandability*—to accommodate increases in data base size, either on existing nodes or by adding new nodes

Several of these objectives—notably performance, reliability, tunability, and expandability—can be obtained through redundancy. Redundancy, however, also introduces the problem of integrity, as we shall see later.

These objectives represent possible user benefits that can be obtained in largest measure through the use of distributed data base systems. Other objectives, which are met by most centralized systems, also must be met by distributed systems; they amount to requirements for any integrated system:

- *Recovery*—The system must be able to recover automatically following an error, a lost message, or a solid failure.
- *Security*—Users must be able to specify access privileges to secure data that the system administrator can enforce.
- *Reorganization*—It must be possible to reorganize the data to improve efficiency, either locally or globally.
- *Efficiency*—The system must use resources efficiently by selecting appropriate algorithms to allow maximum concurrency and a low transaction-rejection rate.
- *Coherence*—The system must maintain consistent multiple copies of data without causing unacceptable updating delays.
- *Deadlocks*—Deadlocks must not prevent the completion of transactions.
- *Fairness*—All locations must have equal priority.

Although these requirements are not listed in priority order, recovery is probably the most important. It is the basic design constraint on present centralized data management systems and will be even more important in distributed systems. The other requirements are also important, and an acceptable protocol must be able to handle all of them. These requirements are clearly made more difficult and complex by the distribution of data. Techniques to meet them in a distributed environment are described below.

Centralized vs. Distributed Data Base Systems

As shown in Figure 19-6, a traditional centralized data base system—which may be considered to include file systems as a special

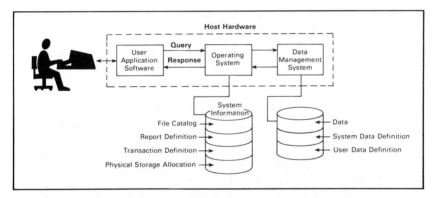

Figure 19-6. Traditional Centralized Data Base System Organization

case in which the data definition and access methods are contained implicitly in the user application programs—consists of:

- Application software
- An operating system
- Data
- Physical storage allocation
- Data management software
- Data definition (system)
- Data definition (user)

The user and his or her application program interface to the data management system through the operating system software, which controls all mass storage. If we follow the CODASYL specification terminology, the data is initially loaded into the data base according to the specification in the data definition language, which also produces the system copy of the data definition, or schema. The user may also define the format of that data in the subschema. The data is manipulated according to the procedures in the data manipulation language, whose statements, in the case of the CODASYL specification, are embedded in a general-purpose procedural language such as COBOL. The data is stored according to the physical storage allocation determined by the operating system.

In a distributed data base system, these data-related components are placed at the nodes of the system. The question of how to distribute the application software, the data, the data management software, and the data definition immediately arises. Conceivably, each of these could be centralized, or distributed in a number of ways, yielding a very large number of possible combinations. When data is stored at more than one node, software capabilities for data definition and management must be available for the accessing and processing of the data. When the user request and data exist at different nodes, data management functions must also be distributed.

Network Data Directory. The integration of data base system technology and a network environment leads to new problems and the need for new functions. One very important need is for a networkwide definition, or directory, of the location and characteristics of all data in the system, including the method of partitioning or replication. Currently, when the system receives a user request to access data, it must first determine the data location. If the data is not local, the originating node must determine the proper node and communicate with it. If the nodes are not compatible, translation functions must be provided to achieve this compatibility, possibly including request translation, data reformatting, or both.

A distributed data system (see Figure 19-7) contains the same functional components as a centralized data system but with additional components: the communications port, the network data directory, and the network data management system. The physical location of the node and the necessary routing information are contained in the communications port, which plays precisely the same role in both distributed and centralized systems. The network data directory must contain the logical information that relates the various units of data to the node(s) on which it resides. The network data management system must manage all aspects of the geographic distribution of data. These management tasks include:

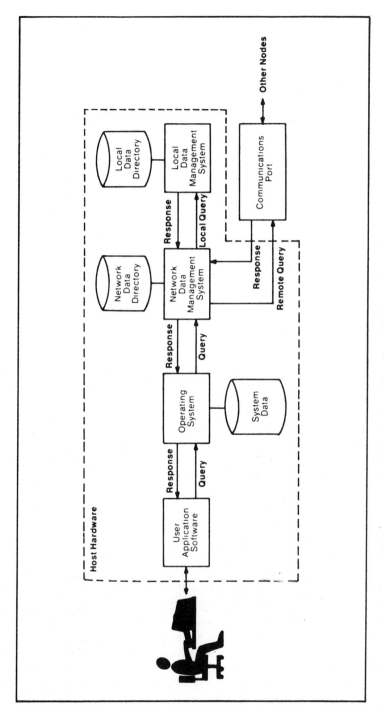

Figure 19-7. A Node Within a Distributed Data Base System

329

- Intercepting the query to determine whether it is to local data
- Accessing the network data directory and routing the request to the appropriate node, if the data is nonlocal
- Coordinating all processing and responses, if multiple nodes are involved
- Interfacing with the user, local and remote data management systems, and system directories
- Providing command or data translation in heterogeneous distributed systems

System Structures for Distributed Data. As mentioned previously, a centralized data base system can have a network, a hierarchical, or a relational data structure. These can be considered design extremes: a continuous spectrum of variations exists between these "pure" approaches. In a distributed data base system the same structural alternatives are available, although the data is placed at the various nodes within the system. It is important to understand that the data structure has no relation to the communications structure. The data structure could be a network (for example, a ring), while the communications structure could be hierarchical; a hierarchical communications structure could support three different data bases—one network, one hierarchical, and one relational.

Other terminology has been used to describe these same basic structures. The horizontal data distribution function[4] is the same as a network, because all nodes are at the same functional level. The vertical data structure is the same as a hierarchy.

Data Distribution Alternatives

There are two basic ways in which to distribute data within a system structure: partitioning and replication.

Partitioned Data. When a body of data is *partitioned*, it is divided into disjoint sets, with one set assigned to each node. Only one copy of each record or data item exists, and it is assigned to some node as its home location at any instant of time. The objective is usually to assign a record to the node that accesses it most frequently, to minimize response time and communications. In general, however, not all accesses at a node can be satisfied by data at that node, so the system data directory must be used to transfer the access to the proper location. Accesses that cannot be handled locally are called *exceptions* or *misses*—terms borrowed from cache terminology that are entirely appropriate in this context. There is a strong analogy between cache storage hierarchies and partitioned data base systems. If the application characteristics are such that the data can be partitioned to make all accesses local (i.e., no misses), this represents an extreme case of partitioning, and the data is said to be *segmented* into completely disjoint sets.

Replicated Data. When data is replicated, two or more copies of the same data exist in the system; as an extreme, every node could have its own copy of some data. Replicating data can provide substantial improvements in performance, cost, tunability, and reliability. These benefits, however, come at the cost of greatly complicated updating to maintain consistency in the copies. The topic of updating replicated data has received considerable attention in the research community because of the benefits of replication; it is treated in more detail below. Performance is a critical issue in the use of replicated data because several of the algorithms used to maintain data consistency require extensive communication among nodes to avoid long delays in update.

Achieving optimum performance in a distributed data base system is a complex issue; performance depends on miss rates, update frequency, number of nodes, amount of data, and communications speed and cost. Some guidelines are summarized in Table 19-1 on page 332.

The most appropriate method of distributing small amounts of data, when real-time update frequency is low, is simply to replicate them because the additional storage cost is low. When the (infrequent) updates occur, they are sent to all locations holding a copy, using a synchronization algorithm. This approach is especially attractive when updates are batched and high performance and reliability are important.

If the amount of data is small and the update frequency is high, replication becomes very unattractive because of the heavy communications burden. If the miss (nonlocal access) rate is low for a partitioned approach (the miss rate applies only to partitioned data since replicated data always has a zero miss rate), the best approach is to partition; even though the update rate is high, most updates are to the local partition. In addition, since only one copy exists, updates to remote partitions require much less overhead and communication than updates to remote replicated data. If both the miss rate and update frequency are high, the best approach is to centralize, regardless of the amount of data.

Table 19-1.   Recommended Data Distribution Methods

Amount of Data	Real-Time Update Frequency	Miss Rate	Recommended Approach
Small	Low	Low	Replicate
Small	Low	High	Replicate
Small	High	Low	Partition
Small	High	High	Centralize
Large	Low	Low	Partition
Large	Low	High	Partition
Large	High	Low	Partition
Large	High	High	Centralize

(The definition of high and low miss rates must be made in the context of the communications cost and delay involved. Generally, a miss rate above 30 percent or a real-time update rate above 10 percent is considerable.) If the amount of data is large, the best approach is to partition unless, again, both a high miss rate and update frequency mandate centralization.

Partitioning and replication represent "pure" or extreme approaches. In practice, a user wants a mixture of the approaches, sometimes for the same data. For example, a data base might be replicated in its entirety at two nodes and partitioned over all other nodes for purposes of tunability. In other situations, a data base might be mostly partitioned, with specific portions replicated at selected nodes for performance and reliability. The design must be based on patterns of use or mass-storage capability at a specific node (some nodes may not have mass storage). Thus, there may be more than one way to reconstruct a complete and nonredundant copy of the logical data from the stored physical data. A collection of physical data that forms a complete, non-redundant copy of the logical data is called a *materialization*.

A complicating factor in partitioning data is the requirement to change the home location of a data element because of changing patterns of access. In principle, this can be done either manually by the data base administrator, or automatically by the system, on the basis of instrumentation data. The method used depends on the dynamics of the application—and the courage of the implementers.

In all situations, users must be shielded from the physical distribution and redundancy of the data; they must be able to interact with the distributed system as easily as with a conventional centralized one. Providing a logically centralized interface to users of distributed systems has been addressed in a number of operating systems now in use or under development (e.g., the National Software Works,[5] the National Bureau of Standards Network Access Machine,[6] and the ARPANET RSEXEC project[7,8]. These projects have a common objective of providing users with a geographically distributed computing network resource that is consistent, logically centralized, and easy to use, in which access is independent of location, although not always independent of system.

Directories. Just as data can be distributed throughout a system, the system data directory necessary for locating it can also be distributed. Just as data can be partitioned, replicated, or made redundant in some combination of these, so can the directory. How the directory is distributed depends on the same considerations governing data distribution. There is no reason to assume, however, that the application characteristics of the directory in a given system will be similar to those of the data it keeps track of. The data might have a high update frequency, while the directory has a low update frequency. In another system, the opposite might be true—as, for example, in a system with partitioned data and dynamic (and frequent) data relocation based on use. With two "pure" methods of data distribution (partitioned and replicated) and three "pure" methods of directory distribution (partitioned, replicated, and centralized) six "pure" combinations exist. Ideally a general-purpose distributed system would support all six "pure" combinations and variations of them, with the final selection made at system generation time.

The directory itself can be treated as ordinary data, with one crucial difference: the location information for the directory must be known to the system nodes *a priori*. This can be accomplished by storing copies of the directory at every node since they are almost never moved.

Treating the directory as ordinary data has another advantage: such normal system functions as storage management, recovery, security and update synchronization automatically become available for the directories.

Update Synchronization of Multiple Data Copies. Because of the advantages of replicated or redundant partitioned data base systems, considerable effort is being made to solve the very difficult problem of update synchronization to maintain data base integrity.

Many applications can function adequately with batch updates. A number of potential problems, however, exist in real-time updates of data with multiple copies. Each node becomes aware of updates originating elsewhere only after some unknown and unpredictable delay. If not controlled, this delay can destroy the internal consistency (integrity) of the data. For example, if multiple copies of an airline reservation data base exist, terminals attached to two different nodes could each sell the last seat on flight XYZ, then reject the update coming from the other location as causing an oversold condition.

In centralized or nonredundant data base systems, mechanisms such as locks can be set to ensure the serialization of updates[9,10]. Serialization of updates ensures consistency of the data. To maintain consistency of data where multiple copies exist, it is necessary to serialize the updates and to apply the serialized updates to all copies in the same order.

Consistency. Two levels of consistency can be defined for multiple copies of data. *Strong consistency* is defined as having all copies of the data updated at the same time. Strong consistency is very desirable since all copies of the data have the same update status at any time: however, processing the update for all copies always entails a considerable delay in response time. *Weak consistency* is defined as having the various copies of the data converge to the same update status over time, although at any instant of time some copies may lag in the number of updates processed. In general, weak consistency will reduce delays and allow more efficient use of resources, but some copies of data will be more up-to-date than others.

We can further define *coherence* as a measure of the differences among multiple copies of data at any instant. We define the *promptness* of a system as the average time delay in completing updates. (Note that formal definitions for the metrics of coherence and promptness have been formulated[11].) A distributed data base system is said to be *convergent* if, when update activity ceases, the coherence approaches unity over time.

A distributed data base system cannot have high coherence and low promptness at the same time; this is a fundamental trade-off that must be made. (This seems to be the information analog of the Heisenberg Principle of Uncertainty in physics, which states that the position and velocity of an object cannot be known simultaneously with arbitrarily high precision.) Some applications require only weak consistency, while others require strong consistency; both types may exist in the same system and possibly require access to the same data, leading to some interesting system design problems.

A number of algorithms have been proposed for controlling concurrent updates to maintain consistency under a condition of weak consistency[11]. In the simplest of these, all update requests are sent from their node of origin to a master node, where they are serialized and given sequence numbers. The updates are then sent to all centers and implemented in sequence number order[12,13]. Other update control techniques are based on a time stamp applied at the node of origin. The time stamps can be made unique at the global level if any single node can create, at most, one update per change of the clock and if the node number is added to the time stamp. These unique time stamps can be used to serialize the order of updates. One way to do this is based on a "majority consensus" value[14]. Each update is voted on for acceptance by all nodes based on updates each node has processed earlier. Updates approved by a majority of nodes are accepted in the order of their time stamps. This approach is immune to failures in communications links or nodes.

Another approach using time stamps classifies updates according to the variables they modify[15]. A specified node is given the responsibility for sequencing updates containing variables of a given class. Potential interference between updates of different classes is resolved by a "conflict graph" created by pre-analysis of the system. This approach quickly identifies situations in which no control is required and reserves careful coordination for updates that could potentially impair integrity.

All these methods and others now under study preserve data integrity. For a given application, there are other important considerations, including:

- Minimizing delay
- Avoiding preferential treatment of nodes
- Minimizing the need to back out updates
- Minimizing communications cost

Each update algorithm must be evaluated in terms of the application of interest to optimize these considerations (appropriately weighted for the application in question).

Deadlock. The same kinds of deadlock problems that arise in centralized multiprogramming systems can also arise in distributed systems. The general methods of solution remain the same on a logical level, but are complicated on a physical basis because of the distribution of physical and data resources. In any approach to deadlock resolution, three basic techniques can be used (whether the system is centralized or distributed):

- Prevention
- Avoidance
- Detection and resolution

Prevention. In prevention, all resources required by a transaction must be requested at the beginning of the transaction. This is very difficult, because the resource requirements are often data-dependent and not known at that time. Acquiring all possible resources at the beginning would be very inefficient, keeping resources idle and decreasing system concurrency.

Avoidance. Deadlock avoidance requires some advance knowledge of the resource use of transactions in order to determine, at each point in time, whether the sequences of actions of incomplete transactions are sufficiently valid that the transactions can run to completion. This approach, like that of prevention, is very unattractive in distributed systems because the advance information necessary to avoid deadlocks is either not available or is distributed so widely that retrieving it causes considerable overhead and delay.

Detection and Resolution. Deadlocks can be detected by searching for cycles in a state graph of resource use; deadlocks have been reduced using this method in practice in centralized systems. In a distributed data system, it is generally not efficient to maintain global state graphs for the whole system, as is done for centralized systems. Two methods not requiring global state graphs have been developed for detecting and resolving deadlocks in distributed data base systems: one is hierarchical, the other, distributed. Either one can detect all deadlocks.

Performance. Unless careful attention is paid to the functions requested and the algorithms used, performance can be a problem in distributed systems. An example of this is a query that requires cross-referencing of data at several nodes—for example, a join. Such a task can incur significant delay because of the need to bring together at one node all the data required for cross-referencing.

One approach to implementing this type of operation is to decompose the query into a sequence of local queries involving only local data, with internode data transfers between local queries[16]. The algorithm consists of a series of steps, each of which is either a data move or local processing of data that has been moved to a single site. An important assumption of this method is that communications cost will dominate processing complex queries in a distributed environment; therefore, at each step, the optimization procedure first attempts to minimize communications cost and then local processing cost. This usually results in doing as much local processing as possible to minimize the amount of data communicated among nodes.

Recovery in Partitioned and Replicated Distributed Data Base Systems. In centralized data base systems, recovery from a system malfunction is accomplished by using a combination of Before and After looks put on an audit trail and checkpoint dumps to establish periodic consistent snapshots of the data. Recovery in a centralized system can be complex and may require manual intervention. Recovery in a distributed system can be much more complex but can also be far more effective if redundant data is used.

Partitioned Systems. In a partitioned data base system with no redundancy, the recovery problem for node failures is logically identical to that in a centralized system, with similar recovery techniques. The only difference is that not all requests are local; however, this is a physical, not logical, difference. Audit trails and checkpoint dumps continue to be used. When a failure occurs, all transactions are suspended while the system tries to recover, using the Before and After looks. Failing this, the audit trail is backed up to the last checkpoint dump. The dump is copied into the data base and processed forward, using the audit trail, to the point of suspended operation. At that point, transactions are again accepted. If fast recovery is important, it may be prudent to maintain an up-to-date duplicate copy of the data; this can speed recovery of mass storage failures (but not processor failures).

In communications failures in partitioned data base systems, the originating nodes fail to get message acknowledgements. The burden of recovery falls on the originating nodes, and access transactions must be queued up until communication is restored.

Replicated Systems. In replicated data base systems, the situation is quite different. If a communications link or a node fails, the rest of the system can continue normal operation; only the transactions originating at the failed node or link are stopped. When the node or link becomes operational again, two options are available. If the outage was short, the most efficient recovery procedure is to obtain the lost updates from the audit trail of another node. If the outage was long, the best approach is to acquire the entire data base from a nearby node, along with a time stamp or ticket number for the last update. This would become, in effect, a very recent checkpoint dump and could be processed forward with the audit trail to the present time.

There would seem to be no need for nodes to take checkpoint dumps in a replicated data base system, since copies at other nodes could serve that purpose. An exception would be if the data base were very large compared to the available communications bandwidth, leading to long transmission times. Each node would require an audit trail, as in nonredundant data base systems.

Lelann[17] describes several protocols for accomplishing recovery in redundant data base systems.

DATA BASE PROCESSOR ARCHITECTURE

Shortly after the invention of the stored-program electronic digital computer in 1946, storage and retrieval of nonnumeric information became an important application. With only a few exceptions, early file access systems (starting in the middle 1950s) and data base systems (starting in the late 1960s) were mapped onto conventional von Neumann computers. Although the desirable way to access nonnumeric data is by value, the von Neumann architecture precludes this. Therefore, a number of artificial methods are used to convert a value into an address. These artificial methods include sequential, indexed, hashed, and set access methods. These access methods have successfully met industry needs until the present time. There has, however, been constant research into file and data base systems in the areas of improved functional ability, performance, and availability.

There was at least one early exception to the use of von Neumann architecture to retrieve nonnumeric data: the UNIVAC File Computer. This system, first delivered in 1954, allowed the addressing of data in mass storage by value, rather than by address. This was done by storing the value of the desired key in a search register, and comparing this value sequentially to values on a drum. With this capability, records of up to 120 characters could be stored anywhere on the drum and retrieved by value; no access method was needed. The importance of this capability is only now being rediscovered.

The 25-year quest for improved functional ability has led to data base systems as we know them today—initially using network structures, and now showing a growing interest in relational structures. The performance requirement was met by brute-force improvements in hardware speed. The one element that did not change was the architecture.

Associative Storage

Accessing data on the basis of value rather than position is fundamental to the concept of a data base computer. Devices that can do this have been called *associative stores, content-addressable memories,* or *search memories.* The term *associative store* has been applied to two quite different kinds of storage units, with a rather unfortunate confusion of terminology. The first storage units with this capability performed a parallel search in a solid-state storage unit of a few thousand bytes in a time on the order of microseconds. The term used here for this technology is *parallel associative storage;* it is typified today by Staran[18]. The only other application of parallel associative storage devices today appears to be the cache, where the term *content-addressable memory* is often used. The association here is within sets of segments of storage, with each set typically having on the order of 1,000 elements.

The second kind of associative store uses a serial storage unit, which can be a disk, bubble, or charge-coupled device. This storage unit is searched serially to find data meeting the search criteria. The term used in this portfolio for this technology is *serial associative storage.* Typically, it can search megabytes in tens of milliseconds. While the parallel associative store is limited to equality searches, sequential storage can use greater-than, less-than, and arithmetic and logical expressions involving operands. One of the earliest sequential associative storage devices was used on the CASSM project.

Data Base Computer Architecture Alternatives

From the early 1970s on, new architectures were proposed to improve the effectiveness of data base systems. These can be classified as:

- Backend systems (using conventional minicomputers)
- Storage hierarchies (self-managed)
- Intelligent controllers
- Data base computers

Backend Processors. Perhaps the earliest new architecture was the backend processor implemented on a conventional minicomputer[6]. The objective was to improve performance and provide a shared data base to several incompatible systems. A number of backend processors implemented on conventional minicomputers have been developed as commercial products.

Storage Hierarchies. The storage hierarchy described by Welch[20] is as old as computers, but the self-managed mass-storage hierarchy first implemented in the mid-1970s was a specific attempt to solve file and data base problems. The first implementation was as virtual disk, where a pool of disks acted as a cache buffer for a tape-cartridge device. A more recent application is the cache disk, where a charge-coupled storage unit acts as a cache buffer for disk (and possibly cartridge) storage. The storage-hierarchy approach depends on substantial locality of reference for data; that is, once a data item is referenced, it or a near neighbor is more likely to be referenced again in the near future. Several experiments performed on a cache disk simulator for a variety of customer files have shown an average hit rate of 75 percent for a 4-megabyte cache buffer. This hit rate is sufficient to cut average access time in half.

Intelligent Controllers. Beginning in the mid-1970s, new architectures were considered that were designed to improve efficiency substantially in accessing a file or data base system through content addressing—that is, addressing by key value rather than location. The approaches were all in the form of back-end attachments to a conventional host over I/O channels or communications lines, and all are considered intelligent-control-unit approaches. These architectures are, at least implicitly, relational in nature because they use flat file storage structures and address information by content. An early example of this kind of architecture is the Content Addressed File System (CAFS). CAFS, an extension of RARES, is based on fixed-head-disk storage, with on-the-fly processing between read and write heads. A single pipeline instruction stream is used. The CAFS work was among the earliest in content addressing; CAFS can be considered the baseline system. It had no significant amount of buffering and no parallel processing.

The Relational Associative Processor (RAP)[21] uses an array of solid-state processing elements, each working on a partition of the entire data base. In RAP, parallel processing was introduced and, with it, the partitioning of the data base into local storage units.

A rather different approach to a data base processor uses a Staran computer[18]. Here, data in a conventional storage unit is sent to an associative register array to be searched for specific key values. The Staran approach is conceptually similar to CAFS, with the fixed-head disk replaced by a random-access main store and the simple comparison logic replaced by a large parallel associative store array. An important difference is that Staran can perform multiple-thread searches against a simple file in one pass.

These three approaches, and several similar ones, greatly improve data base performance, but they suffer from the following drawbacks:

- Mass storage is expensive and, therefore, limited in size
- The entire data base must be resident in the mass store
- The full relational join cannot be performed
- Sorting cannot be performed

Data Base Computers. The next step in the evolution of data base architecture was to move from a data base processor to a data base computer.[22] The mass-storage medium is moving-head disk, which is an order of magnitude lower in cost per stored bit than fixed-head disk. The concept of partitioning the data base into cylinders is introduced, and hashing of the (possibly several) access fields is used to select the cylinders to be searched. The information from a disk track is fully buffered rather than being processed on-the-fly. Parallel processing, in a manner similar to RAP, is used to process data from several tracks at once.

The data-base-computer concept of Hsiao[22] has recently been further extended. The objective remains the same: to support network, relational, or hierarchical data bases on the order of 100 megabytes to 100 gigabytes. The design approach also remains the same, using a backend computer with a general-purpose processor controlling an array of processing elements, an intelligent parallel-transfer disk controller, and a parallel-transfer disk. A limited amount of interprocessor communication, added to permit the join operation and sorting, requires that adjacent processors be able to access the same buffer storage module. A low-cost solid-state serial associative store has been added to identify unique key or sort field values. The resulting data-base-computer architecture (see Figure 19-8) is characterized by six major components:

- A data base processor controller
- Processor elements
- Track buffers
- A content-addressable memory
- A parallel-transfer disk
- A parallel-transfer disk controller

The host interfaces to the data base computer by using high-

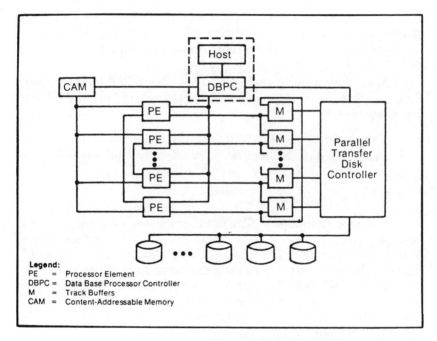

Figure 19-8. Data Base Computer Organization

level commands of, for example, a network or relational nature. These commands are sent to the data base processor controller for analysis. An appropriate set of parameters is then generated and down-loaded to the processing elements. The data base processor controller also generates the necessary I/O commands for the parallel-transfer disk.

The parallel-transfer disk allows the simultaneous reading of all tracks in a cylinder; each track of information is transferred to the associated track buffer, which serves two adjacent processors and holds four tracks of information. When the track buffers are loaded, the processing elements begin operating on the data asynchronously, performing selection, projection, joins, or sorts. Data meeting the criteria is passed back to the data base processor controller and then to the host. Relational and network data base systems can be supported.

These units operate synergistically. The search parameters, for example, are loaded into the processing elements so that all tracks in a cylinder can be searched in parallel. The size of the track buffers is adequate to provide for double buffering. The processing elements control the operation of their track buffers. They are sufficiently powerful to provide equality matches against parameters in the query and to perform the functions: $>$, $<$, $\neq$,

AND, OR, and NOT. Some or all operands can be taken from the record itself ("list all employees where job-title = salesman and bonus $>$ salary").

Somewhat surprisingly, the solid-state technologies of bubbles and charge-coupled storage do not meet the needs of the track buffer because they are too slow by one or two orders of magnitude. A recent survey has shown that a typical record size is about 200 bytes in length. The most common search operation is to look at the first few bytes of the key field to see whether a record is of interest. If it is not, the next operation is to skip 200 bytes to the next record. RAM can do this in about one microsecond, but a charge-coupled store requires 40 microseconds, even at a 5-megacycle shift rate. Bubbles, which are 10 times slower than charge-coupled devices, are even less competitive.

Applications of Data Base Computers. Although data base computers substantially improve the efficiency of accessing and processing data base information, it is important to realize that they are not universally better than present techniques. Two conditions are necessary to make data base computers more effective than present architectures:

- The data base application must be a sizable fraction of the total system load.
- The data access must involve use of several mass-storage accesses with conventional techniques.

If the data base load on the system is only 10 percent of the total load, there is very little point in off-loading it to a data base computer. It is only when the load is appreciable—at least 50 percent and preferably 75 percent—that off-loading becomes attractive. Similarly, if the query can be satisfied by a single mass-storage access, a data base computer cannot improve efficiency as it does in multi-access situations.

A number of experiments and performance estimates have shown that a data base computer can provide performance improvements on the order of 5 to 50 times where the above criteria are met; in areas not meeting these criteria, it simply gets in the way and hurts efficiency.

SUMMARY

Significant progress in data base technology continues to be made at the logical, physical, and architectural levels, spurred by the combination of user needs and advancing technology. The cost/performance ratio of physical devices is improving steadily.

Significant progress is also being made at the logical level, with the development of a common data model that provides for the translation of schemas between network and relational systems. The common data model also demonstrates that either a pointer-based or a value-based storage structure can be used to support either a network or a relational user interface, thus enabling the support of multiple views of a single data base storage structure.

Building on the advances at the logical and physical levels, the architectural improvements embodied in data base computer design promise significant increases in performance at relatively modest cost. Because of the significant improvements in cost, performance, and user interfaces, the future for generalized data base systems looks bright indeed, and we should finally see the end of the need for each user to build his or her own.

Notes

---

1   A. S. Hoagland, "Storage Technology: Capabilities and Limitations." *Computer*, Vol. 12, No. 5 (May 1979), pp. 12-18.

2   M. M. Astrahan, et al, "An Overview of a Relational Implementation: System R," *Data Base Management* (Pennsauken, NJ: AUERBACH Publishers Inc, May 1980).

3   H. R. Johnson and J. A. Larson, "A Common Data Base Architecture." (Internal memo, Sperry Univac Corporation, August 1978).

4   G. M. Booth, "Distributed Information Systems." *AFIPS Conference Proceedings, 1976 NCC*, Vol. 45, pp. 789-795.

5   R. E. Schantz and R. E. Millstein, *The FOREMAN: Providing the Program Execution Environment for the National Software Works*, Report No. 3266. Bolt Beranek & Newman Inc, March 1976.

6   R. Rosenthal, *A Review of Network Access Techniques with a Case Study: The Networks Access Machine*. NBS Technical Note 917 (Washington, DC: National Bureau of Standards, 1976).

7   R. H. Thomas, "A Resource Sharing Executive for the Arpanet." *AFIPS Conference Proceedings, 1973 NCC*, Vol. 42, pp. 155-163.

8   R. H. Thomas, *A Solution to the Update Problem for Multiple Copy Data Bases Which Use Distributed Control*. Report No. 3340. Bolt Beranek & Newman Inc, July 1975.

9   K. P. Eswaran, J. M. Gray, R. A. Lorie and I. L. Traiger, "The Notions of Consistency and Predicate Locks in a Database System."

CACM, Vol. 19, No. 11 (November 1976), pp. 624-633.

10   J. N. Gray, R. A. Lorie, G. R. Putzolu and I. L. Traiger, *Granularity of Locks and Degrees of Consistency in a Shared Database.* IBM San Jose Laboratory Report, 1975.

11   E. Gelenbe and J. Sevcik, "Analysis of Update Synchronization for Multiple Copy Data Bases." *Proceedings Third Berkeley Workshop on Distributed Data Management and Computer Networks,* August 1978, pp. 69-90.

12   P. A. Alsberg and J. D. Day, "A Principle for Resilient Sharing of Distributed Resources." *Proceedings Second International Conference on Software Engineering.* San Francisco, October 1976, pp. 562-570.

13   E. Grapa and G. G. Belford, *Techniques for Update Synchronization in Distributed Data Bases.* Center for Advanced Computation Report, University of Illinois, 1977.

14   R. H. Thomas, *A Majority Consensus Approach to Concurrency Control for Multiple Data Bases.* Report No. 3733. Bolt Beranek & Newman Inc, December 1977.

15   J. B. Rothnie, N. Goodman, P. A. Bernstein and C. A. Papadimitriou, *The Redundant Update Methodology of SSD-1: A System for Distributed Databases.* Technical Report No. CCA-77-02. Computer Corporation of America, February 1977.

16   J. B. Rothnie and N. Goodman, *A Study of Updating in a Redundant Distributed Database Environment.* Technical Report No. CCA-77-01. Computer Corporation of America, February 1977.

17   G. Lelann, "Algorithms for Distributed Data Sharing Systems Which Use Tickets." *Proceedings Third Berkeley Workshop on Distributed Data Management and Computer Networks.* August 1978, pp. 259-272.

18   P. B. Berra and A. K. Singhania, "A Multiple Associative Memory Organization for Pipelining a Directory to a Very Large Data Base." *Digest of Papers, COMPCON 76 Spring.* San Francisco, February 1976, pp. 109-112.

19   G. P. Copeland, G. J. Lipovski and S. Y. W. Su, "The Architecture of CASSM: A Cellular System for Nonnumeric Processing." *Proceedings First International Symposium on Computer Architecture,* December 1973, pp. 121-128.

20   T. Welch, "Memory Hierarchy Configuration Analysis," *Computer,* Vol. 12, No. 5 (May 1979), pp. 19-26.

21   E. A. Ozkarahan, S. A. Schuster and K. C. Smith, "RAP—An Associative Processor for Data Base Management." *AFIPS Conference Proceedings, 1975 NCC,* Vol. 44, pp. 379-387.

22   D. K. Hsaio and S. E. Madnick, "Database Machine Architecture in the Context of Information Technology Evolution." *Proceedings Third International Conference on Very Large Data Bases.* Tokyo, October 1977, pp. 63-84.

chapter 20

The Backend (Data Base) Computer—Part I

INTRODUCTION

A *backend*, described in the most simple terms, is a computer that is electronically attached to another computer called a *host* and that performs data base management services for the host. From another point of view, the backend can be thought of as the product of offloading some portion of a data base management system from the host to an "outboard" computer that is the backend. The term *backend* is chosen because of the obvious analogy to the front end. The latter manages the network or terminals on behalf of the host while the former manages the data base resources including disks, tapes, and possibly other forms of storage. The host is most often thought of as a large, general-purpose computer with user-oriented facilities appropriate for the development, submission, and execution of application programs. In contrast, the backend is typically pictured as a special-purpose mini-computer that is not user programmable—perhaps a glorified controller. The backend is visualized as being in the immediate vicinity of the host and connected to it by a cable. However, these characteristics are not intrinsic to the backend concept. It is the functional relationship between the two computers that establishes their respective roles as host and backend. Furthermore, there is nothing in the definition of the backend that stipulates a particular kind of DBMS. The backend notion is architectural in nature in that it conditions the division of labor between two elements in the computing system, but it does not require specific external features of the DBMS implemented in such an environment. In theory, any of the existing DBMS packages could be offloaded to a backend, and there appears to be little doubt that several systems will eventually be repackaged in this manner with varying degrees of success. Therefore (in theory) the user should be able to evaluate alternative DBMSs using the same criteria he or she now employs and ponder the backend option as a separate issue. In practice, however, the characteristics of the DBMS and its various user languages have a significant influence on the viability and applicability of the backend in which the system resides. This chapter is devoted to establishing terminology; describing the backend; defining the backend's relationship to the computing environment; and identifying important optional implementation characteristics.

OFFLOADING THE DBMS

Communication Between the End User and the Data Base

An *end user* is a person employed by an organization who requires access to stored data and must use this data in order to fulfill his organizational responsibilities. It is assumed here that the data bases are mechanized so that computers are used to access and possibly manipulate needed data. Ignoring any intellectual processes that may be at work, let us start from the point at which the end user interacts directly with the computer, whether this be through a terminal or card reader/line printer. The end user states his requirements through one or more languages, such as job control directives, transaction parameters, and inquiry statements. In return, he may receive output constituting the results of a query or verifying the success of an update. Between these two points, he has caused the computer to invoke a hierarchy of processes that ultimately culminates in a series of read and write operations on data base storage devices. This hierarchy will be called an *information system* for purposes of this discussion. It is useful to think of an information system as a continuum linking the user to a data base, as exemplified in Figure 20-1. Within this continuum, user input is accepted, syntactically dissected, validated,

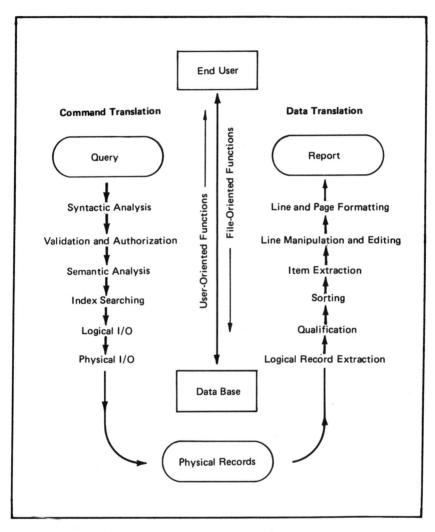

Figure 20-1. Query Processing in a Typical Information System

and interpreted as high-level data base operations. Logical records are derived from physical records, tested, and possibly sorted. Item values are extracted, combined arithmetically, summarized, edited, and finally written in the form of a report.

In a conventional setting, an information system includes a DBMS, as shown in Figure 20-2. It also includes the lower-level system components invoked by the DBMS to access physical storage. Finally, the information system may include software at a higher level than the DBMS itself, although in many cases the DBMSs query language is a sufficient end-user interface. ("Query language" refers here to any self-contained language of the DBMS, and might include updating as well as inquiry facilities.) Figure 20-2 illustrates a typical, traditional information system for which all but the lowest layers are implemented as software in a single computer. Major modules are shown with lines separating them. The solid lines represent the interfaces between these modules or layers, and their labels indicate the "language" or protocol used to effect the interface. The dotted lines suggest that the main modules may in fact consist of smaller ones with their own corresponding standard interfaces.

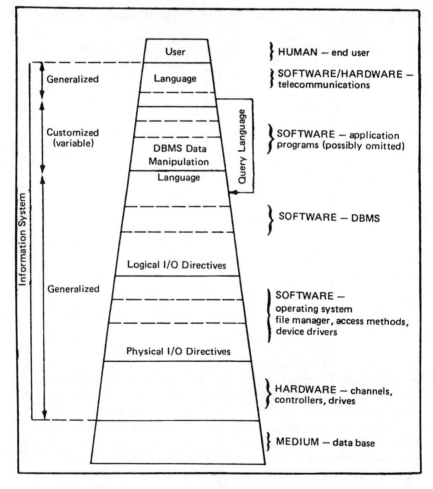

Figure 20-2. Information System: Conventional Architecture

Data Reduction

The information system is depicted as a pyramid to emphasize a fundamental property of such systems known as *data reduction*. In the typical case, the following behavior is observed when a user submits a query to an information system.

- The query is translated to several DBMS calls, which are translated to an even greater number of fetches from data base storage.
- Although many records are read by the DBMS, considerably less data are passed on to the application program. Data reduction at the DBMS level may occur for a number of reasons depending on the particular query and, of course, on the features of the DBMS itself. For instance, the DBMS may extract and pass back only specifically requested items rather than an entire record. The DBMS may perform index manipulation so that only qualified data are returned to the caller.
- Further data reduction may be performed at the application program level. For instance, the program might summarize items obtained from multiple data base records and return only a grand total to the user.

Thus, the various components of the information system contribute to the task of refining a collection of raw data to a relatively small number of values of interest to the end user. Data reduction is frequently an outcome of updating as well, since a single transaction can conceivably cause every data base record to be fetched, modified, and stored.

The intuitive notion of data reduction is sufficient for our purposes, but a mathematical definition is frequently clearer. The Data Reduction Ratio (DRR) for a given user directive against a given data base is D divided by U, where D is the data base traffic (number of characters transferred to or from the data storage devices) and U is the user traffic (number of characters transferred to or from the user). The *expected data reduction ratio* is the average DRR over all user directives issued against the data base.

Backend Architecture

Suppose that a horizontal line is drawn across Figure 20-2, and that all of the information system above the line is implemented in one computer (host) while the remaining lower portion of the system is implemented in another computer (backend). If the necessary hardware and system software is added to effect a link

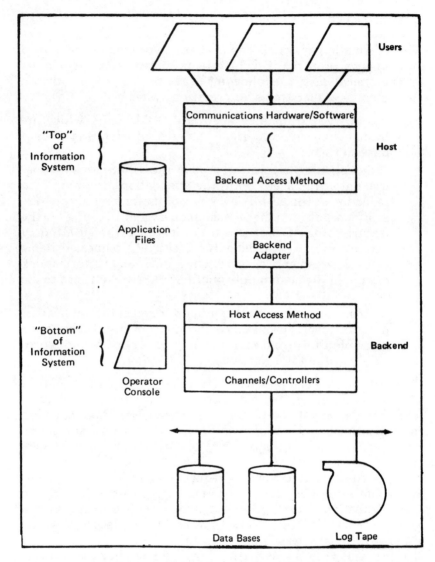

Figure 20-3. Simple Host-Backend Configuration

between the two computers, the result is the host-backend configuration shown in Figure 20-3. Where to draw the line is not pre-
ordained. In theory, it could be anywhere, although we will argue
later that the preferred dividing point is near or at the top of the
DBMS. If the variable portion of the information system (that is,
the application software) is offloaded, then the backend is *user*

programmable. Otherwise it is *nonprogrammable* from the standpoint of the organization's technical staff. The behavior of a nonprogrammable backend can still be influenced externally but not by the introduction of conventional machine code.

In the extreme case in which the entire information system is implemented in the backend computer, the backend is *freestanding,* since the user no longer requires the services of the host in order to access his data bases. It can be argued that, at this point,

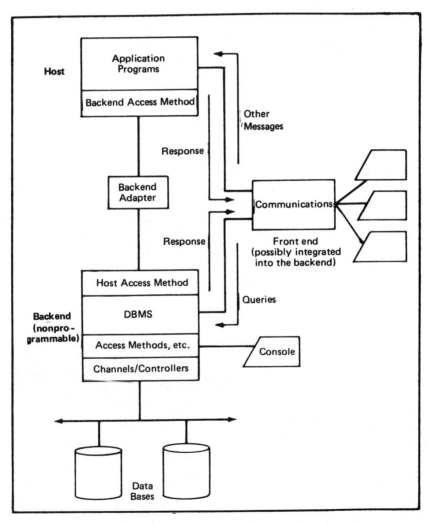

Figure 20-4. Partially Freestanding Backend

the backend has become the host. On the other hand, a freestanding backend need not have most of the facilities ordinarily expected of a traditional host. In fact, it is possible to construct a nonprogrammable backend that is freestanding if the end user's sole interface with his data base is through the query language of the DBMS. In this case, the entire information system is "canned" and offloaded to a dedicated-purpose computer.

An interesting hybrid is the partially freestanding backend depicted in Figure 20-4. A common communications front end examines each incoming request. Those that call for the execution of an application program are routed through the host, which subsequently invokes the backend's DBMS to manipulate the data base. Requests that are queries are routed directly to the backend, and enough of the DBMS must be implemented in the backend to support the query language.

Several variations on this basic theme are possible, including hooking several freestanding or partially freestanding backends together into a geographically distributed network to provide a *distributed data base* like the one shown in Figure 20-5. Each terminal is able to access any data base subset throughout the network of interconnected backend computers. The distributed data base topic is, of course, very important, but it is beyond the scope of this chapter. What needs to be emphasized here is that the emergence of distributed computing systems, both tightly coupled (centralized) and geographically dispersed, is a certainty. A well-conceived and properly constructed backend will be more than an intelligent controller enslaved to a host: it will be a significant building block in a distributed computing environment.

The Data Reduction Ratio (DRR) of the Backend

The DRR of a backend is defined to be D divided by H where D is the data base traffic and H is the traffic over the connection between the host and the backend. Clearly, when the entire information system is offloaded to a backend, the DRR of the backend is equal to the DRR of the information system. At the other extreme, if very little is offloaded, then the DRR of the backend approaches its minimum value:

$$\frac{D}{H} = 1$$

As a consequence of the pyramidal nature of the information system, it is generally true that the backend's expected DRR in-

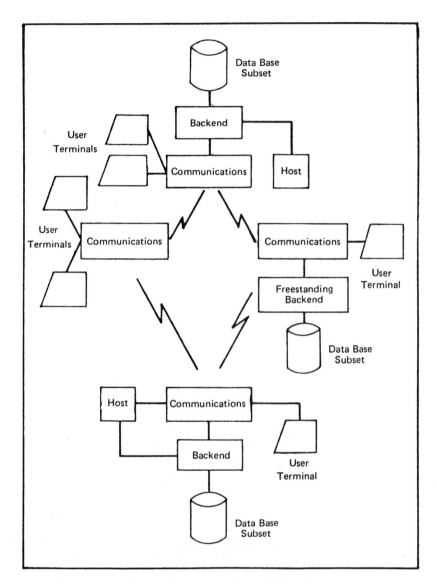

Figure 20-5. The Backend in a Distributed Data Base Environment

creases as more of the system is moved out of the host and into the backend. The expected DRR of a particular backend is a pivotal indicator for its evaluation. It should be observed that the expected DRR is influenced by the intended application as well as by the implementation of the backend itself. That is, certain ways of using a backend will tend to exploit its data reduction capacity more than others.

Multi-threading. A multi-threading backend is one capable of overlapped execution of multiple commands issued from the host, as contrasted with serial execution of such commands. In traditional terms, this implies that the backend operates under the supervision of a multi-tasking monitor that divides the backend's central processor resource among the concurrently outstanding commands. Specifically, while one host-generated command is held up awaiting completion of a data transfer, the central processor can be assigned to another pending command.

A multi-threading backend, in addition to supporting overlapped execution of its work load, is also responsible for resolving conflicting requests originating from the host. For instance, during the time that a data base record is being updated on behalf of one command, the backend may withhold execution of other commands that require access to the same record. Such coordination is necessary to guarantee the consistency of the data base and the accuracy of retrieved data.

Data Security and Integrity

A protective backend is one that includes the controls necessary to protect the data base from accidental or deliberate destruction and unauthorized access.

- A protective backend ensures the *security* of data by requiring the submission of an administratively assigned password prior to satisfying various incoming requests to retrieve or otherwise operate on data base data. In addition, the backend may encode data that is stored in the data base and decode that data when it is retrieved. Various other security techniques may be employed.
- A protective backend ensures the *integrity* of data by means of the appropriate mechanisms for data base checkpointing, backup, and recovery. This facility must be independent of software running in the host.

From an information system viewpoint, a protective backend is the result of offloading the data security and integrity functions normally associated with the DBMS.

Redundancy and Parallel Processing

The backend in Figure 20-3 includes no redundancy of the hardware components and no redundancy of the paths between those

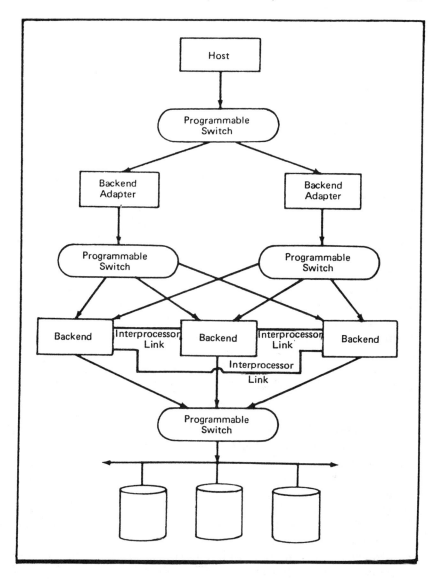

Figure 20-6. Multiprocessing Backend

components. Failure at any point implies failure of the entire backend. We would expect the *multiprocessor backend* of Figure 20-6 to be far more reliable because of the inherent redundancy of the configuration. There are three identical backend processors, each of which can function independently in the event of failure of the others. Similarly, the two backend adapters back each other up. The programmable (automatic) switches essentially reconfigure the system in "real time" as required to sustain ongoing operation. The interprocessor link is a very high-speed data path between each pair of processors. There is nothing special about the degree of redundancy illustrated in Figure 20-6. There might be fewer or more backend adapters and processors, depending upon the desired level of availability of the data base.

In addition to providing improved reliability, the presence of additional processors could conceivably be exploited to provide greater overall computational power by means of *load sharing*— automatic distribution of work among available parallel processors. The three processors in Figure 20-6 could do three times as much work as the single processor of Figure 20-3, although in practice a somewhat lower improvement would be realized because complete parallelism is not achievable. If one of the processors fails, then the incoming work load is distributed among the two remaining processors. The user experiences a graceful degradation in performance rather than hard failure.

Aside from the fundamental choice of software and hardware to effect the derived division of labor between the two computers of Figure 20-3, there are at least two other significant architectural issues confronting the implementer and ultimately the consumer. These are discussed in the following paragraphs, with an emphasis on simply identifying the problem areas, not resolving them. In fact, the problems are important for the very reason that no easy solutions are forthcoming.

The Linkage Problem. Figure 20-3 includes an ensemble of hardware and software used to accomplish the *host-backend link*. The components of the link are the backend access method, backend adapter, and host access method. The implementation of the linkage is not immediately obvious, given that each brand of host has its own way of "talking" to its peripherals. The question can be stated: how does the backend appear to the host? Does the backend emulate a standard peripheral or a special device? In considering the multitude of alternatives, one annoying trade-off becomes apparent: speed versus flexibility. For instance, nearly every computer would be able to interface immediately to a backend that was designed to emulate one or more standard asynchronous (Teletype-like) terminals, but each pseudoterminal could communicate with the host at a speed of at most a few hundred characters per second.

At the opposite end of the spectrum would be a backend that appears to the host as one or more very fast devices such as tape or disk units. These devices attach to high-speed channels of the host that are capable of sustaining data transfers in excess of several hundred thousand characters per second. However, channel interfaces are anything but universal among various manufacturers or even across different models within a host manufacturer's product line. In fact some computers such as IBM's 370/115 have no externally available high-speed channel.

The future holds some promise of stabilization as a result of the recent adoption of the IBM channel protocol as a standard by the American National Standards Institute, but this will not affect the great variety of computers that are currently installed. Therefore, a different channel adapter would have to be engineered for each type of host computer to be supported. Furthermore, the hardware required to interface to a high-speed channel is generally more complex and more expensive than that necessary to connect to a low-speed (telecommunications) channel. In short, if there is a need for a low-cost or very adaptive link between the host and backend, this objective would conflict with a requirement for high throughput across the link.

In view of the preceding analysis, a low-speed link would appear to be the most desirable, provided that the response time requirements of the application could be met. Clearly, the probability that a given interface bandwidth will be sufficient increases in proportion to the expected DRR of the backend. That is, the more the backend "concentrates" data, the slower the link can be. At one extreme, an interactive application that relies on a high-level query language facility contained entirely in the backend will certainly perform adequately with the speed of a telecommunications interface. On the other hand, a channel interface would probably be necessary in a batch intensive environment in which a program issues a very large number of relatively primitive calls to the backend. Backend vendors will very likely offer a wide range of interfaces suited to individual customer needs.

The Storage Sharing Problem. Figure 20-3 differentiates between application files (that is, files not managed by the DBMS) and data bases. The application files, as usual, are on devices native to the host and are accessed through familiar access methods. Data base devices, in contrast, are connected only to the backend and are available only through the backend access method. In this context, there is no need for the data base drives or media to be compatible with the host. Indeed, incompatibility may be advantageous for security reasons. Nonetheless, the expense of dedicating costly mass storage devices to the backend computer might be intolerable in smaller installations, particularly if data bases are on-line only on a part-time basis. Figure 20-7 illustrates one approach to allowing the same set of devices to

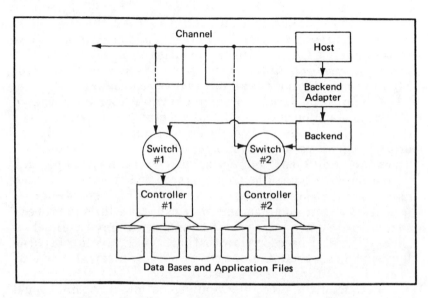

Figure 20-7. Storage Shared by Host and Backend

contain both data bases and application files. Each switch is used to disconnect a set of units (three disks in the figure) from the host and connect them to the backend, or vice versa. These switches could be manual to permit a long-term but flexible assignment of resources to processors. Automatic switches would allow more dynamic sharing, perhaps even on a track or cylinder basis. The manner of switching is not the bone of contention. Once it is agreed that the host and backend can read and write on the same storage devices, then the multiple host problems associated earlier with the high-speed channel interface reappear in a complementary form. Either the shared devices are compatible with a given host type (appear to the host as familiar devices) or they are not. If not, then the host operating system or the controller itself must have special additions to support the new device. Otherwise, the backend's interface to storage must be adapted to the host's standards. In any event, the cost and complexity of accommodating new hosts will put a high price tag on storage sharing. In contrast to the link problem, the shared storage problem is not influenced by the data reduction characteristics of the backend, since the storage interface is at the "bottom" of the information system and the host interface is toward the "top." Neither problem is relevant if the backend is produced by the same company that supplies the host, since presumably there is little incentive to support competing or older host types.

chapter **21**

The Backend (Data Base) Computer—Part II

INTRODUCTION

The backend approach has much to recommend it, especially when contrasted with the prevailing architectural alternatives. Each potential advantage is considered in its turn, usually in a comparison of a partially offloaded information system with a functionally identical counterpart entirely resident in a typical commercial computer. We use "potential" because different users have different, often conflicting needs. More significantly, we have not prescribed all of the implementation characteristics of the backend. Whether a given benefit (or shortcoming) will actually be realized may depend upon whether or not the backend is user programmable, whether or not storage is shared, and how much of the information system is offloaded. The important implementation factors will be highlighted in the discussion of each benefit.

IMPROVED COST/PERFORMANCE

Economy of Specialization

It is often written that substantial savings can be realized by the simple act of moving all or part of an application from a "maxi" to a "mini" because most minicomputers are far less expensive than large mainframes, even considering their reduced capability. The reasons cited include the low maintenance costs of the mini (because it is relatively simple), mass production, and the incorporation of the latest technology (retooling is more frequent). For such reasons alone the attachment of a minicomputer backend to a larger or older host can be expected to cost less than the current market price of host resources (memory, processor time, and channel connect time) that are freed.

Far greater economies are possible because the host is a general-purpose computer and the backend is a special-purpose computer. Just as the front end is tailored for communications, the backend can be customized for data base management, thereby exhibiting greater efficiency than a host-resident information system. For example, the overheads intrinsic to large general-purpose operating systems can be largely eliminated. The backend can make much more efficient use of storage media than is possible with host file systems. The backend might have special firmware or hardware to facilitate its activities. Conceivably, it might be implemented entirely in microcode, like most storage controllers.

- The most dramatic improvements in efficiency require an implementation that goes beyond programming a DBMS in a minicomputer that has a general-purpose instruction set, operating system, and file system.
- In general, a backend that is not user programmable is capable of greater efficiency than one that is.
- The more that is offloaded to the backend, the greater the savings in terms of redeemed host central processor time and host central memory. These unburdened resources translate to actual dollars saved, provided they can be refunded or put to some other use rather than left idle.
- The greatest benefit is obtained when both the host and backend are fully utilized, that is, operating in parallel at full bore. This is best achieved when:
  1. The host is under the direction of a multiprogramming operating system, so one program can be running while another is awaiting responses from the backend, and

2. The backend is multi-threading so that it can execute several directives from the host concurrently, minimizing the probability of idle time due to data base I/O.

- The host's channel is unburdened and its interrupt load is diminished in proportion to the expected DRR of the backend.

Performance Tuning

Performance upgrades in a conventional setting are usually costly and disruptive. Typical alternatives include adding large memory modules, incorporating more channels, replacing the central processor with a more powerful model, or actually obtaining additional computers. These same options can be applied to the backend, only on a much smaller scale than is possible with typical existing hosts and in more manageable and less expensive increments. Furthermore, the backend can be upgraded with less disruption because it is a special-purpose computer. System generation is simpler, and in no case should applications have to be reprogrammed or job control modified to accommodate the new configuration. This desirable limitation of impact upon the organization's technical staff and end users is observed even if an existing backend is replaced by one that is internally (hardware or software) reimplemented but preserves the expected host interface. The backend supplier can exploit advances in processor and memory technology (amortizing the development cost over new users and current users desiring to upgrade) and deliver entirely new backends externally compatible with the old. In other words, for installations that are sufficiently data base oriented, improvements to the backend will be more cost effective, painless, and suitable to actual requirements than host upgrades. The native capacity of the host can be greatly extended through parallelism with the backend, particularly if processors can be added to the backend itself. For instance, a backend with eight processors might be able to transfer data to or from eight disks simultaneously, which is more I/O parallelism than most hosts can handle with standard channels.

- The greatest opportunity for fine tuning backend performance is provided by a multiprocessor backend design that permits the addition and deletion of processors with relative ease.
- The limit to which the backend can be upgraded without outstripping the channel capacity of the host is a function of the expected DRR of the backend.

- It is easier for a backend supplier to offer an improved backend (incorporating the latest processor technology) as a performance upgrade if the backend is not user programmable. Otherwise user programs running in the backend must be converted or the previous environment must be emulated. Modularity and interchangeability are best served by isolating the user-programmable elements of the computing facility.

THE BACKEND AS A "LIFELINE"

The point was made earlier that offloading part of an information system to a special-purpose computer can be a very cost-effective strategy. Once in place, the backend can be gradually enhanced to provide a more graceful and economical alternative to host upgrades. We have implicitly assumed until this point that the need or desirability for a backend is ancillary to the requirement for an information system. In other words we have supposed that the organization already has a DBMS, or has decided to obtain a DBMS, and that the only remaining issue is whether the system is to reside in the host or in an outboard computer. The frequently high initial cost of converting an existing application to use a DBMS has not been considered, since this is constant regardless of the form in which the DBMS is delivered. We now consider the situation in which an organization might adopt a DBMS *primarily* to obtain the backend. This will happen when the backend is viewed as breathing new life into an old or small computer that is on the threshold of obsolescence. Many of the restrictions inherent in these machines can be overcome with the help of the backend, to the extent that useful lifetimes can be significantly prolonged. If this option exists, the cost of a full-scale conversion to a new mainframe must be weighed against the cost of incorporating a backend and adapting existing programs to use it. The medium- and long-term benefits of using a DBMS must also be considered.

- It is to be expected on the basis of past experience with peripherals that backends supplied by a host manufacturer will attach only to that host and probably only to the latest and largest models of the host. Independent backend suppliers are more likely to show an interest in interfacing their equipment to a variety of hosts, old and new.

The following paragraphs indicate typical "lifeline" dilemmas against which the backend can be applied.

Speed Problems

The host's central processor may be too slow to handle an increasing work load in a timely fashion. As a result of using a DBMS, large programs are reduced to relatively small programs that make calls to the DBMS. Since all or part of the DBMS is executed in the outboard processor, the host processor is free to do more computation.

Memory Problems

The host's limited central memory capacity may be inadequate to accommodate larger programs and the need to optimize processor utilization through increased multiprogramming. Again, application programs that call upon the backend's DBMS can be reduced in size, and more of these programs can be resident in the host's central memory at one time. Perhaps of greater importance, sophisticated and powerful data base technology usually associated only with large computers can be brought to computers that were previously considered too limited in memory to execute the required DBMS software.

- The backend can increase the effective central memory and central processor capacity of the host only insofar as the information system is offloaded to the backend.
- The host must be multiprogrammed and the backend must be multi-threaded to maximize overlapped execution of the two computers.
- A multiprocessor backend can prolong the host's life longer than a backend that is limited to a single processor.

Secondary Storage Problems

Since the inception of disk technology, steady progress has been made with respect to increasing the capabilities, reliability, capacity, transfer speed, and characters per dollar of commercially available disks. Other types of direct access devices have been developed and improved as well. Some of the newer storage devices are expected to compete with disks while others are intended to supplement them. Chief among the latter are the very large stores that exhibit much greater average access times than disk, yet are capable of on-line storage in excess of 100 billion characters at considerably less cost per character than is achievable with disk. These large, slow devices are allied with small, fast disks in arrangements called *storage hierarchies* to exploit the best properties of each device type. Storage hierarchies appear to be a particularly attractive vehicle for handling very large on-line data bases.

Because of the constantly improving cost/performance of disk media, and because of the emergence of new storage technology, the pressure to convert or upgrade a currently installed computer often has as its basis the inadequacies of the associated secondary storage. For instance, smaller or older computers may not have the channel capacity or memory speeds to accommodate the transfer rates of new disks. Often the hardware and software prerequisites of interfacing a computer to a new device are beyond the budget or the expertise of the users (or possibly even professional engineering firms). In other cases, the limitation to a certain type or number of devices is arbitrarily imposed by the computer manufacturer in order to encourage upgrades.

The backend represents a compelling alternative to conversion or upgrading to obtain the desired secondary storage capabilities and economies. Conversion, after all, is the act of trading one set of limitations for another—the user is locked into the storage supported by the new computer until he once again feels the pressure to change. The backend potentially solves this problem by separating, once and for all, the characteristics of the host from the characteristics of the data base storage devices. That is, with the backend firmly in place as a filter between the host and storage, either can be varied without affecting the other. This insulation (maximum device independence) could become a fundamental distinction between a backend and a traditional controller. New, perhaps radical, storage technology and storage hierarchies could be introduced without changing hardware or software in the host, because the "logical" level at which the host interacts with the backend is independent of the peculiarities of the devices connected to the other side of the backend. Of course there is no way to avoid transferring existing files from the old devices to the new, but even here the backend might provide standard automated conversion utilities.

The arithmetic is very persuasive: once a backend has been interfaced to a variety of hosts, then the cost of adapting to a new device type is borne only for the backend computer and not for each kind of host. Another crucial point is that the cost of interfacing the backend to a new host should be far less than the cost of directly interfacing a foreign disk to the same computer. This is so because it is sufficient to condition the interface so that the backend appears to the host as a native device, possibly slower and simpler than a disk. In theory, this could also be done with the direct interface to the disk but probably not without comprising any exceptional speed and advanced features the disk may boast. Because of the data reduction property of the backend, a simplified interface to a (slow) host channel need not imply inefficient utilization or reduced functionality with respect to data management.

- A backend supplier committed to the "lifeline" concept must be prepared to support a variety of hosts and, more importantly, keep in step with the state of storage technology. This requires a willingness to build special hardware and software interfaces to old hosts and new devices.
- If the transfer rate of the storage device type exceeds that of the available host channel, then the expected DRR of the backend determines the degree to which the two speeds can be matched (to keep the devices busy).
- A multi-threading backend more fully exploits features of modern disks, such as overlapped seek and rotational position sensing.
- Whether or not a backend offers storage device independence to the host depends somewhat upon how much of the information system is in the backend. In most cases, offloading only the access methods will not be adequate.

THE BACKEND AS A BRIDGE

If an organization uses a DBMS heavily, particularly a DBMS residing in a backend, then the cost of converting an application to run on a different host computer is much less than would otherwise be the case (provided the host portion of the DBMS exists for the new computer). It may appear paradoxical that what has just been touted as a tool to forestall conversion is now being represented as a vehicle to facilitate it, but these two characteristics are not in conflict. It has already been pointed out that the one-time development costs associated with interfacing the backend of a new host should be minor (compared with the cost of connecting a new disk to the host), but they are not necessarily negligible. What has been gained in return for this cost is savings in two areas. First, conversion from one host to another does not require converting existing data bases from one type of storage to another type as is typically necessary. The "distance" between the host and files created by the backend allows, in essence, one host to replace another without disturbing these files. Second, to the extent that the information system is offloaded to the backend, this part of the system need not be reimplemented for each new host.

This represents considerable savings to the implementer and ultimately the user of the information system.

The only software that need be converted is, therefore, that part of the application that remains in the host. It is accepted as generally true that the cost of conversion is more conditioned by the type of language used to develop applications than the sheer number of lines of code. One hundred lines of COBOL are easier to convert than 20 lines of assembly language code. Usually, the higher the level of the programming language employed, the fewer the source statements necessary and the less machine dependent is the resulting program. Since the program or user interface to a DBMS is typically at a very high level, applications that extensively exploit a DBMS are potentially more portable than otherwise, provided that the DBMS is available on a number of computers and operating systems. (Note: This may in fact be true for "CODASYL-like" DBMSs.) In the extreme case, applications that rely primarily on the DBMS query language (which can be regarded as an exceptionally high-level "programming" language) can most easily migrate to new environments. While it is generally true that a conventional DBMS can help the user avoid being locked into a particular host manufacturer, if the DBMS is off-loaded to a backend, then the user is further extricated inasmuch as data bases do not have to be converted. Furthermore, the cost of providing the DBMS itself to several host computers and operating systems is greatly reduced by this strategy.

An application is always bound to the language used to implement it, whether this language is at the assembly, compiler, or DBMS level. The larger the application, the more it costs to convert the application to a new implementation language. What has been stressed here is that the extent and scope of this commitment to a language is determined by the level of that language. If a particular DBMS presents a very high-level language to the user, then the following will be true:

- The characteristics of the operating system, hardware, and storage are transparent to the application, so the scope of the commitment to the DBMS user language does not extend to a commitment to a particular environment.

- Because application programs are smaller when a high-level language is used, the cost of replacing the DBMS user language with another one (that is, replacing the DBMS with another) is usually less than the cost of replacing a lower-level language with another. The use of a high-level language limits the degree of commitment to that specific language.

- As more of the information system is offloaded to a backend, the cost of converting the information system to a new host diminishes correspondingly, since there is less code in the host. Thus, a backend that comprises a substantial portion of the information system is desirable from the standpoint of achieving portability of the application.
- The backend supplier must support interconnection of the backend to a variety of host computers. The DBMS supplier (who might not be the backend supplier) must maintain several versions of the host portion of the DBMS, if any, for each supported host environment.
- A DBMS with a high-level user language is preferable to a DBMS with a lower-level language with respect to minimizing the organization's dependence upon the host hardware, operating system, and the DBMS itself.

DATA BASE SHARING IN MULTIPLE HOST CONFIGURATIONS

Large organizations frequently have several computers, small and large, to handle work loads beyond the capabilities of a single mainframe. Computers in such a collection are defined to be similar if a data base storage device that is supported by one computer is supported by each of the others. Otherwise, the computers are dissimilar. Even though there are some obvious economies in maintaining homogeneity to enchance interchangeability of peripherals, mixtures of dissimilar computers have evolved for various reasons. Different computers are best suited for different applications. Governmental agencies obtain varied manufacturers' mainframes because of federal procurement policies. Frequently one division of a large organization may have different needs or be unaware of recent purchases by another.

Regardless of their individual origins, the time may come when these computers must share data. The problems involved with accomplishing this are enormous for dissimilar computers that are geographically scattered, and they are hardly trivial even when the computers are identical and installed in the same room. The mainframe manufacturer may offer multiple port controllers that permit simultaneous electrical connection between a device and a limited number of similar computers, but this is not a sufficient condition for dynamic data base sharing. The DBMS executing within each machine must be able to communicate rapidly with any concurrently running DBMS in order to effect maximum overlapping of updates to the same data base as well as to maintain the integrity of the data through coordination of update activity.

For the most part, conventional facilities for high-speed intercomputer communications are either very expensive, nonexistent, or not supported by software. The situation is, of course, much worse for dissimilar computers. The manufacturers have developed computers that consist of several processors in the same box but have devoted little effort to engineering express channels between distinct mainframes of the same type, much less those of their competition. Data base sharing among dissimilar computers is particularly troublesome because each variety of computer employs a unique protocol in its interface to storage; formats files in its own style; and uses different representations for data. Most often data "sharing" among dissimilar computers is accomplished by the awkward technique of copying data from disk to tape (perhaps translating data codes in the process), carrying the tape to the target computer, and copying the tape to that computer's disks.

Under the proper circumstances, a backend could provide dynamic data base sharing services to clusters of similar or dissimilar computers. It may even be reasonable to relax the requirement that the computers be in close proximity. The multi-threading backend shown in Figure 21-1 is the vehicle that allows the three hosts to access the same data base. In such a system, the hosts do not have to communicate directly with one another because, by definition, the backend itself is sufficient to properly coordinate the update activity originating in the individual host computers. Furthermore, the multi-tasking monitor in the backend supervises overlapped execution of directives sent by different hosts in order to minimize response times. Each backend adapter is engineered to the characteristics of the type of host to which it is attached. Directives and data coming from the host are translated to a common "language" acceptable to the backend. Conversely, data and status generated by the backend are transformed into representations expected by the host.

The essential point here is that although computer-to-computer interfacing is still required in the form of the software and hardware effecting the host-backend link, this interface need not be as fast as or as complex as the host-to-host link described earlier. As previously mentioned, a sufficiently high degree of backend data reduction will tend to render a teleprocessing interface adequate for the response time requirements of the application. At this point, of course, the hosts in Figure 21-1 can conceivably be remote from the backend. An arrangement of this nature would appear to be particularly practical when the end user's principal access to the data base is through the query language of the DBMS.

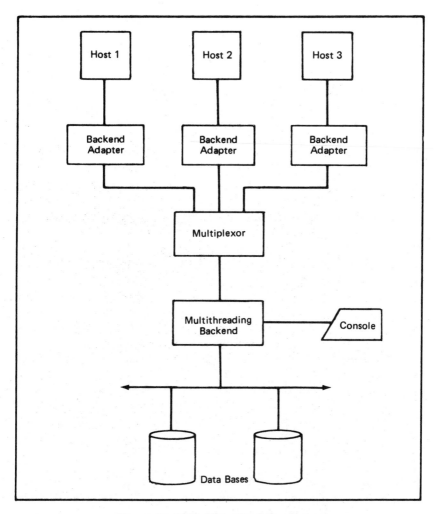

Figure 21-1. Multiple Host Configuration

- A multi-threading backend is a practical necessity in a multiple host environment. In fact a multiprocessor backend would probably be needed to match the aggregate processing speed of a cluster of large hosts.
- The backend supplier must be motivated to furnish backend adapters and DBMS software for each type of host in a cluster of dissimilar computers.
- The greater the expected DRR, the higher the probability that a host in the cluster can be distant from the backend.

ENHANCING DATA BASE SECURITY, AVAILABILITY, AND INTEGRITY

Computers controlled by traditional, general-purpose, multi-programming operating systems are notoriously ill-suited to the task of protecting a data base. The main reason for this is that unrelated user programs are allowed to run in the machine at the same time the information system is active or at least while the data base is on-line to the computer. A clever, malevolent programmer can usually find a way to circumvent the protection mechanisms employed by the information system and, in doing so, gain unauthorized access to data bases. He or she may do this by constructing a program that essentially makes itself part of the operating system and thereby gain access to any of the resources available to the computer. Even the execution of an undebugged but otherwise harmless user program can accidentally result in damage to a data base if it happens to cause a "hard" system crash while the DBMS is in the midst of updating the data base. In a conventional setting, the information system, with all of its protection mechanisms, is subject to the vulnerability of the operating system and computer in which it is encased.

The backend and its data bases are not directly controlled by the host's hardware and operating system. A properly constructed protective backend should be an autonomous filter between the host and the data base. Its independence allows it to screen *every* attempted data base access originating in the host and to gracefully recover a data base when the host experiences hard failure. While absolute security is never entirely achievable, the protective backend *enhances* security significantly by requiring the proper passwords as a condition of access even if the requesting program is in control of the host. There is no path to the files except through the backend. Likewise, while 100 percent data base availability cannot reasonably be expected, the probability of prolonged unavailability can be reduced if the host and backend maintain their own audit trails and each is devised to detect failure in the other.

The basic point to be made here is that two machines should be able to detect an error situation and to contain its effect better than a (faulty) single machine attempting to do self-analysis. The dual audits also provide insurance that the audit trail being used for recovery or rollback has not been corrupted by a faulty machine. These advantages should more than offset the slight decrease in overall system hardware reliability due to additional backend equipment.

- The backend, of course, must be protective if its use is motivated by a requirement for better data protection than is found in conventional systems. That is, the security and integrity mechanisms of the information system must be offloaded to the backend.
- A multiprocessor backend has a lower probability of failure than a single-processor backend because of its built-in hardware redundancy. In a multiple host and multiprocessor backend configuration, overall system availability can be increased to the desired level through the addition of processing elements on either side of the host-backend link.
- A freestanding backend offers an additional measure of data base availability because the data base can be accessed directly through the query language of the DBMS even when the host is down.
- It is impossible for a hostile or undebugged user program to run on a backend that is not user programmable. By confining the user's immediate influence to the host, the nonprogrammable backend can be a more effective barrier to accidental or deliberate destruction of data.
- The protective role of the backend is compromised somewhat if the data base resides on media that are host-readable and more so if direct connection between the host and data base storage devices is possible.

POTENTIAL DISADVANTAGES OF BACKENDS

As with benefits, the possible disadvantages of the backends are relative to traditional information systems and dependent upon characteristics of the backend, the DBMS, and the intended applications. Moreover, the independently supplied backend, while offering the greatest opportunity for radical improvement, also exhibits the greatest potential for creating new problems if improperly designed and supported.

Multiple Vendor Maintenance

When the host and backend are furnished by different vendors, the organization must deal with two companies in the event of failure in the interface between the two computers. Circular finger pointing can become a problem unless there are techniques for clearly assigning fault to a particular piece of equipment. This is easier to do if the backend appears to the host as a commonly

374   CURRENT DIRECTIONS

supported device with respect to interface discipline, speed, and function. It is important to design the backend so that it can be tested and diagnosed in isolation from the host. While difficulties with multiple vendors are certainly not unique to backends, the novelty of the backend may engender more skepticism than usual on the part of the host vendor.

Obsolescence of the Backend (Technical Risk)

In the best case, the backend helps prolong the life of a host when the backend's development keeps pace with new advances in processor and storage technology. In the worst case, the backend is a liability that actually prevents an organization from exploiting new technology. This happens when the backend manufacturer is not responsive to technical change, such as the introduction of new media, faster devices, complex storage hierarchies, or new models of the host computer. The host manufacturer who also builds backends has a theoretical edge over the independent supplier in this regard, since the host manufacturer has advance notice of such anticipated improvements and can correspondingly upgrade its backend ahead of time. On the other hand, the host vendor is more likely to require that the customer upgrade to a new host computer as a condition of obtaining an improved backend or one that is connected to new types of storage. As is often the case, the interests (and the pocketbook) of the user are best served when peripheral equipment is independently and competitively supplied, *provided* that the vendor is committed to long-term customer support and product development.

Cost

The backend is not free. Its cost must be justified in terms of its value to the organization: redeemed host resources, competitive cost/performance in data management, superior data protection, portability of applications, and so forth. If the backend's value is too low or its cost too high, then it is a liability instead of an asset. Since the backend is limited to a very specific role, its value fluctuates as a function of the organization's use of the information system that invokes the backend. If the information system is never executed, then the backend simply takes up floor space. Unlike a general-purpose computer, it cannot be put to work on another kind of task.

Presumably the cost of a backend should be easier to calculate than its value. With respect to cost, however, it is necessary to consider not only the expense of the backend computer but also conversion, training, and maintenance. The data base storage devices connected to the backend may or may not contribute to cost. If the backend can share devices with the host, then these devices are reckoned as part of the host, not the backend. Even if data base storage is dedicated to the backend, it may be possible to return an equivalent amount of the host's storage, particularly if the host hardware is installed on a rental basis. A trade of this nature can only be done if the organization has permanently partitioned its fixed storage resource into the two usage classes: data bases and other application files. On the other hand, where data bases are normally up on a part-time basis, the introduction of a backend will create a requirement to purchase additional storage that will be idle much of the time and not interchangeable with host devices.

From any point of view, it is clear that the utility and net value of a backend is in proportion to the organization's actual or intended commitment to the use of an information system (or DBMS) as a major element in its data processing activity.

Reliability Problems

In a conventional system, the path to storage includes the computer, channels, controllers, and finally the drives themselves. Failure in any link of this chain results in unavailability of all or part of the data base until repairs can be made. Even then, recovery of the data base may be necessary if the malfunction has compromised the integrity of the stored data.

A backend either replaces the controllers or is situated between the host and the controllers. The backend's processor is less complex than the host but more complex than a hard-wired controller, so if all else is equal it will tend to fail less frequently than the host but more frequently than the relatively rugged controllers. Consequently the probability of system unavailability is slightly higher for the single-processor backend configuration. If the proper data base protection features are implemented, then the effects of failure on the data base itself can be satisfactorily contained. Nevertheless the data cannot be accessed while the equipment is down. Additional downtime may not be tolerable in certain types of applications, such as an airline reservation system. In such applications the use of a multiprocessor backend, if supplied, is necessary to ensure continuous availability of the information system. In the extreme case, each processor in the backend must execute the same host directive concurrently and agree on a majority-rule basis as to what data is to be written to storage.

Performance Problems

The performance requirements of a traditional controller are fairly easy to gauge: the equipment must be able to accept data at the rate of the fastest device to which it is attached and simultaneously move this data to the computer. The performance demanded of a backend cannot be readily measured in absolute terms because the backend processes data instead of simply passing a character stream to the host. Today, each organization attempts to evaluate a prospective DBMS in relationship to the specific needs of the end-user community. The complexity and the susceptibility to error of this often subjective judgment will be roughly the same whether the DBMS is in the mainframe or offloaded to a backend.

Suppose that at some time after the information system has been inaugurated, the users discover that system throughput is inadequate, either because the initial judgment was incorrect or because significant growth in the job load was not anticipated. Typical remedies may be applied such as program optimization, redistribution of work loads to smooth out peaks and valleys, or reorganization of data bases. Eventually the organization may choose to upgrade its equipment by obtaining more memory, more channels, or a more powerful central processor.

Promotions of this sort are futile if the throughput bottleneck is the backend or its link to the host. Unless the backend supplier is in a position to upgrade the equipment to the desired level of performance (for example, through the use of multiprocessing), the organization may be motivated to abandon the backend in favor of a mainframe-resident information system (if available). Even if the backend computer is powerful enough to handle its work schedule in a timely fashion, response times may be impaired by the limitations of the host-backend link. This will happen when the observed DRR of the backend is lower than the expected DRR. Perhaps the most frequently executed application program may not be able to exploit the potential data reduction capability of the backend. For some legitimate reason, it may be necessary for the program to retrieve each item of each record in the data base; or maybe the program stores a massive number of new records. In this event, a faster interface between the backend and host is mandatory to clear the bottleneck. However, in the limiting case in which the backend performs no data reduction at all, even the fastest link won't allow the backend to be as responsive as a host-resident information system. This is so because every character transmitted between storage and the program must go through the additional step of being stored in the backend's buffer memory.

However when the expected DRR of the backend is very high and the backend consists of multiple processors and multiple paths to storage, the response times provided are potentially much less than could reasonably be expected of a conventional system.

SUMMARY

It would appear that the backend offers far greater potential for order than for chaos. However, whether an organization can realize the unique advantages of the backend and avoid the possible pitfalls depends on various qualities of the backend, the DBMS, the supplier, and the intended application. The factors involved in evaluating the suitability of a backend are summarized in the following. No weight is assigned to individual factors, as the relevance of each issue will vary from situation to situation. Earlier discussions more thoroughly indicate why and in what cases a particular facet may be important to an organization considering the use of a backend.

Prerequisites of the Application

- Intensive use must be made of an information system (or DBMS).
- A substantial proportion of the total computer resource should be devoted to the information system.
- The application design should permit maximizing whatever data reduction potential the backend may have. For instance, if the backend has a built-in record search and selection function, then this should be used instead of testing records in the application program. If possible, the program should be written to retrieve only specific items of a record rather than the entire record. If the backend supports a self-contained language for query or update, then this language should be used whenever it is practical to do so.
- Backends are better suited for on-line retrieval and maintenance in a multiuser environment than in a single-user, batch environment.

Prerequisites of the Backend Supplier

- The vendor must be responsive to changing customer needs and new technology (particularly storage technology).
- The vendor should be prepared to implement the backend interface and host DBMS software for several host types, old

and new. This range will be limited by the options for connecting peripherals to a given host type. Attachment of a backend is precluded when the host is "sealed in," that is, offers no external path to memory at all. The already recognized need for computer manufacturers to provide and standardize external channels will be intensified by the emergence of the backend.

- Maintenance strategies must be established that ensure quick and decisive isolation of fault in a multiple vendor installation.

Prerequisites of the Backend Computer

- The storage devices connected to the backend should be competitively priced and offer at least the same level of performance as the host devices they displace. In certain cases, it will be desirable to have the backend share storage with the host.

- The link to the host should be durable and fast enough to meet the response-time requirements of the application. There may be a tendency to overkill here, but if "exotic" interfaces are used to attain greater speed, the initial expense and on-going maintenance costs will be greater.

- Most or all of the generalized portion of the information system should be offloaded to the backend. That is, the backend should contain the greatest part of the DBMS and possibly the telecommunications functions as well. Very little real advantage would be gained, say, if only current forms of access methods were offloaded.

- Offloading the variable portion of the information system (i.e., the application programs) is not recommended. The backend is more secure, easier to optimize, and easier to maintain if it is not user programmable. On the other hand the backend supplier might be willing to customize a particular model to suit the specific needs of an organization.

- The backend should be protective, freestanding, and multi-threading. In many applications a multiprocessor backend will be required.

- The potential data reduction capacity of a backend is directly related to its performance and viability in almost any environment.

Prerequisites of the DBMS

The selection of the DBMS is one of the organization's most important data-processing-related decisions. To disregard the DBMS in the interest of obtaining the benefits of the backend is definitely to put the cart before the horse. Because a commitment to a DBMS is essentially a commitment to a specific programming language and data structure, inexpensive options to rescind the original choice are all but foreclosed once the DBMS is broadly used within the organization.

Guidelines for evaluating commercial DBMS products are outlined elsewhere in this book. It is not our purpose here to offer general advice with regard to the selection process. However, the DBMS decision and the backend decision do influence each other in certain limited but important ways. The various end-user and programmer languages associated with one DBMS may be "higher level" or "lower level" than the languages of another DBMS. This notion of "level," while not yielding to a precise definition, is often used to compare the languages of different DBMSs. Language X is said to be higher level than language Y if, on balance, fewer statements are required to state a process in X than in Y. Substituting a higher-level DBMS language for a lower level one is roughly equivalent to moving logic out of the customized application program and into the generalized DBMS. As a result more of the information system becomes generalized and thus more can be offloaded to the backend. When more is offloaded, the potential for data reduction tends to improve. This effect can be visualized as moving the line labeled "DBMS Data Manipulation Language" in Figure 20-2 up toward the apex of the information system. The point is that the importance of offloading as much as possible of the DBMS should constitute a major part of the information system. The different DBMS packages available today differ dramatically in the level of the language available to application programmers. Moreover, the availability of a self-contained (i.e., end user oriented) language for inquiry, update, and report generation establishes an exceptionally high-level DBMS interface and creates the possibility of offering a freestanding backend.

In 1980, INTEL announced the first commercially available backend data base computer, which integrated the SYSTEM 2000 DBMS software line with the hardware products of the parent company, INTEL.

chapter 22

Operational and Technological Issues in Distributed Data Bases

INTRODUCTION

Beginning with the intercomputer communications technology developed by Roberts[1] and continuing through the recent minicomputer explosion, a trend has developed away from the highly centralized systems of the early 1970s to distributed information systems for the late 1970s and early 1980s.

Before discussing the trend toward distributed systems, we must make a distinction between distributed *data* systems and distributed *processing* systems. In a distributed *data* system, subsets of the data base are created over several geographically distinct computer sites, and sufficient accessing power is provided to manipulate these subsets. In contrast, a distributed *processing* system typically has a centralized data base but has software and processing power distributed throughout the linked computer sites.

This chapter will focus exclusively on distributed data systems. The purpose is to investigate the emerging area of distributed data base technology and to indicate some important technological and operational issues.

The overall goal of a distributed data system is the controlled access to and the sharability of the data distributed across a computer network. The key terms in this formulation—*controlled access, sharability,* and *computer network*—need to be defined. Controlled access means the degree of security necessary to protect the data from unauthorized user access. Sharability refers to multiple and diverse users accessing data from different, perhaps remote, computing facilities. A computer network is a collection of heterogeneous computing facilities connected by means of high-speed communication.

In order to provide sharability of data, the various accessing mechanisms and DBMSs must cooperate with one another. This creates distinct problems for the specific facilities such as data translation, cooperating data base operating systems, and data integration. It appears that the distributed data base technology necessary for the achievement of this goal has yet to be realized.

Specific goals, which are, in some cases, analogous to those of the decentralization concept in data processing, include reliability and backup, efficient use of existing resources, distribution of data volume, partitioning to increase response time, and localization of data base controls.

It is interesting to observe that the basic issues to be resolved in the area of distributed data bases are similar in form and substance to those that DBMS implementors have faced for the past 10 years. The many distributed data base issues tend to fall into two categories: technological and operational. In the technological category are the mechanisms required to achieve integrated access and processing functions. These include data translation, description, and information translation; language translation encompassing manipulation and interrogation; and data directory. The operational issues address the software design considerations and the performance implications of the distributed system. Included in this category are the issues of multiple data base synchronization, concurrency problems (such as update and deadlock), and distribution/partitioning problems.

DESIGN ISSUES IN DISTRIBUTED DATA BASES

A survey of the large volume of technical literature on distributed processing reveals a diversity of distributed data base issues. Unfortunately, the research on this broad range of issues has been uneven—the majority of the results reported are in the area of modeling data distribution strategies. Very little is reported on the solutions to existing operational problems. The purpose of this section is to formulate the design issues and review the related research results.

Horizontal vs. Vertical Design

In an excellent survey on distributed information systems, Booth[2] defined two types of distributed processing design strategies— horizontal and vertical. Horizontal system design involves the connection of processing nodes that are at the same functional level. These nodes may be located with the same computing facility or between different facilities. The important point is that no one node has greater control of the system than another.

Figure 22-1 gives an example of a horizontally distributed system in which four information processors are located remotely from each other and are linked by communication facilities. Communication is provided by data exchange across the communication facility; a distributed data base is not necessarily needed to support this type of system. One would be used, however, if each site maintained copies of the same information.

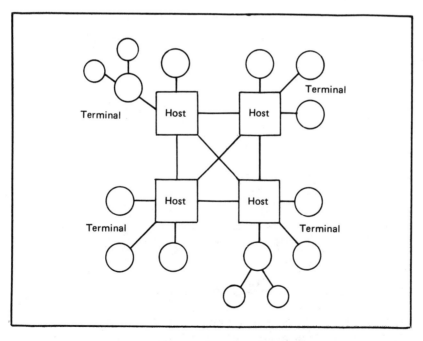

Figure 22-1. Horizontally Distributed System

Vertical (or hierarchical) system design involves the connection of processing nodes when one or more nodes exert control over the others. Figure 22-2 illustrates a vertical system design. An example of vertical system design would be a large-scale information processor maintaining a master data base used for overall scheduling and control. Several satellite processors (indicated by triangles) might be minicomputers, each having its local portion of the master data base and/or other information not contained in the master data base. Satellites may also handle different parts of the manufacturing process and, in this case, the master data base would be updated nightly or weekly from the local data bases. Another level that is controlled by the satellites and that monitors and controls factory equipment may exist. A vertically designed system forms a hierarchy of nodes and is often called a hierarchical system.

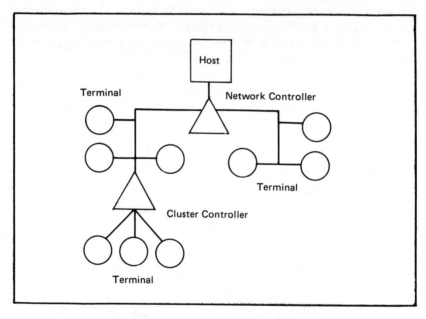

Figure 22-2. Vertically Distributed System

Partitioning vs. Replication Data Design

Another design issue confronting the DBA deals with the distribution of the data base. Sutherland[3] pointed out that there are fundamentally two different types of data distribution. A data base may be maintained identically at many sites, or it may be composed of many non-overlapping segments that, when taken together, contain all of the data in the data base. The former method is called replication, and the latter is termed partitioning.

Partitioning can be done with horizontally or vertically distributed systems. For example, a bank may have two large information processing centers, one in San Francisco and the other in Los Angeles, and therefore partition its data base by geographic location. The information accessed most often by northern users would be located in the San Francisco center; information accessed most often by southern users would be located at the Los Angeles center. However, both information processing centers could obtain information from the other.

An example of a vertically partitioned system is the data base partitioned according to an organization's structure. The master data base exists at corporate headquarters and distinct subsets are resident divisional data bases. There is no duplication of data among the divisional data bases, but at corporate headquarters the data base contains all the information. It should be noted that information can and must flow in both directions in this type of system.

The replication of data at individual nodes of all or part of a data base also creates a distributed data base. In a vertically replicated banking system, a central information processor maintains records on all customer accounts while local branch processors maintain information only about customers at that particular branch. The central data base is updated each night with the day's transactions, and each local data base is subsequently re-created with the new information. It should be noted that few systems are at either one extreme or another; most exhibit some combination of partitioning and replication.

Several researchers have investigated methods for partitioning the data base. The pioneering work in the area of physical data distribution is Chu's[4] investigation of a linear programming solution to optimize the allocation of files in a network. Positing certain assumptions—that the number of file copies is known; queries are routed to all files; query patterns are known; and a Poisson queuing discipline is used—he formulated a zero-one linear programming solution. It is well known that such a solution is valid only for small problems, since the number of variables and constraints increases rapidly as the number of nodes in the problem increases.

Whitney's[5] Ph.D. dissertation addressed the broader problem of computer communication system design but applied Chu's approach to the optimal allocation of files. Casey[6,7,8] relaxed the limitations set by Chu's model and showed that the proportions of update traffic to query traffic determine an upper bound for the number of file copies that are maintained in the network.

The distribution of data in a network is not independent of the programs that use the data. Accordingly, Levin[9] extended the data distribution strategies by considering the effect of programs. He formulated a model that considered the effect of the dependencies between programs and data and their optimal allocation in a network.

The allocation problem was partitioned into three levels. The first level assumed that the access patterns were static and known over a period of time. A zero-one linear programming solution was developed for the optimal allocation of files. In the second level, the assumption that the access request patterns were known was relaxed, and a dynamic programming solution approach was formulated. The third and final level addressed the situation in which the access request patterns are initially unknown. A statistical procedure for estimating these patterns was developed and incorporated into the file allocation model. This would be useful in the adaptive reassignment of files in the network.

The replication of data at individual nodes in a distributed data system raises the problem of maintenance of the multiple copies. In a recent paper, Johnson and Thomas[10] developed a method for synchronizing multiple updates in a multiple-copy data base environment. Under the assumptions that each data base manager is responsible for updating his copy of the data base and that complete communication exists among the data base managers, they employed a time-stamp solution. The key feature of their approach to maintaining consistency and synchronization of the data base was the attachment of a quintuple to each element of data that contained information such as time created, time last modified, site originating change, etc. This approach allows several sites to maintain multiple copies of a data base in a consistent state. It should be noted, however, that the time designation used refers only to the originating site. (The network has no time synchronization of clocks, as yet.) The potential exists, therefore, for updates to be lost. Johnson additionally placed some severe restrictions on the types of modifications allowed.

Researchers at the University of Illinois are investigating the problem of maintaining multiple data base copies in a network environment.[11,12] Three primitive operations are proposed and several algorithms are provided as solutions. Algorithms involving clock synchronization or modification constraints have been avoided as much as possible. Also under study are the problems concerning network failure recovery; several causes of failure are identified and several solutions proposed.

In a related effort (also at Illinois), resilient protocols for computer networks are being analyzed.[11,12] The purpose of this study is to determine how network communication protocols can be designed and implemented so that they are resilient to failures and abuse by aberrant or malicious software. Analysis of the ARPANET file transfer protocol has structured the area and decreased complexity. A layered approach to protocol resiliency has been employed whereby all underlying protocols involved are assumed to be resilient. One other assumption permits a protocol process to assume that all errors are due to the communication media or to the remote process. Initial findings have identified several problem areas concerning protocol resiliency. Included among the problems are connection termination, format inconsistencies, the restart facility, and message synchronization.

Standardization vs. Integration

Since many different DBMSs and corresponding data models are available, another design decision that must be made is whether to allow more than one DBMS in a distributed data base system. Two situations exist: the standardized approach, which uses only one DBMS and data model; and the integrated approach, which allows many. The standardized approach is best suited to the vertical or hierarchical design. The master data base is either partitioned or replicated across many nodes; the existence of more than one DBMS or data model creates many problems with centralized control. The integrated approach allows multiple DBMSs within the network but requires translation mechanisms to provide some type of commonality; this implies a much higher degree of distributed data base technology.

Development of a data base translation technology has been the focus of research at the University of Michigan.[13,14] A series of increasingly general data translators that validate the data description language approach has been developed. These translators provide the capability to *convert* data from one hardware environment to another and to restructure the data to fit different data models. Following this technology, Bakkom[15] proposed an integrated distributed data base system model. Two modules, the Data Request Emulator (DRE) and Data Restructuring Manager (DRM), allow many different DBMSs and data models.

In an Infotech report, Cashin[16] referred to the integrated approach as "database interworking." He cited network file transfer and file access as examples of interworking, since users express requests in terms of a local host system and are protected from the access languages and conventions of the remote system. The major focus of discussion is the problem of translating between both query languages and data models. Cashin proposed formulating a common query language data model to be used as a communication mechanism between data base systems. The relational model of data is suggested as a possible common data model.

In addition to the standardized and integrated approaches, Shoshani[17] introduced still another—the centralized approach—and discussed the relative merits of all three approaches. One important advantage of the centralized approach is that the translation of data and languages is unnecessary. There are several disadvantages, however, including the performance bottleneck of a single system and the compromise of using just one type of system. On the other hand, with the standard approach, failure of one node could not cause failure of the entire system. Shoshani concurred that the integrated approach would require the greatest technology and incur the burden of translation. Development of a common data management system language is proposed as a workable solution to the translation problem.

OPERATIONAL ISSUES IN DISTRIBUTED DATA BASES

In addition to the design issues in distributed data base development, there are several operational issues that must be addressed before a distributed data system can become operational. This section reviews the issues related to directory management, data control, system reliability and data integrity, deadlock, and security and privacy.

Directory Management

The location and content of the data dictionary in a distributed data system is an extremely important issue. The location of the directory controls the accessibility of the distributed data; the content dictates the structure and type of the data to be distributed. Some of the early work in this area was contributed by Aschim,[18] who classified distributed data systems by two methods. The first was a classification according to the geographical location of files and directories; the second was according to the distribution and types of data management systems used in the network.

The following important issues relating to the directory classifications were discussed by Aschim:

- Centralized files, central directory
- Distributed files, distributed directory

- Distributed files, centralized directory
- Centralized files, distributed directory

Aschim also enumerated the problems resulting from a distributed DBMS approach and investigated them in light of standard and non-standard interfaces between systems. Several other issues involving translation between host computers were also discussed.

There is a great deal of work being done in directory management. Wesley Chu at UCLA is working on the location of the data directories in a distributed data system. This research is directed toward the analysis of directory location schemes under various situations. Kimbleton at the Information Sciences Institute of the University of Southern California has developed an "optimal" assignment algorithm based on the minimization of process execution costs. The resulting assignment algorithm, he claims, is inexpensive and easy to implement.

Sutherland,[3] at Bolt, Beranck, and Newman (BBN), has envisioned the data directory function as a binding between names of "entities" and their location within the distributed data system. Two approaches to this issue have been discussed: the "full access name" and the cataloging function. The full access name accomplishes the binding simply by providing a distributed data system location field within every file name, thereby explicitly specifying the location. The cataloging function provides for a distributed data sharing system to maintain the name-to-location bindings internally, in such a way that a user need not know the location of the file.

Distributed Data Control System

Another operational issue that needs to be considered is the control mechanism to achieve data integration and access. A distributed data system is dependent upon functions provided by operating systems, data base management systems, and computer network systems. Research in any of these areas, therefore, is applicable to the area of distributed data bases.

The research by Sutherland[3] for BBN touched upon several important issues. One of the issues investigated was network transparency as a means to provide a uniform access to all network resources. Sutherland proposed that this could be achieved by using a network control system with a high degree of automation to reduce or remove explicit network interactions by a user. A concept based on the trapping mechanism of the TENEX system was advanced as one solution for implementation.

Several other issues in Sutherland's study dealt with the maintenance and update of multi-image files on the system. One suggested solution involved the collection of global system update information. Persistent process (which ensured the eventual completion of tasks assigned to temporarily nonfunctioning machines) and time stamping of data were also investigated as possible solutions.

System Reliability and Data Integrity

A distributed data system must be designed to ensure that a failure in one component does not shut down the entire system. Sutherland[3] has given four criteria for designing reliable systems: redundancy, simplicity and modularity, persistence, and active monitoring. Sutherland demonstrated that multiple components of data ensure to a greater degree the availability of needed data and the continuation of system operation. Simplicity and modularity of design allows not only redundant data but also redundant interchangeable components. When redundancy is not desirable, a persistent process can be initiated that completes tasks when resources become available. Active monitoring can help to spot and correct trouble before it becomes serious. Sutherland's reliability system allows for some redundancy of data and components, simplicity of component design, persistent tasks, and active system monitoring.

A distributed data system that cannot ensure the correctness of the information stored in the data base is of limited value to the user. Integrity refers to the protection of data against improper alteration or destruction. For example, if data is stored redundantly in a distributed data base system, an alteration of the data at one location must cause the same alteration at all other locations at which the data is stored. Research is needed in the area of data integrity and validation in a network environment. Sutherland[3] pointed out that data redundancy requires mechanisms for keeping redundant data equivalent. Cataloging features, access protocols, and selection strategies are proposed.

Deadlock

The deadlock situation occurs when concurrent processes need exclusive use of a shared resource. The process that accesses a resource first "locks out" the other processes from accessing it and goes on to access another resource. Now if this resource has been locked out by another process, and the other process also needs to access the first resource, the deadlock situation occurs; neither process can free the resource needed by the other process. For example, in the data base situation, suppose there are two processes, 1 and 2, and four data elements, A, B, C, and D. Process 1 requires data elements A, B, and C, and process 2 requires data elements B, C, and D. A deadlock occurs when process 1 locks A and B and is waiting for C, and process 2 locks C and D and is waiting for B.

Chamberlin, Boyce, and Traiger[19] suggested three categories of deadlock solutions:

- Detection, in which deadlocks are discovered and remedied
- Avoidance, in which only "safe" requests are granted
- Prevention, in which deadlocks cannot occur because of the basic design of the system

Chamberlin, Boyce, and Traiger also pointed out four problems associated with deadlock that are unique to, or complicated by, a shared data environment: non-unique resource names, non-static resource categories, interdependent locks, and increased complexity. To overcome these, a system of "protocols" and an algorithm have been proposed for deadlock detection in a shared data environment.

Chu and Ohlmacher[20] investigated deadlock prevention and detection mechanisms in distributed data bases. They proposed three methods of deadlock protection. The first is a simple prevention mechanism that allows resource access only when all requested resources are available. The second method—the process-set-prevention mechanism—permits a process to access resources as needed except when a deadlock possibility is detected. The third method provides deadlock detection based on the analysis of process and resource lists. Chu and Ohlmacher concluded that the simple mechanism is superior in most applications; however, the process-set-prevention and detection mechanisms provide for efficient file utilization and greater flexibility and may therefore be preferable in some cases.

Aschim[18] also investigated deadlock problems associated with exclusive file lockout. In cases when individual files are not logically interrelated, two solutions were proposed: a two-stage reservation system that requires the assignment of unique priorities to all users or processes, and a fixed-sequence reservation system that requires assignment of unique numbers to all resources.

Security and Privacy

The security of a data base refers to the protection of the data base against unauthorized disclosure, alteration, or destruction.

The problems of security in a host system are severely intensified when extended to networks. In his BBN report, Sutherland[3] pointed out that the goals of network transparency and ease of access conflict with the goals of security and privacy. Sutherland favors the implementation of a uniform user identification scheme. To this end, he investigated the concept of "authentication sites" that would verify a user's identity. In a network, one insecure machine can endanger the security of a user's data on all machines. Therefore, upon successful log-in, an authentication process would be assigned for the duration of the session and would control access to network resources.

STATE OF THE ART AND FUTURE DIRECTIONS

The previous sections have reviewed the operational and technological issues pertaining to distributed data systems. In this section, we will discuss the state of the art and indicate some directions to pursue.

Current Theoretical and Practical Results

The goal of data sharing in a multi-computer network increases the many problems that already exist in data management and introduces a new class of distributed management problems. The existing approaches to the single-system data management issues of privacy, integrity, concurrent access, user interface, data model, data organization, etc., are challenged by the distributed nature of the data. The complexities and interaction of the numerous components introduce new issues at all levels in the system design process.

When we examine the approaches to distributed data systems, we find that several methods and techniques are being pursued, and classification schemes have already been developed:

- In the area of program and data distribution, theoretical results have indicated several approaches to data and program allocation; however, application to existing systems is difficult because of the problems involved with measuring user/process access patterns and interdependencies of data.

- A fairly complete analysis of distributed file system designs has been provided, but actual implementations are dependent upon technological advances in the area of computer networks in general. The major difficulty in this area concerns the update problems resulting from multi-image files.
- The issue of deadlock is fairly well understood, and several algorithms have been proposed to solve this problem in a distributed data sharing system.
- Few research efforts have been directed toward the topic of security and privacy other than to acknowledge the serious problems involved in a distributed system.
- The concept of directory management has been researched in light of the master file location dictionary or directory. Research has yet to examine closely the aspects of the network relation space (a data structure that permits relations across file boundaries) or the creation of a master data schema.
- Several research efforts have touched upon the role of a master distributed data control system but as yet do not agree upon the principal functions of such a system.

In the area of software implementation, the work at BBN has produced two operating systems to support distributed data systems. RSEXEC, the Resource Sharing Executive system, is representative of the state of the art of practical software implementation. RSEXEC is an experimental distributed executive system that functions to integrate the operation of ARPA network TENEX hosts. Several advanced concepts of distributed resource sharing have been implemented. One major feature of RSEXEC is a distributed file system that spans host computer boundaries and supports uniform file access and automatic maintenance of multi-image files (subject to the constraint that all files are operational at the moment of update). It also supports the concept of device binding in such a way that all references to a device are, in fact, directed to a remote host.

RSEXEC is used by the TIPS on the ARPA network to provide information services to network users. The design involves a "broadcase" initial connection protocol (for selecting a host for services) and a mechanism by which multiple file images are consistently maintained. The important aspect of this implementation is that the feasibility of using large hosts to provide extended capabilities to smaller hosts has been demonstrated.

McROSS, another BBN software implementation, simulates and analyzes air traffic situations. It is a system capable of executing multiple processes distributed among a number of host computers. McROSS also has the capability to redistribute its operational parts among network hosts without interfering with the simulation. This capability evolved from the application of techniques for dynamic reconfiguration developed in an earlier software effort, CREEPER, a demonstration program that could migrate from computer to computer within the ARPA network.

Future Directions

Although some techniques and solutions have been developed for special cases involving a common operating system and computer, research is needed to develop a coherent methodology for the design, implementation, and management of distributed data bases. An intensive research program is needed to cover areas discussed in the following sections.

Analysis of the Essential Components of Distributed Data Systems. The area of distributed data sharing lacks a firm logical structure upon which research may be based. Previous attempts to structure the area have succeeded only in revealing the high degree of integration involved. As a result, subsystems are difficult to define and identify. Specific investigations should be directed toward providing functional definitions for operating systems, DBMSs, communications networks, resource sharing executive systems, and distributed data base management systems. These functional definitions will aid in the identification of basic subsystem responsibilities and should provide insights to the natural structure of the area.

Development of Translation Technologies. Optimization schemes that involve dynamic resource allocation will depend on the ability of the distributed system to store data and execute programs at any network node. Since the integration of different systems is the most sophisticated approach to distributed data sharing systems, the ability to move data and programs from node to node will, in turn, depend on translation technologies in data translation, query translation, data model translation, programming language translation, and operating executive command language translation.

The areas that specifically demand further investigation are data query and model translation, since these technologies must be developed to achieve integration of DBMSs, an initial goal of distributed data sharing systems.

Design of an Integrating Schema. Several research efforts have been directed toward the concept of a master catalog system to identify and locate data files in a distributed system. Further investigation is required to develop search strategies and optimal configurations.

An additional area that demands investigation concerns the concept of a master or integrating schema that describes the logical structures of all data files existing in the distributed data base. This feature, in conjunction with the master directory, permits the determination of a data file's logical structure as well as its identity and location; it could be essential to the development of query and data model translation schemes. The existence of a master schema also permits the logical relation of data across file boundaries. All files in the network could then be considered as areas within a single large data base. The concept of a multi-image file could be extended in such a system to provide for multi-image records that are common to several different data files. Efforts should be initiated to determine the full ramifications of such an approach.

Design of an Integrated Data Base Control System. The objective of a distributed data management system is to provide powerful resource sharing capabilities without compromising the basic functions currently provided by single-host systems. Current investigations indicate problems in the area of multi-image files. Research is, therefore, needed to determine the ramifications of multi-image files upon basic DBMS functions. Functions that require investigation include:

- *Data definition*—specifications must be developed to describe multi-image file structures.
- *Interrogation*—selection schemes are needed to determine which file copy to use for a given application.
- *Update*—problems with synchronization, deadlock, and data integrity must be investigated. This is a critical area.
- *Security*—ramifications of the network upon security must be evaluated. This is also a critical area.
- *Creation*—specifications must be developed to describe expected access requirements to the system.

Furthermore, the complexity of the distributed data sharing design demands research and development of an integrating control system. The object of such a system would be to coordinate and control the functions of systems subordinate to itself, such as operating systems, DBMSs, network communication systems, and translation systems. All functions required of a distributed data sharing system would be accomplished by the individual subordinate processes under control of the integrating system. In some respects, research has already discovered the need for such a system. Additional research should be directed toward this area to permit efficient and optimal operation of the distributed system once the underlying technologies become available.

Analysis of Design Strategies. The advent of distributed data sharing technologies will call for the development of sophisticated techniques to measure and analyze system performance relative to different optimization strategies. The evolution of these techniques is a critical factor in the evaluation of both static and dynamic distributed system configurations. Evaluations of this type are required by systems designers (as well as operating system procedures) to select resource and job configurations for the distributed data sharing system.

Critical Areas. Further investigation into the area of multi-image file maintenance (with special emphasis on update, data integrity, and security/privacy) is critical because computer network technologies have developed sufficiently to allow practical implementations of distributed file systems. In addition, translation techniques and master schema concepts will play important roles in the development of integrated data base control systems in the next few years and should be investigated. Furthermore, integrating data base control system designs should be investigated as a technique to coordinate and control the subsystems within the resource sharing network.

SUMMARY

The area of distributed data base technology is relatively new and requires much more research and development to become economically feasible in most applications. There is no question that this technology is being developed, however. It is recommended, therefore, that management become familiar with the technological trade-offs involved in distributed data bases. It is further recommended that research and development continue in the areas outlined here.

Notes

1   L. G. Roberts, "Access Control and File Directories in Computer Networks," *Proceedings of the 4th Annual IEEE International Conference on Communications*, March 1968.

2   G. M. Booth, "Distributed Information Systems," *Proceedings 1976 NCC*, Vol. 45 (Montvale, NJ: AFIPS Press) pp. 789-795.

3   W. R. Sutherland, "Distributed Computation Research at BBN," Vol. III, *BBN Technical Report 2976*, December 1974.

4   W. W. Chu, "Optimal File Placement in a Computer Network," *Computer Communications Networks*, N. Abramson and F. Kuo, eds, (Englewood Cliffs, NJ: Prentice Hall, 1973), pp. 82-94.

5   V. K. M. Whitney, "A Study of Optimal File Assignment and Communication Network Configuration," (Ph.D. thesis, The University of Michigan, 1970).

6   R. G. Casey, "Allocation of Copies of a File in an Information Network," *Proceedings of the Spring Joint Computer Conference, 1972*, AFIPS Press Vol. 40, 1972.

7   R. G. Casey, "Design of Tree Networks for Distributed Data," *AFIPS Conference Proceedings 42*, 1973, pp. 251-257.

8   R. G. Casey, "Design of Tree Structures for Efficient Querying," CACM 16, 1973, pp. 549-556.

9   K. D. Levin, "Organizing Distributed Data Bases in Computer Networks " (Ph.D. dissertation, University of Pennsylvania, 1974).

10 P. R. Johnson and R. Thomas, "The Maintenance of Duplicate Databases," NIC #31507, January 1975.

11 P. A. Alsberg et al, "Preliminary Research Study Report," Research in Network Data Management and Resource Sharing, Center for Advanced Computation, University of Illinois at Urbana-Champaign, Urbana, Ill. May 19, 1975.

12 P. A. Alsberg et al, "Survey Report," Research in Network Data Management and Resource Sharing, Center for Advanced Computation, University of Illinois at Urbana-Champaign, Urbana, Ill. May 19, 1975.

13 A. G. Merten and J. P. Fry, "A Data Description Approach to File Translation," *Proceedings 1974 ACM SIGMOD Workshop on Data Description, Access and Control*, Ann Arbor, Mich. May 1974, pp. 191-205.

14 E. W. Birss and J. P. Fry, "Generalized Software for Translating Data," *Proceedings 1976 NCC*, Vol. 45 (Montvale, NJ: AFIPS Press, 1976), pp. 889-899.

15 D. Bakkom, "A Model for Study of Distributed Data Base Systems," Data Translation Project Working Paper, 1976.

16 P. G. Cashin, "Data Base Interworking," *Network Systems & Software*, Report #24, Infotech Information Ltd., 1974.

17 A. Shoshani and I. Speigler, "The Integration of Data Management Systems on a Computer Network," NIC #15717, 1973.

18 F. Aschim, "Data Base Networks—An Overview," *Management Informatics*, Vol. 3, No. 1 (February 1974), pp. 12-28.

19 D. D. Chamberlin, R. R. Boyce and I. L. Traiger, "A Deadlock-Free Scheme for Resource Locking in a Data Base Environment," *Information Processing 74* (Proceedings IFIP Congress, Stockholm, Sweden, August 5-10, 1974), pp. 340-343.

20 W. W. Chu and G. Ohlmacher, "Avoiding Deadlock in Distributed Data Bases," *Proceedings ACM National Conference*, November 1974, pp. 156-160.

chapter **23**

The Technology of Data Translation— An Overview

INTRODUCTION

The computer field is a rapidly expanding area marked by stunning technological developments. These developments, together with increasing user demands, have brought about a great many changes. For example, the General Accounting Office issued a 1977 report in which it estimated that the federal government spent 450 million dollars on conversion efforts during the previous fiscal year.[1]

Rapid growth within the computing industry has also caused data and data formats to proliferate; this makes it very difficult to transfer data from one environment to another or within an environment that has undergone change. (A change in the environment is defined informally as a change in the hardware, software, or applications systems.) Introducing a DBMS, for example, causes a (software) change in the environment. In this case, the DBA must create and/or integrate existing files into data bases. This can involve converting computerized files from other installations (foreign files), restructuring and reformatting existing data bases, or translating data into various forms required by different applications. Even with DBMS technology, introducing

399

new processing or information requirements necessitates change. Typically, this requires restructuring existing data bases to adapt to the new requirements.

APPROACHES TO THE CONVERSION PROBLEM

There are essentially two technical solutions to the problem of conversion translation: specialized manual conversion programs and generalized translation.

The use of specialized programs is the more common technical approach. Unfortunately, it has several serious disadvantages. Special translation programs are usually written for each required translation. Expending such effort on programs that are used only once is a costly proposition. Moreover, special programs may be unreliable for restructuring complex data bases because of the probability of program error or data misinterpretation. This process is even more complex if conversion between hardware/software systems is also being performed.

There are, however, advantages to using the special conversion approach. Because they are customized, such programs generally execute efficiently. They usually involve fairly simple procedures and are, therefore, readily available to any enterprise with a programming facility. Coordinating the use of these procedures, however, can be difficult even with simple restructuring.

By comparison, the general purpose approach solves many of the problems inherent in the special-purpose program approach. Its most important advantage is its generality—one program is used to execute multiple translations. Such packages may also be designed for portability and reliability since the additional development effort is not wasted.

Nevertheless, such an approach is not without problems. For example, the initial research and development costs are high because the software is apt to be fairly large and complex. Once developed, the software may not execute efficiently because it is so generalized. Furthermore, this approach depends heavily on a language to describe the source and target data structures and a language to describe the restructuring specification itself. Such languages may be difficult to design and can be cumbersome to use. Finally, the development of generalized capabilities is hardly an insignificant obstacle; thus, it may be difficult to generalize to different hardware and software systems.

Fortunately, most of the problems associated with the generalized approach are technological in nature and are not inherent in the approach itself. In the long run, therefore, a generalized approach to data translation is superior to the manual approach.

In the middle of this volatile situation, the DP manager must satisfy user demands while maintaining an economic operation. To take advantage of the economic benefits of new hardware/ software capabilities and DBMSs, the DP manager and the DBA need a variety of data base conversion tools. A new software technology called data translation has recently been developed. Several groups have been developing data translation methodologies at the University of Michigan, IBM Research, the University of Pennsylvania, and Bell Laboratories.

CONVERSION TERMINOLOGY AND CONCEPTS

As with most technical disciplines, key terms in translation technology are often ill defined. This section provides some basic definitions of key terms that are used in the remainder of this chapter.

A *data conversion process* is the alteration of a *data base structure*. Such a change can take place at any level in the data base structure; two principle components have been identified:[2]

- *Logical Structure.* A logical structure is composed of data items, the grouping of data items into record types, and relationships among record types (sets). A logical structure is described by a *data description* written in the *data definition language* (DDL) of a particular system. The logical structure of a data base is frequently referred to as the *schema*.

- *Physical Structure.* A physical structure is an arrangement of the data in the logical structure on physical storage devices. This system-specific implementation is composed of item encodings and access methods to facilitate access and processing by the system.

Corresponding to the levels of a data base structure are two types of conversion processes. *Restructuring* is a conversion process that modifies the logical structure. *Data conversion* is a conversion process that occurs at the physical structure level and does not change the logical structure; in the simplest case, it is often referred to. as *file conversion*. (For the purposes of this discussion, the difference between a file and a data base lies in the complexity of the logical structure. A file has a simple, homogeneous record structure; a data base usually has a complex interdependent record structure.)

The technical term used to define a family of conversion processes ranging from restructuring to data conversion is *data translation.* The major components of data translation methodology are algorithms for transforming data, techniques for implementing these algorithms in software, and languages to specify data transformation requirements.

There are two classes of data translation. *Static translation* occurs when the entire source data base is converted into the target data base in a single operation. This is analogous to traditional batch-oriented processing. *Dynamic translation* is a real-time process in which only a portion of the source data base is translated into the target data base.

Two other concepts are important in discussing the implementation of data translators: independence and generality.

In terms of software architecture, independence can be defined as the ability to insulate one system component from the implementation details of another. If a system supports *device independence,* application programs can process files independent of the device on which they reside. *Machine independence* means that a program can be run in more than one hardware environment. *Data independence,* which is very important in the conversion process, has two aspects. *Physical data independence* is the ability to change the physical structure of a data base without affecting the logical structure or the application programs. *Logical data independence* is the ability to change the logical structure without adversely affecting application programs. Achieving logical data independence is an expensive process; it has been implemented to various degrees in different systems.

Generalized software is software that is capable of performing a range of tasks rather than one specific task. Data translators can be generalized in terms of the number of different source and target systems between which data can be converted.

DATA TRANSFORMATION MODEL

The data translation process consists of several different levels of data transformations. Figure 23-1 provides a model of these data transformations. The model consists of five transformations and two intermediate formats of the data base. The format and load data transformations are the inverses of the reformat and unload transformations respectively; the former concepts are not discussed in the following sections because all pertinent concepts are covered by the discussion of reformat and unload.

The model is meant to show only a sequence of data transformations; it is not meant to prescribe a data translator architecture or methodology. Considerations of generality and performance have motivated designers to follow various approaches in implementing data translators.

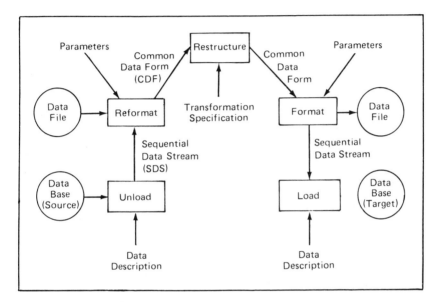

Figure 23-1. A Data-Driven Conversion

Unload/Load and the Sequential Data Stream

The purpose of the unload data transformation is to reduce the complex physical structure of the source data base to a very simple physical structure, the sequential data stream. The source data base contains not only the information in which the user is interested but also a large amount of control information that is specific to a particular system. This control information is used by the system for such data management functions as overflow chaining, index maintenance, and record blocking. In many systems, when a record is to be deleted, it is marked or flagged but not actually deleted. During the unload transformation, this system-specific information is deleted.

One factor that leads to a high degree of complexity in the physical structure is the use of pointers. Pointers are used for two basic purposes: to represent relationships that exist between record instances and to implement alternative access paths to the data. During the unload transformation, the second class of pointers may be discarded without losing information. The first class of pointers, however, does maintain information that must be preserved during the transformation.

As the name implies, the sequential data stream is a linear representation of a physical structure. It requires very little control information, is relatively simple to manipulate, and can be described by a simple data definition.

There are several approaches to preserving relationships in the sequential data stream that are implemented by pointers in the source data base. One method is to make relationships implicit in the ordering of the data. In many data base systems, physical pointers are used (that is, pointers that are functions of the physical address of the record). During the unload transformation, physical pointers are replaced by logical (device-independent) pointers.

In general, the unload transformation may be conceptualized as a process in which the physical structure of a data base is mapped into a linear version of the data base. Figure 23-2 shows an example of an unload transformation. In this example, the source data base contains records of types A and B. A relationship between the records is implemented by a pointer chain. The pointers are functions of the physical device on which the record exists. After the unload process, the relationship is represented by the order of the records in the SDS.

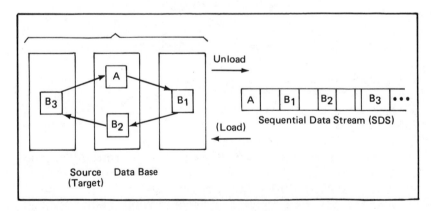

Figure 23-2. Unload Transformation Example

Reformat/Format and the Common Form

The purpose of the reformat transformation is to create a common data form representation of the source data. Since the logical structure of the sequential file is relatively straightforward, the file conversion process enters the data transformation model at this point. Typically, most files have a simple physical structure; this means they are in a format similar to the sequential data stream. The reformat transformation is a one-to-one mapping of data items in the sequential data stream to the common data form.

During mapping, several levels of data conversion may be required. At the lowest level is a change in storage space constructs (that is, a change in the byte size or word size used by a machine). A change in character code may be required; in this case new record ordering may be required to accommodate a change in the collating sequence. A third component of reformat transformation is the reencoding of items (for example, changing packed decimal items to binary, or floating-point to character string). Other considerations during the reformat process are the boundary alignment of items, as well as the justification, padding, and the like of data values.

A persistent and difficult problem in reformatting is caused by the use of nonstandard, application-specific encodings. For example, an application program may use the high-order bits of a zoned decimal number even though these bits are not used by the system. The specification of nonstandard item encodings is a difficult problem in data translation.

There are two approaches to the development of a common data form: system specific and system generic. In the former case, a particular internal format (sometimes called a translator internal form) is designed to facilitate the restructuring process on a particular machine. If the data translator has a distributed architecture (for example, in a heterogeneous computer network), a system-generic format has to be developed to handle the diverse data representation. This is by far the most difficult kind of format to design and may cause significant processing problems because of its generality.

Restructuring

While the unload and reformat transformations occur at the physical structure level, the restructuring transformation occurs at the logical structure level. A wide range of restructuring transformations is possible, including the addition of new item types into records, the merging of item types from two different record types into a third record type, and the addition of new interrecord relationships.[3]

Rather than attempt to classify restructuring transformations further, we will look at one example. Figure 23-3 contains the schema of a source data base composed of two record types (PRODUCT and PART) and one relationship (IS-USED-IN). The restructuring transformation is an inversion of the logical structure to the target schema also shown in Figure 23-3. The schema-level view of a restructuring transformation can be misleading unless one realizes the instance-level impact of the transformation.

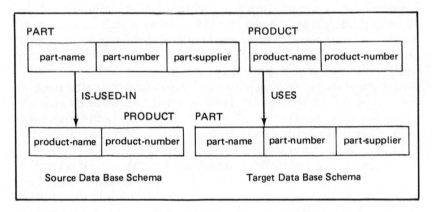

Figure 23-3. Schema-Level View of Restructuring Transformation

Figure 23-4 shows two instances of the IS-USED-IN relationship in the source data base and one instance of the USES relationship that would result from the transformation.

The restructuring example in Figures 23-3 and 23-4 shows that to build one instance of the target relationship, several instances of the source relationship had to be accessed. This suggests a further requirement for the common data form. If complex restructuring transformations are to be supported, the CDF should be structured to facilitate the rapid retrieval of records.

The purpose of the transformation model is to show the wide range of data transformations that may occur in a data translation. Depending on the purpose of the data translator, only some of the transformations may be required. Also, for the sake of efficiency, several transformations may be performed concurrently.

TECHNICAL APPROACH

In the later 1970s, a general approach to the data base conversion problem has been proposed.[4,5,6,7,8,9,10] It is interesting to observe

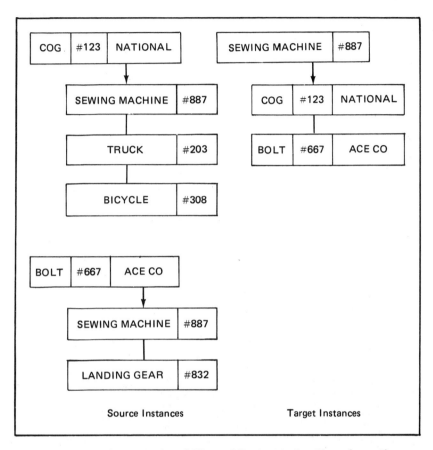

Figure 23-4. Instance-Level View of Restructuring Transformation

that these efforts involve some degree of generality and are based on a descriptive approach (i.e., both the source and target data bases and the transformations to derive the target from the source data base are described in a high-level language).

The approach proposed by the University of Michigan[4] is representative of others and consists of two steps:

1. User specification of the necessary descriptions
2. Execution of the data translator based on these descriptions (see Figure 23-5)

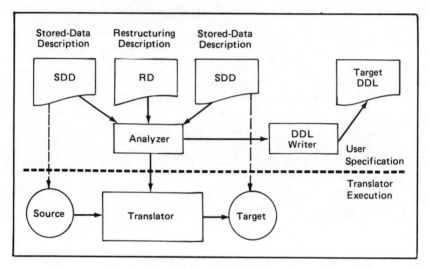

Figure 23-5. Data Description Approach

The user supplies descriptions of the logical and physical aspects of the source and target data bases. The user also provides specifications for the restructuring transformations that are needed to map source data into the target data. Two languages were developed to provide these descriptions: a stored-data definition language (SDDL), used to describe the source and target data bases; and the translation definition language (TDL), used to describe the restructuring transformations.

The SDDL is a high-level language based on a powerful model of data. At first glance, the SDDL appears similar to the data description language of a DBMS. A closer look, however, reveals several important differences. The stored-data definition language, based on common data definition practices, is actually an extension of the logical DDL to the more physical implementation aspects. Not only does the SDDL describe the logical structure of the data, it also describes the:

• Mapping of the logical structure to the physical storage structure

• Mapping of the physical storage structure to storage devices

• Access paths to the data

The translation definition language, on the other hand, deals primarily with logical transformations of data and describes the translation of source instances to target instances. This language was developed at the University of Michigan. It began as a simple association list of source item names and target item names; it has since developed into a powerful restructuring language.

The SDDL and TDL descriptions are processed by an Analyzer, which is similar to a compiler. Instead of producing object code, however, the Analyzer generates tables. It produces a stored-data description table (SDDT) and a restructuring description table (RDT), respectively. These, in turn, are used to drive the translator.

The DDL Writer, an auxiliary module that need not be generalized, uses the stored-data definition table of the target to construct a data definition of the target data base. This definition is written in the language of the target DBMS. There are several advantages to be derived by using this module. For one, application programs can use the data base immediately. In addition, the user can verify the target description. The DDL Writer allows users to verify that the target data description is consistent with their view of the target data base. What is more, the DDL does this in a language with which the users are familiar.

The second step in the translation process is the physical transformation of source data into target data. Driven by the data descriptions prepared in the first step, the second step employs three components: a Reader, a Restructurer, and a Writer (Figure 23-6). The Reader accesses the source data base; the Restructurer transforms the source data into a form suitable for the target; and the Writer creates the target data base.

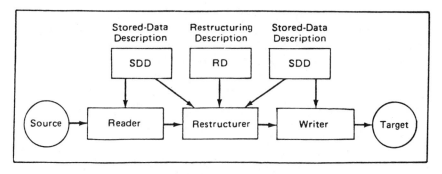

Figure 23-6. Components in the Translation Process

The Reader module, driven in part by the source SDD table, performs many functions. It

- Sequentially accesses physical records
- Physically deblocks these records
- Logically identifies their components
- Automatically creates the translator internal form (TIF), which is processed by the Restructurer

In dealing with complex data base structures, the Reader must keep a record of the access paths among these unblocked records; in this way, the Restructurer is provided with an accurate representation of the source data base.

The Restructurer module accesses the source TIF and transforms it to a representation of the target data base, the target TIF. The conversion from source to target is a transformation of the logical structure. The conversion is directed by the RD which contains the restructuring specifications.

The Writer, driven in part by the target SDD table, creates the target data base by constructing target data derived from the target TIF.

The data description approach to data translation provides the basis for two implementation approaches. The *interpretive approach* is based on a generalized processor driven by a set of tables. In contrast to the interpretive approach, the *generative* approach emits a specific object code to perform each translation (Figure 23-7).

The approach used by the University of Michigan (described previously) is an interpretive translation approach in which the stored-data descriptions are encoded into tables that direct the generalized processing algorithm. (The operational version of the Michigan Translator has been implemented on the Honeywell H6000 and is being used by the WWMCCS-user community.) The generative approach, used in the work at Penn[5,11] and IBM Research,[12,8] creates specialized PL/1 programs to perform each translation. (The XPRS system developed by IBM Research is available to users of 360/370 equipment on a joint study contract with IBM. There is, of course, a hybrid approach. In the hybrid approach, the components of the interpretive approach model produce an executable code while other components remain interpretive. The interpretive approach was chosen by Michigan because it can be a good research tool, and it facilitates the building of series of data translators.

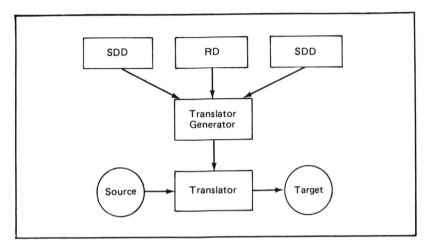

Figure 23-7. Generative Data Translation

Notes

1 "Millions in Savings Possible in Converting Programs From One Computer to Another." Office of Management and Budget, National Bureau of Standards. FGMSD-77-34, September 15, 1977.

2 J. P. Fry and E. A. Sibley, "Evolution of Database Management Systems." *Computing Surveys* 8, 1 (March 1976), pp. 1-42.

3 N. C. Shu, B. C. Housel and V. Y. Lum, "CONVERT: A High-Level Translation Definition Language for Data Conversion," *Comm. ACM* 18, 10 (1975), pp. 557-567.

4 J. P. Fry, R. L. Frank and E. A. Hershey III, "A Developmental Model for Translation," *Proceedings 1972 ACM SIGFIDET Workshop on Data Description, Access and Control,* ed. A. L. Dean, pp. 77-106.

5 J. A. Ramirez, "Automatic Generation of Data Conversion Programs Using a Data Description Language (DDL)" (Ph.D. dissertation, University of Pennsylvania, 1973).

6 A. G. Merten and J. P. Fry, "A Data Description Approach to File Translation." *Proceedings 1974 ACM SIGMOD Workshop on Data Description, Access and Control,* pp. 191-205.

7 D. E. Bakkom and J. A. Behymer, "Implementation of a Prototype Generalized File Translator." *Proceedings 1975 ACM SIGMOD International Conf. on Management of Data,* pp. 99-110.

8 N. C. Shu, et al, "Express: A Data Extraction, Processing, and Restructuring System." *Transactions on Database Systems,* 2, 2 (1977).

9 A. Shoshani, "A Logical-Level Approach to Data Base Conversion." *Proceedings 1975 ACM/SIGMOD International Conf. on Management of Data,* pp. 112-122.

10 A. Shoshani and K. Brandon, "On the Implementation of a Logical Data Base Converter." *Proceedings International Conference on Very Large Databases,* 1975, pp. 529-531.

11 J. A. Rameriz, N. A. Rin and N. S. Prywes, "Automatic Conversion of Data Conversion Programs Using a Data Description Language." *Proceedings 1974 ACM SIGFIDET Workshop on Data Description, Access and Control,* pp. 207-225.

12 V. Y. Lum, N. C. Shu and B. C. Housel, "A General Methodology for Data Conversion and Restructuring." *IBM R & D Journal,* Vol. 20, No. 5 (1976), pp. 483-497.

Bibliography

ACM/NBS. "Data Base Directions: The Next Steps." *Proceedings of the Workshop of the National Bureau of Standards and the Association for Computing Machinery held at Fort Lauderdale, Florida, October 29-31, 1976*. NBS Special Publication 451, U.S. Department of Commerce, Washington, DC, September 1976.

Albrecht, H.R., and Ryder, K.D. "The Virtual Telecommunications Access Method: A Systems Network Architecture Perspective." *IBM Systems Journal*, Vol. 15, No. 1 (1976), 53-80.

Altshuler, G.P., and Plagman, B.K. "A User System Interface Within the Context of an ICDB." *NCC Proceedings*. May 1974.

Andersen, G.A., and Jensen, E.D. "Computer Interconnection Structures: Taxonomy, Characteristics, and Examples." *Computing Surveys*, Vol. 7, No. 4 (December 1975).

Astrahan, M.M., et al. "System R: Relational Approach to Database Management." *ACM Transactions on Database Systems*, Vol. 1, No. 2 (June 1976), 97-137.

Bachman, C.W. "The Evolution of Storage Structures." *Communications of the ACM* Vol. 15, No. 7 (July 1972), 628-34.

Bakkom, D.E., and Behymer, J.A. "Implementation of a Prototype Generalized File Translator." *Proceedings of the 1975*

ACM SIGMOD International Conference on Management of Data. W.F. King (ed.), San Jose, CA (May 1975), 99-110.

Bakkom, D.E., and Schindler, S.J. "Operational Capabilities for Database Conversion and Restructuring." Technical Report 77 DT 6, Database Systems Research Group, University of Michigan, Ann Arbor, 1977.

Bandurski, Ann Ellis. "Associative Memories: A Trend in Data Base Technology." *AUERBACH Data Base Management.* Portfolio 24-01-12, 1978.

Bedford, G.G. "Technology Summary." Research in Network Data Management and Resource Sharing, Center for Advanced Computation, University of Illinois, Urbana-Champaign, May 19, 1975.

Bernard, D. "Intercomputer Networks—An Overview and Bibliography." Master's thesis, Moore School of Electrical Engineering, University of Pennsylvania, 1973.

Birss, E.W., and Fry, J.P. "Generalized Software for Translating Data." *Proceedings of the 1976 National Computer Conference*, Vol.45, Montvale, NJ: AFIPS Press 889-899.

Blanc, R.P. "Review of Computer Networking Technology." NBS Technical Note 804, January 1974.

Bobeck, A.H.; Bonyhard, P.I.; and Geusic, J.E. "Magnetic Bubbles—An Emerging New Memory Technology." *Proceedings of the IEEE*, Vol. 63, No. 8 (August 1975), 1176-95.

Booth, G.M. "The Use of Distributed Data Bases in Information Networks." *Proceedings of the First International Conference on Computer Communication.* Washington, DC, October 24-26, 1972. Published as A. Winkler (ed.), *Computer Communication Impacts and Implications*, 371-376.

Canaday, R.H., et al. "A Back-end Computer for Data Base Management." *Communications of the ACM*, Vol. 17, No. 10 (October 1974), 575-582.

Canning, Richard. "The 'Data Administrator' Function," *EDP Analyzer*, November 1972.

Carbonnell, J.R. "On Man-Computer Interaction: A Model and Some Related Issues." *IEEE Trans. on Systems Science and Cybernetics*, Vol. SSC-5, No. 1 (January 1969), 16.

The Cautious Path to a Data Base, EDP Analyzer, Vol. II, No. 6 (June 1973).

Champine, G.A. "Four Approaches to a Data Base Computer." *Datamation*, Vol. 24, No. 13 (December 1978), 100-106.

Chang, Ernest. "A Distributed Medical Data Base: Network Software Design." Working Paper, Computer Science Department, University of Waterloo, July 1975.

Chang, Ernest, and Linders, James. "A Distributed Medical Data Base." *Methods of Information in Medicine* (October 1974), 221-225.

Chou, W., and Frank, H. "Routing Strategies for Computer Design." *Proceedings of the 22nd MRI Symposium on Computer-Communications Networks and Teletraffic*. Brooklyn, NY: Polytechnic Press, 1972.

CODASYL Programming Language Committee. *Data Base Task Group Report*. New York: Association for Computing Machinery, 1971.

CODASYL Systems Committee. *Data Base Task Group Report*. New York: Association for Computing Machinery, April 1971.

CODASYL Systems Committee. *Feature Analysis of Generalized Data Base Management Systems*. New York: ACM, 1971, 520.

Cohen, L.J. "Making the Data Base Decision: Facing Cost/Benefit Realities." *GUIDE*, November 1973.

Collier, W.W. "Asynchronous Interactions on Shared Data." *IBM SIGOPS*, 1974.

Construction Management Action Group. "Requirements for a Data Base Management System." June 1971.

Cullum, P.G. "The Transmission Subsystem in Systems Network Architecture." *IBM Systems Journal*, Vol. 15, No. 1 (1976), 24-38.

Cuozzo, D.E., and Kurtz, J.F. "Building a Base for Data Base: A Management Perspective." *Datamation*, October 1973.

Data Base Administration Committee, Data Base Project, Integrated Systems Division. *Establishment of a Data Base Administration Function*. SHARE, Inc., June 4, 1974.

Data Base Administration Project of the Information Management Group, Information Systems Division. *The Data Base Administrator*. GUIDE International, November 3, 1974.

Data Base Systems. Infotech State of the Art Report, 1975.

Datacomputer Project. *Datacomputer Version 0/11 User Manual*. Working Paper No. 10. Cambridge, Mass.: Computer Corporation of America, December 1974.

Datacomputer Project. *Datalanguage*. Working Paper No. 3. Cambridge, Mass.: Computer Corporation of America, December 1973.

Datacomputer Project. *Further Datalanguage Design Concepts*. Working Paper No. 8. Cambridge, Mass.: Computer Corporation of America, December 1974.

Datacomputer Project. *Semi-Annual Technical Report*. Cambridge, Mass.: Computer Corporation of America, June 1975.

Data Translation Project. *University of Michigan Stored-Data Definition Language Reference Manual for Version II Translator*. University of Michigan, Ann Arbor, 1975.

Date, C.J. *An Introduction to Data Base Systems,* 2nd ed. Reading, Mass.: Addison-Wesley Publishing Company, 1977.

Day, J. "A Proposed File Access Protocol Specification." NIC #16819, June 1973.

Dean, Joel. *Managerial Economics*. Englewood Cliffs, Prentice-Hall, Inc., 1951.

Deppe, M.E. "A Relational Interface Model for Database Restructuring." Technical Report 76 DT 3, Data Translation Project, University of Michigan, Ann Arbor, 1976.

The Diebold Group, Inc., *Organizing for Data Base Management*. Document #516, December 1971.

Donnelly, J.E. "A Distributed Capability Computing System (DCCS)." Working Paper, Lawrence Livermore Labs, February 1976.

Edelman, J.A.; Jones, E.E.; Liaw, Y.S.; Nazif, Z.A.; and Scheidt, D.L. "REORG—A Data Base Reorganizer." Bell Laboratories Internal Technical Report, April 1976.

Emery, Dr. J.C. *An Overview of Management Information Systems*. Society of Management Information Systems, Special Report, September 1972.

Engles, R.W. *A Tutorial on Data Base Organization*. San Jose, Calif.: IBM Corporation, June 1969.

Eswaran, Kapali P. "Placement of Records in a File and File Allocation in a Computer Network." *IFIP Proceedings*. 1974.

Farber, D.J., and Heinrich, F.R. "The Structure of a Distributed Computer System—the Distributed File System." *Proceedings of the First International Conference on Computer Communication*. Washington, DC, October 24-26, 1972. Published as S. Winkler (ed.) *Computer Communication—Impacts and Implications,* 364-370.

Fiedler, Fred E. *A Theory of Leadership Effectiveness*. McGraw-Hill. 1961.

Fiedler, Fred E. "Style or Circumstance: The Leadership Enigma." *Psychology Today*. Vol. 2, Issue 10 (1969), 39-43.

Frank, R.L., and Yamaguchi, K. "A Model for a Generalized Data Access Method." *Proceedings of the 1974 National Computer*

Conference. Montvale, NJ: AFIPS Press, 437-444.

Frank, T. "Minis in Business, Part 4." *Computerworld,* January 8, 1975.

Fry, J.P., and Deppe, M.E. "Distributed Data Bases: A Summary of Research." *Computer Networks,* Vol. 1, No. 2 (November 1976), 1-13.

Fry, J.P., and Jeris, D. "Towards a Formulation of Data Reorganization." *Proceedings of the 1974 ACM/SIGMOD Workshop on Data Description, Access, and Control.* R. Rustin (ed.). New York: ACM, 83-100.

Fry, J.P. "Distributed Data Bases: A Summary of Research." The University of Michigan, Data Translation Working Paper, DE 801, August 1975.

Fry, J.P.; Frank, R.L.; and Hershey, E.A., III. "A Developmental Model for Translation." *Proceedings of the 1972 ACM SIGFIDET Workshop on Data Description, Access, and Control.* A.L. Dean (ed.), Denver, Colo. (November 1972), 77-106.

Fry, J.P.; Smith, D.C.P.; and Taylor, R.W. "An Approach to Stored-Data Definition and Translation." *Proceedings of the 1972 ACM-SIGFIDET Workshop on Data Description, Access, and Control.* A.L. Dean (ed.), Denver, Colo. (November 1972), 13-55.

Fry, J.P. "Introduction to Storage Structure Definition." *Proceedings of the 1970 ACM-SIGFIDET Workshop on Data Description, Access, and Control.* E.F. Codd (ed.), Houston, Tex., November 1970.

Gerritsen, R., and Morgan, H. "Dynamic Restructuring of Databases with Generation Data Structures." *Proceedings of the 1976 ACM Conference.* New York: ACM, 281-286.

Ghosh, S.P. "File Organization: The Consecutive Retrieval Property." *Communications of the ACM,* Vol. 15, No. 9 (September 1972).

Goguen, N.H., and Kaplen, M.M. "An Approach to Generalized Data Translation: The ADAPT System." Bell Telephone Laboratories Internal Report, October 5, 1977.

GUIDE Information Management Group. *The Data Base Administrator.* November 1972.

GUIDE International Inc. "User Language System Requirements." *GUIDE Secretary Distribution,* 1973.

Habermann, A.N. "Prevention of System Deadlocks." *Communications of the ACM,* Vol. 12, No. 7 (July 1969), 364-377.

Habermann, A.N. "Synchronization of Communication Processes." *Communications of the ACM,* Vol. 15, No. 3 (March 1972), 171-176.

Head, R.V. "Management Information Systems: A Critical Appraisal." *Datamation*, May 1967.

Heart, F.E., et al. "A New Minicomputer/Multiprocessor for the ARPA Network." *Proceedings of the National Computer Conference, 1973.*

Helgesen, W.B. "Trends Affecting Distributed Processing and Databases." Working Paper. Billerica, Mass.: Honeywell Information Systems, 1975.

Hendrix, G.G.; Sacerdoti, E.D.; Sagalowicz, D.; and Slocum, J. "Developing a National Language Interface to Complex Data." *ACM Transactions on Database Systems*, Vol. 3, No. 2 (June 1978), 105-147.

Hobgood, W.S. "The Role of the Network Control Program in Systems Network Architecture." *IBM Systems Journal,* Vol. 15, No. 1 (1976), 39-52.

Holler, E. "Files in Computer Networks First European Workshop on Computer Areas." *IRIA Frame,* May 1973, 381-396.

Housel, B.C., and Shu, N.C. "A High-Level Data Manipulation Language for Hierarchical Data Structures." *Proceedings of the 1976 Conference on Data Abstraction, Definition, and Structure.* Salt Lake City, 155-169.

Housel, B.; Lum, V.; and Shu, N. "Architecture to an Interactive Migration System (AIMS)." *Proceedings of the 1974 ACM SIG-FIDET Workshop on Data Description, Access, and Control.* R. Rustin (ed.), Ann Arbor, Mich. (May 1974), 157-169.

Housel, B.; Smith, D.; Shu, N.; and Lum, V. "Define: A Non-Procedural Data Description Language for Defining Information Easily." *Proceedings of the 1975 ACM Pacific Conference.* San Francisco, Calif., April 1975, 62-70.

Hume, Gerald E. "The Data Base in a Critical On-Line Business Environment." *Datamation,* September 1974.

Joint GUIDE-SHARE Data Base Requirements Group. *Data Base Management System Requirements.* New York: SHARE, Inc., 1970.

King, P. F., and Collymeyer, A.J. "Database Sharings—An Efficient Mechanism for Supporting Concurrent Processes." *AFIPS* *42* (1973), 271-275.

Labetoulle, J., et al. "Analysis and Simulation of a Homogeneous Computer Network." *Computer Communications Network Group Report E-30,* University of Waterloo, January 1975.

Lefkowitz, Henry C. *Data Dictionary/Directory Systems.* QED Information Sciences, February 1977.

Licklider, J.C.R. "Man-Computer Symbiosis." *IRE Trans. on Human Factors in Electronics,* Vol. HFE-1 (March 1960), 4-11.

Lin, S. C.; Smith, D.C.P.; and Smith, J.M. "The Design of a Rotating Associative Memory for Relational Database Applications." *ACM Transactions on Database Systems,* Vol. 1, No. 1 (March 1976), 53-75.

Lochousky, F.H., and Tsichritzis, D.C. "User Performance Considerations in DBMS Selection." *Proceedings of the Third International Conference on Very Large Data Bases.* Tokyo, 1977.

Lowenthal, E.I. "Computing Subsystems for the Data Management Function." *Proceedings of the Third Texas Conference on Computing Systems.* IEEE, November 1974.

Lyon, John K. *The Database Administrator.* New York: John Wiley and Sons, 1976.

McFadyen, J.H. "Systems Network Architecture: An Overview." *IBM Systems Journal,* Vol. 15, No. 1 (1976), 4-23.

McGee, W.C. "Informal Definitions for the Development of a Storage Structure Definition Language." *Proceedings of the 1970 ACM-SIGFIDET Workshop on Data Description, Access, and Control.* E.F. Codd (ed.), Houston, Tex., November 1970.

Madnick, S.E. *Design of a General Hierarchical Storage System.* Report CISR-6, MIT Sloan School of Management, March 1975.

Madnick, S.E. "INFOPLEX—Hierarchical Decomposition of a Large Information Management System Using a Microprocessor Complex." *Proceedings of the National Computer Conference,* 1975.

Management of Data Elements in Information Processing. Edited by Hazel E. McEwen. U.S. Department of Commerce, National Bureau of Standards, NTIS. Springfield, Va., April 1974.

Manning, E.G., and Peebles, R.W. "A Homogeneous Network for Data Sharing—Communications." *Computer Communications Network Group Report E-12.* University of Waterloo, March 1974.

Marill, T., and Stern, D. "The Datacomputer—A Network Data Utility." *AFIPS Conference Proceedings 44,* 1975.

Martin, James. *Security, Accuracy and Privacy in Computer Systems.* Englewood Cliffs, NJ: Prentice-Hall, 1973.

Meltzer, H.S. "Current Concepts in Data Base Design." Presented at the Association for Systems Management International Systems Meeting, May 15, 1973.

Miller, J.G. "Adjusting to Overloads of Information." In *Organizations,* Vol. II. Edited by J. Litter. New York: John Wiley and Sons, 1969.

Minami, Warren N. "Data Administration: The Key to Better Management of a Neglected Corporate Resource," *Journal of Systems Management,* May 1976.

Mullery, A.P. "Computer Networks and Data Sharing: A Bibliography." Working Paper, IBM Watson Research Center, January 1972.

Muntz, C.A., and Cashman, P.M. "The File Handling Facility for the National Software Works." Working Paper, Massachusetts Computer Associates, February 1976.

Navathe, S.B. "A Methodology for Generalized Database Restructuring." Ph.D. dissertation, University of Michigan, 1976.

Navathe, S.B. "Schema Analysis for Database Restructuring." *Proceedings of the Third International Conference on Very Large Databases.* New York: ACM, 1977.

Navathe, S.B., and Fry, J.P. "Restructuring for Large Data Bases: Three Levels of Abstraction." *ACM Transactions on Database Systems,* Vol. 1, No. 2, New York: ACM, 1976, 138-158.

Navathe, S.B., and Merten, A.G. "Investigations into the Application of the Relation Model of Data to Data Translation." *Proceedings of the 1975 ACM SIGMOD International Conference on Management of Data.* W.F. King (ed.), New York: ACM, 123-138.

Newell, A.; Shaw, J.C.; and Simon, H.A. "Elements of a Theory of Human Problem Solving." *Psychology Review,* Vol. 65 (May 1958).

Nolan, Richard L. "Computer Data Base: The Future is Now." *Harvard Business Review,* (September-October 1973).

Nolan, Richard L. *Managing the Data Resource.* New York: West Publishing Co., 1974.

Owens, R.C. "Evaluation of Access Authorization Characteristics of Derived Data Sets." *Proceedings of the ACM-SIGFIDET Workshop on Data Description, Access, and Control.* San Diego, Calif., November 11-12, 1971.

Panigrahi, G. "Charge-Coupled Memories for Computer Systems." *Computer,* Vol. 9, No. 4 (April 1976), 33-42.

Peebles, R. "Design Considerations for Distributed Data Access Systems." Ph.D. dissertation, Moore School of Electrical Engineering, University of Pennsylvania, May 1973.

Peebles, R.W., et al. "Simulation Studies of a Homogeneous Computer Network for Data Sharing." *Computer Communications Network Group Report E-19,* University of Waterloo, March 1974.

Plagman, B.K., and Altshuler, G.P. "A Data Dictionary/Directory System Within the Context of an Integrated Corporate Data Base." *AFIPS Conference Proceedings,* Vol. 41, Montvale, New Jersey, 1972.

Plagman, B.K., and Altshuler, G.P. "An Integrated Corporate Data Base Concept and Its Application." *ACM SIGFIDET Workshop Proceedings.* November 1972.

Plagman, B.K., and Hong, B.L. *Principles of Data Dictionary/ Directory Systems.* New York: John Wiley and Sons, 1981.

Rameriz, J.A. "Automatic Conversion of Data Conversion Programs Using a Data Description Language." *Proceedings of the 1974 ACM SIGFIDET Workshop on Data Description, Access, and Control.* R. Rustin (ed.), Ann Arbor, Mich. (May 1974), 207-225.

Roberts, L.G. "Access Control and File Directories in Computer Networks." *Proceedings of the Fourth Annual IEEE International Conference on Communications.* March 1968.

Roberts, L.G., and Wessler, B.D. "Computer Network Development to Achieve Resource Sharing." *Proceedings of the Spring Joint Computer Conference, 1970.* AFIPS Press, Vol. 35, 1972.

Ross, Ronald G. *Data Base Systems: Design Implementation & Management.* AMACOM, 1978.

Sagolowicz, D. "IDA: An Intelligent Data Access Program." *Proceedings of the Third International Conference on Very Large Data Bases.* Tokyo, 1977.

Schontz, R. "A Multi-Site Data Collection Facility." NIC #31440, December 1974.

Shemer, J.E., and Collymeyer, A.J. "Database Sharing: A Study of Interference, Roadblock, and Deadlock." *ACM SIGFIDET Workshop on Data Description, Access, and Control* (1972), 141-163.

Shoshani, A. "A Logical Level Approach to the Data Base Conversion." *Proceedings of the 1975 ACM SIGMOD Conference.* W.F. King (ed.), San Jose, Calif. (May 1975), 112-122.

Shoshani, A. "Data Sharing in Computer Networks." NIC #12623, October 1972.

Shoshani, A., and Bernstein, A.J. "Synchronization in a Parallel-Accessed Database." *Communications of the ACM 12* (November 1969) 604-607.

Sibley, E.H., and Taylor, R.W. "A Data Definition and Mapping Language." *Communications of the ACM,* Vol. 16, No. 12 (December 1973), 750-59.

Sibley, E.H., and Taylor, R.W. "Preliminary Discussion of a General Data to Storage Structure Mapping Language." *Proceed-*

ings of the 1970 ACM-SIGFIDET Workshop on Data Description, Access, and Control. E.F. Codd (ed.), Houston, Tex., November 1970.

Simon, H.A. *Models of Man.* New York: John Wiley and Sons, 1957.

Simonson, W.E., and Alsbrooks, W.T. "A DBMS for the U.S. Bureau of the Census." *Proceedings of the First International Conference on Very Large Data Bases.* ACM, 1975.

Smith, Daniel S. "Data Base Management System Selection Procedure." *Proceedings of the 19th Annual College and University Machine Records Conference,* May 5-8, 1974.

Smith, D.C.P. "A Method for Data Translation Using the Stored Data and Definition Task Group Languages." *Proceedings of the 1972 ACM SIGFIDET Workshop on Data Description, Access, and Control.* New York: ACM, 107-124.

Smith, D.C.P. "An Approach to Data Description and Conversion." Ph.D. dissertation, Moore School Report 72-20, University of Pennsylvania, 1972.

Stieger, W.H., "Data Administrator Functions." Unpublished manuscript, CODASYL Systems Committee, July 1970.

The Stored-Data Definition and Translation Task Group. *Stored-Data Description and Data Translation: A Model and Language.* Information Systems, 1976.

Swartwout, D. "An Access Path Specification Language for Restructuring Network Databases." *Proceedings of the 1977 SIGMOD Conference.* New York: ACM, 81-101.

Swartwout, D.E.; Deppe, M.E.; and Fry, J.P. "Operational Software for Restructuring Network Databases." *Proceedings of the 1977 National Computer Conference,* Vol. 46. Montvale, NJ: AFIPS Press, 499-508.

Swartwout, D.E.; Wolfe, G.J.; and Burpee, C.E. "Translation Definition Language Reference Manual for Version IIA Translator, Release 3." Data Translation Project, Working Paper 77 DT 5.3, University of Michigan, Ann Arbor, 1977.

Taylor, R.W. "Generalized Data Base Management System Data Structures and Their Mapping to Physical Storage." Ph.D. dissertation, University of Michigan, 1971.

Taylor, R. W. "Generalized Data Structures for Data Translation." *Proceedings of the Third Texas Conference on Computing Systems.* Austin, Tex., 1974, 6-3-1.

Thomas, R. "Comments on File Access Protocol." NIC #17454, June 1973.

Tsichritzis, D., and Klug, A., ed. *The ANSI/X3/SPARC DBMS Framework Report of the Study Group on Data Base Management Systems.* New Jersey: AFIPS Press, 1977.

Uhrowczik, "Data Dictionary/Directory Systems." *IBM Systems Journal,* Vol. 12, No. 4 (1973).

U.S. Department of Commerce. *Technical Profile of Seven Data Element Dictionary/Directory Systems.* NBS Special Publication 500-3, National Bureau of Standards, February 1977.

U.S. Department of Health, Education and Welfare. *Records, Computers and the Rights of Citizens.* Report of the Secretary's Advisory Committee on Automated Personal Data Systems, July 1973.

UNIVAC. *UNIVAC 1100 Series Data File Converter.* Programmer Reference UP-8070, Sperry Rand Corporation, March 1974.

Weinberg, Gerald M. *The Psychology of Computer Programming.* New York: Van Nostrand Ltd., 1971.

Westin, Alan F. *Databanks in a Free Society.* New York: Quadrangle Books, 1972.

Westin, Alan F. *Privacy and Freedom.* New York: Atheneum, 1970.

Whitney, V.K.M. "A Study of Optimal File Assignment and Communication Network Configuration." Ph.D. thesis, University of Michigan, 1970.

Yamaguchi, K. "An Approach to Data Compatibility, A Generalized Access Method." Ph.D. dissertation, University of Michigan, 1975.

Young, J.W., Jr. "A Procedural Approach to File Translation." *Proceedings of the 1970 ACM-SIGFIDET Workshop on Data Description, Access, and Control.* E.F. Codd (ed.), Houston, Tex., November 1970.

Index